Penal Policy and

Also by Barbara A. Hudson and published by Macmillan

Justice through Punishment

Penal Policy and Social Justice

Barbara A. Hudson

First published 1993 by
THE MACMILLAN PRESS LTD
Houndmills, Basingstoke, Hampshire RG21 2XS
and London
Companies and representatives
throughout the world

ISBN 0–333–49575–6 hardcover
ISBN 0–333–49576–4 paperback

A catalogue record for this book is available
from the British Library.

Printed in Hong Kong

For Harry and Adam

Contents

Preface

This book started life as a research project with Middlesex Area Proba-. tion Service, and I am grateful to the management and staff there for encouragement to undertake the original sentencing survey, and for agreement that the questions it seemed to generate were interesting to people other than myself, as well as for practical help with data collection. The latter stages of the book's development have been enriched by a new partnership with Northumbria Probation Service, and again I am grateful to colleagues at all levels of the service for sharing with me some of their hopes and their concerns about the way penal policy is affecting criminal justice practice.

A grant from the Leverhulme Trust enabled me to have some time between leaving Middlesex and commencing my duties with the University of Northumbria, and this was crucial in allowing me some space to further analyse the original data and develop the theoretical ideas which enabled me to see what was happening in the Middlesex courts as part of a much more general trend. In turning a collection of data into a book with wider themes, I have been much assisted by comments by Maureen Cain and Carol Smart on my first proposals, and by the patience and timely advice of Steven Kennedy and Frances Arnold at Macmillan. For help with bringing it some way down to earth again, I am indebted to the anonymous reviewer used by the publisher. In providing evidence to support my central contention that whatever the differences in penal policy with respect to crimes, the same groups of people are penalised everywhere, I am grateful to Dick Whitfield for his list of contacts, and to Inkeri Antilla, David Biles, Else Holm, Jacqueline de Plaen and Knut Sveri for the helpful material they so generously sent to me.

For encouraging me to believe that I had something worth saying and had better get on and say it, thanks to Andrew Ashworth, Dee Cook, Tony Jefferson, Roger Matthews and, especially, Pat Carlen. Between carrying out the original research which prompted the book and finally getting down to writing it, I have moved from being a researcher, employed by the probation service, back into teaching. Colleagues at Newcastle have been supportive, students have been challenging; Heather Scott and Mat Curran in particular have managed not to look too bored when hearing for the umpteenth time about problems with this or that chapter, and their convivial friendship has been sustaining throughout.

This book has had an embarrassingly long gestation period. Changing jobs, moving from one end of the country to another, as well as the often bewildering speed of developments in the penal policy field, made it difficult to settle down to the task of writing. New people to get to know, new courses to write, the beauty of the Northumbrian countryside and the acquisition of a large garden have all proved unchallengeable excuses or irresistible temptations not to work on the book, but I can only hope that the final result is the better for having a longer than envisaged time for reflection between the original idea and its realisation.

Above all, and as ever, I am grateful to Adam and Harry for love and patience. They have both assisted in countless ways: thanks Adam for doing the ironing and helping with tedious chores like checking references; thanks Harry for always listening (or at least convincingly pretending to) and for keeping the sherry flowing.

Barbara A. Hudson

Introduction

One afternoon in the mid-1980s, a very senior Home Office official addressed an audience of senior probation officers who were gathered in the autumn sunshine of a south coast resort to consider how best to develop probation practice in the light of evolving penal policy. He told them that the need was to adopt styles of work focusing on offending and acknowledging themselves as punishment; the days of probation as social work were over, the service must recognise its role as unequivocally part of the penal system. Its special purpose was, he said, to provide appropriately constructive but none the less punitive programmes that would encourage sentencers to allow offenders whose crimes were in the middle range of seriousness to remain in the community, thereby helping the Home Office achieve its objective of ensuring that only the most serious offenders were sentenced to imprisonment. In fact, he was outlining the policy that is now well known as *twin-tracking*, the main strategy for the achievement of which is increased provision of punishment in the community. When the staff conference ended, managers and probation officers set about this task of devising and implementing strategies to increase the number of people convicted of medium-serious crimes (such as burglary) on their caseloads, and reduce the number of first offenders.

This scene was being enacted up and down the country. Probation services rapidly developed offending behaviour groups, intensive probation programmes, alcohol and addiction courses, and they accepted in large measure the role allotted them by government of being the principal 'transmission mechanism' for translating penal policy into penal practice. Like juvenile justice in the early 1980s and American probation in the mid-1970s to mid-1980s, probation services in England and Wales seemed to accept that it was their clinging on to outmoded social work models, their lack of target hardening, their lack of offence focus in court reports and in post-sentence work, that enabled the courts to send so many non-violent, non-serious offenders to prison. All the probation services in England and Wales drew up statements of objectives and priorities which prioritised local reductions in imprisonment rates, and raising the criminality profile of their probation and community service caseloads.

As a probation service research officer I, together with others in the

1

same role, was engaged in devising instruments to monitor the implementation of these objectives, and to assist in their achievement. The
main contribution of probation researchers at this time was the introduction of the 'risk of custody scale', a predictive instrument designed
to help probation officers target recommendations for the more interventive new forms of probation on those who would be most likely
otherwise to go to prison. My own contribution to this endeavour was
to precede the introduction of a risk of custody scale in the service for
which I worked by a sentencing survey. It seemed to me worth checking
out that the factors that were put forward as general risk of custody
indicators really were correlated with imprisonment in our own courts,
and to spot any others that were significant, at least locally, and so
should be included.

The contrast between the sentencing survey findings and the scene
described in the opening paragraph provided the initial impetus for this
book. Sitting in courts to test whether the information I was asking
probation officers to enter on to the survey forms was readily obtainable,
the people I saw going into custody were very different from the serious
offenders who so monopolised the attentions of managers and policy-
makers. A mentally disturbed man was refused entry by a psychiatric
hospital late at night and threw a brick through the hospital window –
outcome, imprisonment, with the magistrate expressing regret that he
could think of nowhere else to send him where he would receive psychiatric assessment and treatment. A woman urinating in a public
park, a homeless man starting a small fire to keep himself warm – again,
sent to prison by apologetic magistrates. These people were all first-
time 'criminals', so under new probation targeting guidelines had not
qualified for pre-sentence reports, let alone recommendations for probation orders. At a Crown Court I saw a man go to prison for the crime
of writing a cheque (for less than £50) that he knew would not be
honoured because the bank had informed him that it would no longer
redeem his cheques and had instructed him to destroy his cheque
guarantee card. By the time the case came to court, he had repaid
the money to the shopkeeper, and although he had no offences during
the preceding eight years, he was sentenced to imprisonment on the
grounds that as he had already had a suspended sentence (for a first
offence, nine years previously), he had used up all his chances. He was
black, as was the would-be psychiatric patient.

It is the relationship between these two scenarios that is the subject
matter of this book. The cases I witnessed are by no means unusual or

exceptional. I came across similar events in all the courts I visited, and anyone working in the courts today could relate incidents of the same kind. In all the courts covered by the survey, I found black defendants being given high tariff alternatives to custody in circumstances where white offenders were given conditional discharges or probation orders. In run-of-the-mill property cases, where an employed offender would be fined, a corresponding unemployed black offender would be given suspended sentence or community service, but if white, would be given conditional discharge or probation. Black offenders were receiving 'last chance' alternatives to custody for first-time property offences where white offenders were receiving 'first rung on the ladder' disposals; for minor offences against the person, black offenders were being sent to prison but white offenders were being given fines or probation. Mentally disordered offenders being sent to prison because of lack of facilities for assessment and treatment in the community is not unusual either: in 1986, the first year of my survey and so the year in which my pilot observations were made, a Home Office survey suggested that about 1500 male prisoners were suffering from some form of mental disorder (NACRO, 1986).

I found variation between courts, and in the same court at different times, in the offences which produced the highest rates of custody. In one court where sentences correlated very strongly with current offence rather than previous convictions, in the first round of my survey it was burglary which produced the most custodial sentences, in the second round it was DSS fraud, and in the third it was driving with excess alcohol. In other courts, shoplifting from a nearby shopping centre resulted in a crop of custodial sentences following a campaign in the local newspaper. What I found, in short, was disparity and temporal variability in the offences producing imprisonment, but consistency and stability in the vulnerability to custody or other inordinately severe penalty of the homeless, the mentally ill, the unemployed, and especially unemployed black offenders. Evidence from other countries shows that this is a general phenomenon. Whatever criminal justice policies and institutional arrangements are adopted; whatever regional and national differences there might be in opinions about which offences deserve custody, the poor, the disturbed, the migrant, disadvantaged ethnic minorities are consistently overpenalised and overimprisoned.

The Home Office minister expounding penal policy aims to a probation audience was also part of a pattern. A series of white papers, green papers, circulars and regulations has culminated in the 1991 Criminal

Justice Act, whose main aims are to make punishment proportional to
the seriousness of the current crime, and to reserve custody for the most
serious offences. The green paper *Punishment, Custody and the Community* (Home Office, 1988) which laid down the principles which
would be incorporated in the Act, stated very clearly the commitment
to making punishment fit the crime; to making present offence count
much more in sentencing than previous convictions; to making restriction of liberty a common element in custodial and community penalties;
and to making the probation service responsible for the administration
of 'punishment in the community'. Again, this development is by no
means unique to Britain. Federal sentencing guidelines in Australia,
Canada, the USA, and the new penal code in Sweden, as well as amend-
ments to legislation, policy and practice in several other European
countries, are all in the direction of making the punishment fit the
crime. On an international scale usually only seen in times of occu-
pations or their aftermath (the introduction of the Napoleonic Code;
post-war revisions of penal codes in countries which had been occupied by Hitler and other dictators), there has been a flurry of penal
policy activity in the 1980s and going into the 1990s. It has all been in
the direction of making the punishments proportional to the gravity of
offences; of making fair punishment the main penal aim rather than
reform or rehabilitation of offenders; and it has been concerned to
reserve imprisonment for serious offences, substituting community
penalties for short prison sentences for non-violent offences.

The relationship between the two scenarios described in the opening
paragraphs, then, should be that the first will make the second less likely.
As penal policy is implemented, it should no longer be such a regular
occurrence that black people receive prison sentences or up-tariff alternatives for minor offences, that homeless or mentally disordered
petty offenders receive prison remands or sentences because there is
nowhere else for them to go.

Realism, critique and abolitionism: theories of crime, the state and punishment

My aim, then, is to review penal policy developments, and to present an
analysis of the deeper structures of the relationships between crime, the
state, and strategies of punishment which will reveal, not only the likely

impediments to the success of contemporary penal policies, but the closures and limits on the vision of 'justice' which has been espoused.

In order to develop this analysis, I have drawn on traditions which are usually separate from each other. Questions about penal discrimination against black people, against the poor and unemployed, have usually been asked from within a sociological–criminological frame of reference. The work of Steven Box, for instance, and his American and European counterparts, drawn upon in Chapter 2, demonstrates the connections between race, unemployment and imprisonment. Arguments about the proper purposes of punishment, debates about issues such as disparity in sentencing, whether penal purposes can best be achieved through sentencing legislation, councils or judicial discretion, are usually raised within a legal theory–law in context perspective, exemplified by the work of Andrew Von Hirsch in the USA, Andrew Ashworth and David Thomas in England. I have drawn freely on these traditions, and hope in some ways to bridge the gap between them.

With imprisonment, too, there is usually a distinct boundary between works which question the social role of imprisonment (Foucault, 1977; Mathiesen, 1990; Reiman, 1979) and those which deal with practical problems of imprisonment – overcrowding, destructive regimes – whilst accepting its continued existence, albeit seeking contraction in the use of imprisonment as well as regime reforms (Morgan, 1984; King and Rutherford, 1980). Again, I draw on both these traditions, my own position being that while prisons are likely to be with us for at least the foreseeable future, the abolitionist perspective is necessary to make us question some of the taken-for-granted assumptions about the inevitability of imprisonment as a standard response to crime.

The legal perspective on crime and punishment is very much in the ascendancy. Not only does penal policy reflect the influence of legal thinkers – passages in *Punishment, Custody and the Community* read very much like the formulations of just deserts theorists such as Von Hirsch whilst other parts parallel the ideas of incapacitation advocates such as James Q. Wilson – but the crime–punishment frame of mind dominates much of our thinking about social problems in a more general sense. In the treatment of the homeless and the mentally ill, for example, we see not just a lack of facilities so that magistrates like the ones in the cases cited here have nowhere to send people except prison; we also see that problem events are more likely to be seen as crime-events rather than as illness-events or social needs-events. Inner city disturbances are talked of in terms of lawlessness and wickedness; the response to the events in Newcastle, Oxford and Cardiff in the summer of 1991 was to provide for tougher sentencing of the 'new' crime of aggravated car theft rather than to initiate programmes to create jobs and recreation facilities; it is the *crimes* of the poor, the *crimes* of the young people sleeping rough, the *crimes* of the mentally ill that we care about, rather than their plight of itself. To understand this, we need to go beyond both legal theory and conventional criminology. In other words, whilst legal theory might be able to tell us what is the appropriate punishment for the crime before the court, and whilst criminology might be able to tell us that, and even sometimes why, the black defendant is more likely to end up in prison than the white defendant, we need to transcend these perspectives if we are to be able to understand why the mentally disturbed man and the homeless woman are more likely to be arrested and brought to court than to be given treatment or accommodation.

In order to understand both the lack of facilities for the mentally ill, the homeless and others in need of help or treatment outside the prisons and the wider criminal justice system, and the tendency to prioritise crime over other social problems (and to interpret events such as a sick man throwing a brick through a hospital window as crimes rather than as indicators of need for treatment), one must go beyond legal theory and criminology, and situate these questions within a critical theory of the contemporary state. In his Cobden Trust Human Rights Day lecture, Stuart Hall described political–ideological currents as '*Drifting into a Law and Order Society*' (Hall, 1980), and this conception has influenced critical analysis of public policy developments in the Thatcher–Reagan era. The 'new right' political goals are social authoritarianism and economic libertarianism, which at its simplest means increased regulation of people and their social relationships, which we can see in examples such as increased repression of homosexual relationships, making social security benefits available to young people only if they are in training, etc.; whilst at the same time there is a withdrawal of government intervention in the economy, and reduced levels of public expenditure:

> Social authoritarianism, as the phrase suggests, relied heavily on regulation via the rule of law. Also it required other pragmatic changes in order to carry through an authoritarian programme. These included massive pay rises for the police and the military; a much-publicized clampdown on welfare fraud and the development of Special Claims Control Units to investigate the 'scroungers'; the introduction of

the openly punitive 'short, sharp, shock' regime for young offenders; and eventually, the expansion of British prisons, longer sentences and restricted parole. Together with the attack on welfarism at all levels and the introduction of work-schemes for the unemployed ('long, dull, thud') these initiatives represented collectively a major structural change. (Scraton, 1987, vii)

Understanding of this structural context in which criminal justice is enacted, helps us understand why the people described in the second vignette are in court at all, and also throws some light on why the first scene was happening: not only have welfare agencies contracted as penal agencies have expanded, but the rhetoric of law and order, crime and punishment has prevailed over the rhetoric of help and treatment. My intention is to analyse the penal policy that has emerged from this drift to law and order, and further to analyse it in terms of its likely effect on the disadvantaged. In this, I am allying myself with one of the defining traditions of critical social science, that is to be working on behalf of those on the downside of power relations.

If critical social theory provides understanding of the wider currents of which penal policy developments are a part, critical criminology and critical legal studies are the frameworks within which I hope to contribute to understanding of the specifics of penal policy. Just deserts approaches to penality claim, above all, to be fair to offenders (Ashworth, 1991 *inter alia*). Deserts theorists are therefore much concerned with disparities in sentencing (disparity in the sense of giving different sentences for similar offences), they are concerned about excess penalisation of black people that cannot be explained by the crimes they have committed, and they dislike approaches to penality which imprison people for offences they may (but may not) commit in the future rather than offences which they have already committed. What legal reasoning itself cannot encompass is that penal policy is pursuing fairness in a system which is itself partial: only critical criminology can show us the penal system as the social control subsystem which regulates the behaviour of the poor. Although legal theory can put forward ideas which promote consistency and proportionality of punishment, it cannot tell us why, of all the many problems associated with criminal justice, disparity and lack of fit between crimes and punishments are the two that have engaged official as well as academic concern. We need to go beyond legal theory and penology in order to understand why penological thinking is so dominant compared with welfare thinking, and why some penological themes are vigorously addressed in debate and legislation, whilst others are neglected. If penal policy 'is less the outcome of implementing new ideas than of a discursive process through which aspects of existing practice are selected, emphasized, refined and formally discussed, while other aspects are ignored, subordinated dispersed and relegated to the informal' (Milanovic and Henry, 1991, p. 206), we need to go beyond its own terms to understand which themes are selected and which are rejected, as well as to understand why penal policy as a whole has received so much priority.

Critical social science is, then, a tradition of investigating ideological and structural shifts, of which the paradigm case is the Frankfurt school's studies of the rise of fascism in Germany in the years leading up to the Second World War. The tradition continued with studies by Frankfurt school social scientists in Germany after the war and in the countries to which they had fled during the rule of Hitler, notably Marcuse's investigations of the welfare–warfare economy in post-war USA. In England, the critical approach has been used to understand the development of new right policies, especially around the themes of racism and repression (for example, Centre for Contemporary Cultural Studies, 1982). In the sphere of crime and criminal justice, the key issues that have been addressed within the critical perspective are *criminalisation* and *paramilitarism*. Corresponding broadly to Marxist ascriptions of ideological and repressive functions to the criminal law, critical criminologists have concerned themselves with the projection of disadvantaged groups as criminal in order to promote divisions within subordinate groups – rough/respectable, deserving/non-deserving, scrounger/genuine claimant – and to shift the blame for unemployment and homelessness on to the victims themselves. The unemployed become the unemployable, the homeless become the shiftless, and the state is absolved of responsibility towards them. At the same time, crime is promoted as a more urgent social problem than unemployment, lack of health and welfare facilities, and urban decay. Paramilitarism has become a characteristic of social regulation as problem populations become (or are perceived as) more difficult: paramilitary policing accompanies police preoccupation with urban disorder; paramilitarism becomes necessary in prisons as prisoners serve longer sentences, with little prospect of parole or remission. To these basically Marxist formulations have more recently been added concerns and methods informed by post-Marxist thinkers such as Foucault, and feminist theorists. The collection of papers included in the volume *Law, Order and the*

Authoritarian State (Scraton, 1987) is a good example of this approach to criminal justice.

Critical theory is

> an approach which starts with internal criticism of existing theories in terms of their own criteria and then proceeds to generate the conceptual equipment necessary to overcome the deficiencies and closures discovered in the theories examined, and at the same time to understand social origins of the influence wielded by the theories criticised. It is thus concerned to understand the historical nature of these theories and the conditions which affect the possibility of the emergence of an alternative theory. (Hunt, 1987, p. 14)

This is exactly the approach I have taken to contemporary penal policy, moving from an examination of its major themes, through investigation of the context in which it is developed and implemented, to its closures and limitations, and considering alternative approaches such as the abolitionist agenda. My key concerns are, first, to examine the content of penal policy, and, second, to analyse its dominance over competing perspectives such as the social work/psychiatric discourse.

Much recent criminological writing has been from the so-called 're-alist' perspective: the right realists such as Wilson who are advocating tough penalties for crime, and the left realists. Left realists such as Jock Young and Roger Matthews have distinguished themselves from those whom they define as 'left idealists' by insisting on the reality of crime. Crime, they say, is a serious problem, and in particular it affects the lives of the underprivileged and subordinated groups with whom the left idealists profess themselves to be concerned. In this insistence on the reality and seriousness of crime as a social problem – rather than just the criminalisation that is the focus for critical criminology – they might be described as realists in the sense of being pragmatists, but they are also realists in the epistemological sense of being concerned with the real as opposed to the ideological. Realist epistemology contends that there is a factual world, but that understanding of it is distorted by ideological misrepresentation; the Marxist distinction between appearance and reality is the basis of this approach (Keat and Urry, 1982). Thus, realist criminologists seek to establish the reality of crime by conducting surveys of victims, and they seek to promote law enforcement and criminal justice strategies which respond to 'real' causes of crime rather than being based on the uncaring and uncomprehending reactions of the new right. Although I might disagree with some of the causal connections expressed in some left realist writings and although I might worry about some of the penal strategies they appear to accept with equanimity, my main difference from their work is that the questions I seek to address here are questions which are begged by their description of the criminological enterprise rather than encompassed by it:

> there undoubtedly exists a disproportionate number of blacks and ethnic minorities in the prison systems of most western countries. To an extent such disproportionality would be alleviated by a justice which was colour blind, but it would scarcely tackle the fact that poor people (and hence blacks) are under greater pressure to commit the crimes which are at present the focus of the criminal justice system and prisonization. (Young and Matthews, 1992, p. 5)

Whilst I would be in complete agreement with this statement, I am concerned as to why criminal justice professionals and so many reformers and theorists seem to be content with this 'extent' to which overimprisonment might be reduced by deserts sentencing. Secondly, I am exploring the ways in which the crimes of the poor are made the focus of the criminal justice system, rather than demonstrating the circumstances which propel them into criminality. Moreover, the left realists have taken as their task the reduction of crime: 'Let us state quite categorically that the major task of radical criminology is to seek a solution to the problem of crime and that of a socialist policy is to substantially reduce the crime rate' (Young, 1986, p. 28). I might well disagree with this, or at least think that even if it were the *major* task, it is certainly not the *only* one – investigation of state practices and ideologies seems to me a legitimate and necessary function of social science, especially academic social science. That is not the point, here, however. I would certainly not dissent from realist opinion as to the strategies that should be adopted to reduce crime:

> the endemic problems of society at large, namely, gross economic inequality and patriarchy – that is, *structural* problems – are of greater importance in the creation and control of crime than unfairness and injustice in the *administration* of justice. Intervention to control crime must, therefore, prioritize social intervention over

criminal justice intervention. (Young and Matthews, 1992, pp. 3–4)

My focus is on why England and Wales, the USA and to a lesser extent Western European countries, have done exactly the opposite of this – that is they have prioritised criminal justice policy and expenditure over other spheres. To a large extent, this book is addressed to the question of why, especially in England and Wales, the law-and-order, crime–criminal justice frame of reference is quite so dominant, and on that question, the critical theory concept of criminalisation is more relevant than the work of the realists. The probation service is highlighted in particular because it represents this 'drift to law and order' so closely. In spite of everything probation officers know about the structural problems facing their 'clients' and their consequent need for help, they have largely jettisoned their social work ethos and taken on the juridical discourse. In the wake of the 1991 Criminal Justice Act, probation officers of all grades are receiving training in sentencing aims, criteria for custody and the judicial perspective on sentencing; there is no reciprocal training of judges and magistrates in sociology, psychology and social policy.

Another interesting question begged by the realists' statement of purpose is why, when penal intervention is given priority over social intervention, the penal theory that gains most assent is the one theory which makes no claims for effectiveness in crime reduction. Incapacitation theory claims crime reduction efficacy by keeping likely reoffenders out of circulation; deterrence theory claims that exemplary punishment will stop potential criminals from crimes they might commit if they thought the punishment would be worth the likely gain; deserts theory, on the other hand, makes no such claims, and deserts theorists admit that 'more can probably be achieved through various techniques of situational crime prevention, social crime prevention, and general social and educational policies' (Ashworth, 1991, p. 13).

That the drift to law and order has led to pre-eminence of one of the few forms of penal policy that justifies itself in terms of fairness to offenders rather than effectiveness in reducing crime, is a nice irony, worthy of exploration. The more that criminalisation of subordinated groups is pursued, the more that penal provision takes precedence over social provision, the more dominant becomes legal reasoning, and what contemporary policy represents more than anything is the triumph of legal thought. Legal ways of looking at problems; the use of law to regulate social relationships; the recourse to law by citizens as well as the state when they have troubles to be dealt with; the prevalence of legal concepts such as rights and obligations over social concepts such as help and need, are recognised by the relational theory of law which has been developed within the critical legal studies tradition:

> relational theory facilitates the recognition and exploration of the degree and forms in which legal relations penetrate other forms of social relations. This point does not just involve the well-known thesis that modern law increasingly reaches its regulatory arm into more and more social relations. It also embraces the idea that the 'presence of law' within social relations is not just to be gauged by institutional interventions but also by the presence of legal concepts and ideas within types of social relations that appear to be free of law. (Hunt, 1987, p. 17)

It is not just, then, that the criminal justice/penal system has been given much more scope and resourcing than the health/welfare system, but that legal reasoning has come to dominate penal thinking, and also thinking in other spheres such as mental health and child welfare.

Critical legal studies and critical criminology, then, have given me the basic framework for my analysis, and I intend the work as a contribution to the critical exploration of regulation of problem populations in the Thatcher–Reagan, Major–Bush era.

Penal policy and social justice

Underlying the whole work is a belief that penal policy has as its ultimate justification that it contributes to social justice. The social injustice endured by the groups with whom penal policy and criminal justice are primarily concerned has been put aside by penal theorists, who by and large have taken the view that they cannot do anything to redress wider social injustices, what they can do is protect the people with whom the courts come into contact from the additional injustice of unfair punishment: 'Whatever is "just" in the sentencing aim of "just deserts" is not a wider social justice, but the justice of reflecting sound principles of state punishment' (Ashworth, 1991, p. 13). By insisting on 'due process', by legal forms and legal safeguards, legal injustice can be avoided, even if penal policy has no concern with social inequalities. A contrary view, expressed by some Marxist legal theorists and by penal abolitionists, is that there can be no legal justice in a socially unjust society, and that therefore the whole notion of law and rights needs to be abandoned, or at least the criminal and justice penal system should be dismantled.

My view is that both the juridical denial of a necessary relationship between the penal realm and wider social policies, and the position of total denial of the possibility of justice, are unhelpful. There is of necessity a relationship between penal policy and social justice, since there is a relationship between all public policy and social justice. My argument is that penal policy must recognise itself as an element of public policy and not claim to be somehow separate from, and the guardian of virtues superior to, other domains of public policy. It must acknowledge that contributing to social justice is the justifying objective of any policy subsystem.

It is ironic that at the same time that penal policy has eschewed the aspiration of 'doing good' it has avowed that of 'doing justice', as though the two are somehow different. Since publishing my earlier critique of the justice model of penality, I have frequently been asked how I can possibly be 'against justice'? I am not, but I am against very narrow conceptions of (legal) justice dominating our engagement with people and their problems, so that insights which might bring about more socially just solutions are excluded. Commensurate punishment is not always the 'just' solution: there are occasions when not to punish might be just; when treatment might be a requirement of humanity rather than a presumption of 'needology'; when including someone on a caseload might be safety net-providing rather than net-widening. There may, as the jurists say, be 'one right answer' in every case, but the central contention of this book is that the right answer can only be arrived at with the contributions of several ways of thinking.

Organisation of the book

This book, then, is a reflection on the relationship between penal policy and social justice. Chapter 1 presents an overview of penal policy over the last twenty or so years, a time of unprecedented activity in policy reformulation and practice innovation. The story that is told is of a gradual clarification of policy from reactive, crisis-driven innovation to clear, openly articulated principles, with some principles having emerged as dominant over competing trends. Chapter 2 looks at the relationship between penal policy and social structure, and discusses the various theories that have been proposed to explain that relationship. The question which concerns that chapter is whether the reforms of penal policy aimed at reducing disparity have any potential for reducing discrimination. In Chapter 3, I am concerned with the connections between penal policy and social policy, especially policy towards the mentally ill. I review the literature on decarceration and transcarceration, and also look at discursive aspects of the increasing tendency to punish the badness of the mad, rather than treat the madness of the bad. Chapter 4 looks at the effects of penal policy on penal practice and criminal justice agencies. In particular, the problems of prison crowding and conditions, and penal inflation and aggregation in non-custodial sanctions are discussed.

Having analysed the existing relationship between penal policy and social justice in these chapters, Chapter 5 looks at proposals put forward by penal reformers, criminologists and the like – proposals which have come to seem more acceptable to the official mind in the light of ever rising costs, the difficulties of translating their policies into practice, and dramatic events like prison riots. This chapter draws heavily on the work of Pat Carlen (1989) and Roger Matthews (1989). The final chapter considers the possibilities for these reform proposals being successful, and argues that it is legal theory itself, the dominance of jurisprudential assumptions in our thinking about crime, that presents the most formidable obstacle. Abolitionism and feminist critiques of law are enlisted to help see the limits of jurisprudence for dealing with crime in ways consistent with ideals of social justice. In clarifying my own position on these issues I was greatly assisted by the publication of Valerie Kerruish's analysis of the ideological nature of jurisprudence, and I have adopted Nicola Lacey's formula for the rationing of punishment (Kerruish, 1991; Lacey, 1988).

The obvious omission in all this is a discussion or definition of social justice itself. I do not wish to engage in esoteric philosophical debate, first and foremost because what I mean by social justice seems to me well understood and commonly shared by almost all those whom I have met working within the probation service, juvenile justice, in policy-making and academic circles, and whose books and papers I read. Social justice, for me, denotes a society governed by consent rather than coercion, with rights and benefits evenly distributed among citizens. This simple form of words involves, of course, a complex reality, with government acting in the interests of all rather than favouring sectional interests; with government interference in the lives of citizens limited to preventing harm and providing welfare goods which individuals cannot provide individually but must arrange collectively; with sex-, race- and class-derived social inequality eliminated and with material inequality restrained by equality of opportunity; with legal definitions of criminal behaviour corresponding to general sentiments; and with the weak protected and the predatory restrained, a reality which present society is very far from embodying. However far from the ideal actual society might be, my argument is that all forms of public policy should acknowledge the obligation to contribute towards the achievement of this ideal.

Denying the relationship between penal policy and social justice is wrong on at least two counts. First, penal policy is bound to have some effect, for good or ill, on social justice:

> Although it is true that no change in criminal justice practices would be sufficient to eliminate the structural inequalities in our society, it is also true that changes in criminal justice practices can do a great deal to make matters worse. Every movement towards stronger repression through the criminal justice system widens and deepens the gulf between our stated commitment to overcoming racism and inequality and the realities of our current social and economic practices.
>
> Criminal justice issues cannot be separated from issues of social and distributive justice. It is crucial to acknowledge that given current realities, punishment designed to protect and affirm existing social order also reinforces inequalities in opportunity and status. Honoring our commitment to true justice requires that we stop acting as if the goal were just to get tougher, when those who will feel the sting most are those who already suffer the most from the absence of broader social justice. (Harris, 1987, p. 216)

A straw is just a straw, but penal policy ought to ensure it is removing straws from the camel's back of inequality, rather than adding them. Secondly, it is through its claims to contribute to the just society that criminal law, penal policy and the infliction of punishment derives legitimacy. Questions of the right to punish, the duty to obey the law even in an unjust society are considered in the final chapter, for now it is enough to say that without its necessity for the achievement of a just society, there is no basis for criminal law and so for penal policy to dissociate itself from problems of social injustice is (definitionally) absurd. The notion of justice I have sketched is fully compatible with the 'justice as fairness' formulation of John Rawls, a conception of justice which is echoed in deserts theory. Rawls theory, however, distinguishes between the 'original position', prior to any social contract, when people are equal, so equal that they do not have any idea of their position in society, and tells us that it is only in this (imaginary) position that a citizen could propose truly impartial laws. If someone was aware of themselves as rich, he explains, they would naturally propose laws that would favour the rich, for instance they would be against taxation for the provision of welfare, whereas if they were aware of themselves as poor, they would favour high taxation (Rawls, 1972, pp. 18–19). In the actual position, when social benefits are very unequally divided, then justice as fairness requires that any redistribution of benefits by social institutions should be in the direction of bestowing greater benefits on the least advantaged. By the definition of justice which has found most favour among contemporary legal theorists, therefore, social inequalities should be taken into account in the allocation of benefits and pains in criminal justice. Other contemporary philosophical reflections on the nature of justice which have been taken up by penologists and legal scholars, for example Gewirth's *Principle of Generic Consistency*, also lead towards taking account of all the circumstances surrounding an offence. In particular, Gewirth's principle seems to urge us towards widening the scope of our ideas of culpability and adopting a weaker definition of freedom of choice than that which lies behind present representations of free will and the reasoning criminal, since the principle (which essentially combines the Kantian moral imperative – do that which you could wish to be universalised – and his command to treat people as ends not means, with the modern phenomenological precept of reciprocity of perspectives) requires us to appreciate others' conditions of action along with our own (Gewirth, 1978).

I am not proposing, therefore, any new theory of social justice, but insisting, by taking seriously jurisprudence's own conditions of existence, by taking seriously the definitions of justice and the justifications for criminal law and the existence of punishment that legal theorists themselves espouse, that penal policy cannot ignore the reciprocal effects of its own practices and those of other areas of social policy.

1 Developments in Penal Policy during the 1980s

At the beginning of the 1980s, crime and criminal justice were widely held to be in crisis – crisis of dramatic and urgent dimensions in the USA and England and Wales, and crisis to a somewhat lesser extent in other Western countries. This crisis was many faceted: crime rates were rising, imprisonment rates were rising, policy responses were unclear and inadequate, public anxiety and media attention were aroused to a degree uncomfortable and unaccustomed for politicians and criminal justice professionals (Bottomley and Coleman, 1980). The crisis was thus variously described as a crisis of management, a crisis of legitimation, and a crisis of effectiveness (Matthews, 1988, p. 4). Furthermore, things looked set to get worse rather than better, with consequential rises in prison overcrowding, soaring public expenditure, and further loss of public confidence (Bottoms and Preston, 1980). It looked intractable: just as the problem of rising crime had not been solved by the expansionary, social-democratic social policies of the 1950s and 1960s (Taylor, 1981), and the problem of rising interventiveness and extensiveness of punishments had not been solved by the liberal-democratic penal policies of the 1960s and 1970s (Austin and Krisberg, 1981; Cohen, 1985; Thorpe *et al.*, 1980) so it seemed that prison populations were not falling in response to the reductionist, liberal-conservative fiscal and social policies of the late 1970s and 1980s (Scull, 1984). Rather than a reduced criminal justice system ambit, what seemed to happen was that the penal net widened, strengthened and tightened as the social welfare net narrowed and loosened, that rather than witnessing decarceration we were seeing 'transcarceration' (Lowman, Menzies and Palys, 1987), manifest particularly in the apparent transfer of the mentally disordered from hospitals to prisons, and of young people from children's homes to penal establishments.

Policy responses were fragmentary, often contradictory, and lacked any clear rationale. Initiatives were rarely aimed at fundamentals: one penalty might be substituted for another, relative powers of courts might be adjusted, fines might be raised in line with inflation; often changes were in nomenclature rather than in substance, for example changing the name of 'borstals' to 'youth custody establishments' and then to 'young

17

offender institutions'. There did not seem to be policy emerging that was
the result of deep analytical thinking about penal purposes, despite the
setting up of impressive sounding advisory councils, royal commissions,
presidential enquiries and the like. No clear goals or major objectives
could be derived from reading of statutes or from observations of criminal justice decision-making (Hogarth, 1971), and it was even suggested
that legislatures appeared to view definition of goals as politically undesirable or, at least, impossibly difficult (Kittrie, 1980).

Responses to crime varied greatly with time and place. 'Justice by
geography' became a catchphrase of the 1970s and early 1980s (Krisberg,
undated) as statistics were produced showing wide variations in penal
practices – especially in the use of imprisonment – within countries and
between ostensibly similar nations such as the member states of the
European Community (Kress, 1980; NACRO, 1988). 'League tables'
showing per capita rates of imprisonment such as those compiled by
the Council of Europe concerning the prison populations (Table 1.1) in
member countries in 1988 received wide publicity.

The NACRO report which publicised these figures pointed out that
the differences in imprisonment rates could not be explained by differences in crime rates, quoting David Faulkner, Deputy Under-Secretary at
the Home Office, as saying of crime rates:

> the situation in the rest of Western Europe is very much the same as
> ours – some countries have a bit more burglary or a bit less trouble
> with motor vehicles, but by and large you cannot say you are any
> better or worse off in France, Holland or the Scandinavian countries
> than you are in England and Wales. (Faulkner, D., 1987, quoted in
> NACRO, 1989, p. 2)

Similar series demonstrated differences between the member states in
the federal nations (USA, Canada, Australia, West Germany*) and between towns and regions in the unitary states (e.g. Austin and Krisberg,
1985; Biles, 1986).

Rates of imprisonment are constructed from a complex network of
penal practices, and although they are used by reformers to argue for
countries' comparative punitiveness, the proportion of a population which

---

*The terms West Germany or Federal Republic of Germany have been retained when
referring to situations, policies, research, statistics etc. obtaining or carried out before
reunification.

Table 1.1

Country	Number of prisoners per 100 000 population
Luxembourg	103.4
United Kingdom	98.2
Austria	96.0
Finland	93.0
France	92.0
Turkey	90.2
West Germany	86.7
Portugal	84.0
Switzerland	77.6
Belgium	70.5
Spain	69.2
Denmark	69.0
Italy	62.0
Sweden	61.0
Ireland	56.0
Norway	47.0
Greece	42.9
Cyprus	42.0
Iceland	41.3
Holland	36.0
Malta	19.7

SOURCE: NACRO, 1989, p. 1

is imprisoned at any one time is at best a very crude indicator of national propensities in attitudes towards crime and punishment (Lynch, 1988). Aggregate figures like these conceal important constituents of the prison population such as usage for remand or for sentenced prisoners, lengths of sentence and numbers of receptions, social composition of the prison population, the purposes which a prison sentence is meant to serve, and the offences for which it is considered the appropriate response. Nations (and states/regions) also differ greatly in their ranges of alternative, non-custodial penalties, their rules for who is eligible or not for non-custodial sanctions, regulation regarding parole, remission, sentence substitution, etc. 'Justice by geography' is therefore a catchphrase which conceals many complexities, and cross-national comparisons in criminal justice are hazardous and may be misleading. None the less, during the last twenty or so years there has been considerable and growing interest by policy-makers and criminologists in their neighbours' penal practices.

In looking at comparative systems and policies, we gain an impression of disparity of outcome based on diversity of legislation, institutions, procedures and practices. As well as the broad division into common-law-based systems (the Anglo-Saxon countries) and code-based systems (most of continental Europe), countries can be classified by the prominence they give to different penal purposes. Although in modern times all advanced industrial nations have embraced the aim of reform/ rehabilitation/resocialisation of offenders, this has variously been combined mainly with retribution (USA, England and Wales, West Germany), deterrence (the Scandinavian countries) and incapacitation (France, Italy), with the result that, among other things, offences such as theft and burglary with a largely intentional character have been associated with extensive use of imprisonment in England and the USA, whereas offences such as drinking with excess alcohol which frequently have unintended but serious social consequences (death and injury to other road users) usually (and mandatorily, for example in Norway) lead to custody in Scandinavia and the Netherlands. The likelihood of reoffending estimated on social–personal characteristics of offenders is a strong correlate of imprisonment in countries with a 'social defence' penal tradition which aims to protect society by reforming those deemed susceptible to reform and incapacitating through isolation and incarceration those who are judged poor prospects for reform. In Belgium, for instance, non-custodial penalties are discouraged for 'those lacking the necessary qualities' for reform. Qualities cited as presumptions against community penalties include vagrancy, habitual offending, sadism, perversion and mental illness (Bishop, 1988, p. 50).

The 1970s and early 1980s: frantic innovation

Although major differences exist in traditional penal philosophies, institutional arrangements, procedural conventions, ranges of available sentences, etc., some significant trends emerged during the 1970s and 1980s which could be discerned in most Western countries. These trends had coalesced by the end of the 1980s into an emergent penal orthodoxy offering a clearer, more widely accepted rationale for the distribution of punishments generally, and for the imposition of imprisonment in particular, than has been apparent for very many years.

One of the first manifestations of this development was the proliferation of so-called 'alternatives to custody' in the 1970s and 1980s.

Although most countries still have fewer possible sentences than the United Kingdom, most have experimented with one or more of suspended sentences, intermittent or part-time custody, enhanced probation, community service, curfews, and have tried to extend the scope of standard penalties, for example raising the levels of fines, so that they can be seen as sufficient punishment for more serious offences, or relating them to income so that they become feasible for more offenders. Whilst the criminal justice system in England and Wales has tried or is trying all these disposals except intermittent custody (which has been proposed several times but withdrawn following opposition by somewhat unlikely alliances of radical reformers and traditionalists such as the Magistrates' Association (Hudson, 1985)), most countries have shown more restraint. Suspended sentences, often combined with fines, are available widely, and community service is one of the most highly regarded innovations, having been adopted for instance in Canada, Australia, New Zealand, and The Netherlands. Most states in the United States have developed enhanced probation programmes, often involving community service, curfews (electronically monitored in some states) and in combination with what in England are seen as separate sentences, such as suspended prison sentences and fines or compensation.

This search for alternatives to custody is generally taken to reflect growing disillusionment with the efficacy of prison for reforming criminals, as well as alarm at the costs of mass imprisonment. The development of prisons with a reformative mission has been well documented (*inter alia* Foucault, 1977; Garland, 1985; Ignatieff, 1978 and Rothman, 1971), and whilst this has been taken to have occurred in all the industrialising countries from the late eighteenth and twentieth centuries, disillusionment with prison as a suitable arena for reform and rehabilitation, though persistent, has been more piecemeal and sporadic. Wholesale disbelief in the value of imprisonment has been shown to occur in particular combinations of time and place (Rutherford, 1984) or to affect particular societies because of configurations of experience and intellectual tradition (De Haan, 1990), or to be voiced by particular groups or individuals within societies (for example, American Friends Service Committee, 1972; Mitford, 1974), but it is only recently that it has been reasonable to claim that 'the scepticism concerning the prison as a place of treatment has now become a part of formal criminal policy in virtually every European country' (Bishop, 1988, p. 47).

The decline of rehabilitation as a primary principle of penality has been extensively written about (Bean, 1976; Gaylin *et al.*, 1978; Hudson,

1987), but its replacement by an alternative penal policy has in most places followed rather than preceded the expansion of alternatives to imprisonment. In the 1970s and at least the early 1980s rehabilitation was still an important – if not pre-eminent in more than a very few jurisdictions – penal aim, and so loss of faith in the rehabilitative potential of imprisonment was an initial stimulant to the expansion of alternative sanctions. (Imprisonment indeed can be held to fail according to most conceivable aims of punishment (Mathiesen, 1990) and so it is not surprising that the search for acceptable alternatives has been shared by so many people in so many places.) The search for alternatives to custody in most jurisdictions has been specifically concentrated on the replacement of short custodial sentences. These are generally held to be damaging in that they disrupt the offender's employment and training, personal and social relationships, without giving time for any education or therapy to take place within the institution. In addition, there is the widely deplored 'contagion' effect, whereby offenders not yet irrevocably motivated towards a life of crime come into contact with more hardened, more committed criminals. A United Nations sponsored study on the development of non-custodial penalties in Europe remarked on this widespread desire to replace short custodial sentences with fines, community service, or to suspend such sentences. In surveying the arrangements for apportioning penalties the study reports that in many countries short sentences of up to six or twelve months imprisonment are usually suspended or replaced by fines (Kalmthout and Tak, 1988, p. 3), whilst in other countries they are expected to be avoided altogether in favour of community sanctions. There is variation in whether alternatives to custody are prescribed, encouraged or merely provided, and although most countries discourage the use of short sentences, either by legislation or persuasion, there are exceptions to this. A survey of the use of non-custodial sanctions in Europe by the Helsinki Institute for Crime Prevention and Control (an institution sponsored by the United Nations) quotes a Dutch criminologist summarising the situation:

> four groups [of countries] can be distinguished. The first is formed by countries which accord official priority to alternatives in their legislation. This is done, for example, by imposing restrictive conditions on the application of custodial sentences, thereby encouraging the use of alternatives. This category includes those countries which permit the body responsible for executing sentences to replace the custodial sentence imposed by a fine or other sanction. The second

group seeks the solution in more radical methods. Punishments below a given minimum are excluded. The minimum varies from 14 days to one month. The third group is that in which the alternatives to custodial sentences are provided by the legislature without any special encouragement being given to the courts to make a particular choice. The legislature confines itself to providing options. Finally, there are countries which, far from seeking to solve the problem by creating alternatives or encouraging the use of alternatives, actually preach the benefits of short custodial sentences in the hope of thus raising the threshold to long custodial sentences. (Stolwijk, 1986, quoted by Bishop, 1988, pp. 59–60)

Examples include Italy, where short custodial sentences may be (and often are) replaced by fines, Greece, where they are usually suspended or replaced by fines, and Austria and Germany, where the legislation requires that fines should be substituted for sentences of up to six months, unless there are special considerations of prevention which indicate otherwise (Bishop, 1988, p. 102). By and large, countries which emphasise the denunciatory and general deterrence functions of punishment favour replacement or suspension of sentences once pronounced, whereas those emphasising retribution and individual deterrence have concentrated more on the development of community-based alternative sanctions.

In the United Kingdom, we have wavered between these various positions. Mandatory suspension of prison sentences up to six months was introduced in the 1968 Criminal Justice Act but soon repealed, the reason usually given being that the judiciary undermined the legislative intent by giving very few such short sentences in order to get around mandatory suspension. The result of the introduction of suspended sentences in England has been held to be an increase rather than a decrease in overall imprisonment; first, because of longer sentences being given to avoid mandatory suspension, and second, by imprisonment being imposed for breach of suspended sentences (Bottoms, 1981).

Suspended sentences have never been popular in England, and it is noteworthy that they have not been made available for juveniles, the group for which there is the most generally shared view that custody should be avoided. This dislike of suspended sentences seems to be carried forward in the 1991 Criminal Justice Act, which provides that courts may suspend custodial sentences for offenders aged 21 and over in 'exceptional circumstances' (Criminal Justice Act 1991, Section 5(1)), and stipulates that suspended sentences should be combined with a compensation order and/or fine (Home Office, 1992).

The community service order, introduced into England and Wales in the Criminal Justice Act 1972, was clearly intended by the Home Office as an alternative to short prison sentences: 'The community service order was introduced with the primary purpose of providing a constructive alternative for those offenders who would otherwise have received a short custodial sentence' (Home Office, 1978, p. 21) – but this was not buttressed by any legislative restrictions on its use. The 1972 Act did make the proviso that it was only to be used for imprisonable offences, but this is, of course, a very wide category, and does not say that it should be restricted to cases where a prison sentence has actually been deemed appropriate. Lack of legislative guidance and differences in the views of many sentencers as to the proper use of community service has meant that although it soon became a very popular sentence, it does not seem to have had much effect in reducing prison populations (Bottoms, 1987). Again the 1991 Criminal Justice Act continues the language of sentences being 'available' to courts in referring to all the community sentences which it provides, and in referring specifically to community service says that 'there is no longer any suggestion that this order is an alternative to custody' (Home Office, 1992, p. 24).

Not only have we not made suspended sentences available for young offenders, but as recently as the 1980s we experimented with the short detention centre sentence, with no rehabilitative content, with the aim of administering a 'taste of custody' to young people. Similar adherence to the shock value of a short period of incarceration is evident in the USA, where in many states probation is combined with a prison sentence of up to a year rather than being an alternative to custody, and where a probation order is made as a sentence in its own right, it may well commence with a few days' 'shock' incarceration (Kress, 1980). In Canada, too, studies of appeal decisions show short sentences of imprisonment for such offences as breaking and entering and petty theft being upheld on the grounds that they 'teach (especially young) people a lesson' (Jobson, 1980).

Another strategy to avoid short sentences is the introduction of criteria for the imposition of custodial sentences. First offenders, non-violent offenders, and offenders participating voluntarily in treatment programmes are candidates for non-imposition in most countries, and

here in the UK we have mixed the taste of custody message by introducing criteria for imposing custody on offenders under the age of 21,
and on those who have not previously served a custodial sentence.
Introduced in 1982, the criteria were so worded as to allow for imprisonment under most circumstances, the criteria of seriousness of the offence, danger to the public or failure to respond to previous disposals
being left unspecified, and therefore available for invocation almost at
judicial will (Burney, 1985). The criteria were extended in 1988, by
adding the words 'history of', to the failure to respond to previous
disposals criteria, which meant that having had a previous disposal such
as probation or community service would not make custody inevitable
for a further offence. With the emphasis on current offence being the
main principle of the 1991 Criminal Justice Act this clause is removed
and the new criteria listed in section 1 are:

(a) The offence and, if appropriate one other offence associated with
    it, is so serious that no other form of penalty would be justified.
(b) The offence is a violent or sexual offence, and the court is of the
    opinion that the public must be protected from serious harm from
    the individual.
(c) The offender has refused a community sentence which requires
    his or her consent.

In addition to developing wider repertoires of penalties, many countries in the 1970s and early 1980s made efforts to divert people not
only from custody, but also from sentences and even court appearances
altogether. Innovations such as police cautioning schemes and dis-
continuance of prosecutions were meant to divert some people out of
the criminal justice system altogether, whilst ideas such as reparation
by offenders to victims, and mediation between victims and offenders
were introduced for use in some cases instead of prosecution, in other
circumstances instead of punishment. Such schemes have undoubtedly
had some success in that the rate of young people – on whom they are
principally targeted – being prosecuted or imprisoned declined in many
places, and their extension to adults is being urged on the basis of their
effect in the de-escalation of criminal justice intervention in the lives
of young people. Prosecutors in West Germany, for example, have wide
powers to dismiss cases for both juvenile and adult offenders – even for
reasonably serious offences provided that supervisory, therapeutic or

voluntary treatment is undertaken – and to order reparative measures (Feest, 1991), much of the reduction in imprisonment achieved there being ascribed to this non-prosecution policy. The low detention rate in The Netherlands is also associated with the practice of wide prosecutorial discretion to dismiss cases (Muncie and Sparks, 1991, p. 96). None the less, there has been considerable criticism, especially of the early variants of these schemes, in that they had expansionary rather than reductionary affects and were used for people who, without their existence, may not have been formally processed at all (Austin and Krisberg, 1981, 1982; Lemert, 1981).

Whilst all this activity to reduce the use of imprisonment has been under way, most countries have seen prison populations rising (Table 1.2), and have been adding to rather than subtracting from prison capacity.

We can see that even countries which are traditionally parsimonious in their use of custody, such as Sweden and The Netherlands, have not been immune from this trend. There are differences regarding which segment of the prison population has been rising, for instance, the figures below are aggregates of sentenced and remand populations, and are made up of rises of 2 per cent in the remand population and 18.3 per cent in the sentenced population in France, but in Sweden on the other hand the remand population rose by 5 per cent whilst the sentenced population fell by 2.3 per cent, and in England and Wales the sentenced population rose by .03 per cent as against a rise in the remand

Table 1.2   Changes in prison populations from 1 February 1986
to 11 February 1987

Country	% increase
Belgium	8.5
France	10.2
Greece	9.8
Ireland	3.2
Netherlands	5.1
Spain	10.1
Sweden	2.8
England and Wales	3.0

SOURCE: Council of Europe, 1987, p. 24

population of 13.0 per cent. A prison capacity of 4900 cell places in The Netherlands was expected to rise to 7000 by 1990–1, and it has been noted that as cell capacity rose so did prison populations (ibid., p. 38).

There are many reasons put forward for this general rise in the use of custody, amongst them rising unemployment (Box and Hale, 1982, 1985), rising rates of violent crime (Michalowski and Pearson, 1987), the break-up of social institutions such as the family and the community (Kalmthout and Tak, 1988). In England and Wales, rising rates of violent crime have been particularly favoured as an explanation (Baldock, 1980). The number of offenders sentenced for violence against the person rose from 48.4 thousand in 1979 to 55.7 thousand in 1989; the number sentenced to immediate custody for violence against the person rose from 7.1 thousand in 1979 to 9.1 thousand in 1989 (Home Office, 1990a).

Prison crowding became an issue in many places. Responses to the problem have been summarised by Kalmthout and Tak in their survey of sanctions in the member states of the Council of Europe:

– automation of the administration of the prison system in order to optimalise the occupation rate in prisons (Sweden);
– building new penal establishments and re-opening closed ones (France, the Netherlands, UK);
– a general amnesty or pardon (France, July–August 1981, 12,000 prisoners, Italy, December 1986, approx 8,000 prisoners); setting priorities for the use of pre-trial detention (Netherlands) or reducing the use of pre-trial detention (France);
– privatising the execution of prison sentences (France);
– making greater use of conditional release (Netherlands, Denmark). (Kalmthout and Tak, 1988, p. 7)

In England and Wales, pre-trial detention reduction has also been attempted through strengthening the presumption for bail, bail information verification schemes and bail hostels. Conditional release for short-sentenced, non-violent offenders has been made near automatic, and privatisation is now being introduced, at least experimentally. Most of the solutions listed above are in use in the USA; there are very few states which by the mid-1980s had not introduced guidelines or policies of some sort to regulate the use of imprisonment.

There is now an extensive literature on the development of guidelines in the USA (Hudson, 1987; Wasik and Pease, 1987 *inter alia*). Although some were formulated to reflect clear penal philosophies, the most celebrated being the desert-based Minnesota guidelines, and some – Minnesota again – had regard to prison capacity, more were concerned simply with reducing disparities in terms of imprisonment given or actually served (Kittrie, 1980; Nagel, 1990). The existence of guidelines does not necessarily imply a penal philosophy, but it does involve some thought being given to the proper use of imprisonment. Studies of the various guidelines and determinate sentencing laws have discerned behind them principles of desert, public protection, or simply the reduction of disparity through legislating averages of terms typically being served.

Whilst it is now (almost) common ground among professionals and reformers that too many non-violent offenders are imprisoned for short, non-productive sentences, and whilst prison statistics of many nations reveal a preponderance of non-professional property offenders amongst inmates, reduction of such imprisonment has been less marked than the trend towards increased average prison terms, and increased numbers of long-term prisoners. These trends certainly apply to England and Wales. Whilst the proportion of offenders sentenced to immediate imprisonment for theft and handling stolen goods fell by only 1 per cent from 10 per cent in 1980 to 9 per cent in 1989, and the proportion sentenced to immediate imprisonment for fraud and forgery was exactly the same in 1989 as in 1980 (13 per cent), the proportionate use of immediate custody for drugs offences rose from 7 per cent in 1980 to 16 per cent in 1989 (Home Office, 1990a). Between 1979 and 1989 the proportion of adult males sentenced to terms of over four years increased from 22 to 37 per cent, and for females the proportion sentenced to over three years increased from 16 to 42 per cent (Home Office, 1990b). During the latter half of the 1980s, the number of people in prisons in England and Wales serving sentences of over four years doubled, from 6077 in 1984 to 12 178 in 1990 (*Criminal Law Review*, editorial, April 1992). In France, the proportion of sentences of up to three months declined by 2 per cent from 1980 to 1988, but longer sentences increased during the 1980s (Table 1.3).

A Dutch study has similarly reported the trend for prison populations to contain increasing proportions of people serving long terms for serious offences (Brand-Koolen, 1987), whilst a world-wide survey reported a general trend towards more life sentences (Eratt and Neudek, 1992). Regardless of any desire to reduce sentence lengths, several factors mitigate against this. First, there has been the removal of the

Table 1.3   Prison population in metropolitan France: rate of increase over seven years

	1.1.81	*1.1.88*	*% change*
5 years up to 10	2822	3058	8.4
10–20 years	1850	2783	50.4
Life	349	415	18.9

SOURCE: Faugeron, 1989

death penalty in progressively more countries and in some states of the USA, and the tendency to impose life sentences or long prison terms in some countries (Greece, for example) where the death penalty remains on statute. Secondly, there has been a marked growth in crimes of a very serious nature which cross national boundaries, and where federal and international agreements have resulted in more lenient jurisdictions standardising upwards to a harsher level. Terrorism, especially airline terrorism, drugs trafficking and international company fraud are prime examples. Whilst most countries would agree that people involved in such crimes deserve the most severe penalties available, the penalties becoming standard look harsh in the traditions of the UK and Indiana, where presumptive sentences given for classes of crimes of different seriousness range from 30 to 60 years or death for murder, 20 to 50 years for class A offences (including kidnapping and rape), 6 to 20 years for class B offences (including armed robbery and arson), 2 to 8 years for class C offences (unarmed robbery), to 2 to 4 years for class D offences (theft, incest), rather than harsh in the traditions of The Netherlands or Minnesota. According to the Minnesota guidelines, the presumptive term for burglary with three previous offences is eighteen months if a prison sentence is deemed necessary – the in–out line incorporated in the guidelines suggests that a non-custodial sentence would normally be given in such cases, as it would for theft with less than six previous convictions (Hudson, 1987, pp. 73–7).

New levels of consciousness have led to certain offences being taken more seriously, resulting sometimes in more prison sentences, sometimes in longer sentences. Driving with excess alcohol, for example, has long been an offence frequently punished by imprisonment in Scandinavia, but one that usually produced a fine in the UK. The proportion of such cases resulting in imprisonment in England and Wales has risen steadily in the last years of the 1980s, with much public support. In 1980, 9 per cent of motoring offences resulted in immediate custodial sentences and in 1988 this had risen to 15 per cent; in 1980, 71 per cent of motoring offences were punished by fines, but in 1988 this figure had dropped to 50 per cent (Home Office, 1990a). Unless the offence is repeated or produces death or injury, sentences are usually short, and this is probably one of very few crimes where the 'short, sharp shock' is (increasingly) thought appropriate. Sentence lengths have increased considerably for rape in the UK and elsewhere, again to general public approval; five years is now generally regarded as a 'starting point' (Samuels, 1987). Part of this increased punitiveness can be attributed to the success of feminist groups in challenging interpretations of consent, and to the discrediting of judgments which allow for victim connivance or precipitation through provocative dress, going out unaccompanied, etc. (Box-Grainger, 1986). As well as this increase in normal sentence lengths for rape, the proportionate use of imprisonment for sexual offences as an overall category increased from 18 per cent in 1980 to 35 per cent in 1988 (Home Office, 1989a). Domestic violence, violence against children generally, and racial violence have begun to be taken more seriously, again with the support of 'progressive' opinion. As already mentioned, the 1991 Criminal Justice Act formalises these trends by making violence and sexual offending criteria for custody.

Whilst few would argue against the use of relatively long prison sentences for the most serious violent or professional crimes, there remains much argument that the overall scale of penalties should be reduced, especially in the UK and much of the USA, and it has seemed over the last fifteen or so years that the whole range of sentences is being pulled up in the wake of the most severe. Speaking of the situation in France, but applicable much more generally, one commentator has pointed out that 'every time repression against serious crimes is intensified, punishment of petty crimes by prison sentences seems to intensify as well' (Faugeron, 1989, p. 237).

What, it is well to ask at this point, did all this criminal justice tinkering amount to? A sense of crisis throughout the 1970s and 1980s led to a flurry of innovation. New forms of crime demanded new, internationally mandated severe penalties, whilst the rise in violent street crime, especially in the UK and USA but also in other parts of the Western world, gave credence to the 'get tough' movement (Van den Haag, 1975; Wilson, 1975) which proposed swift, certain, harsh punishment and an end to 'soft option' rehabilitative penalties such as casework centred probation, suspended sentences and moderate fines. Prison was to be the norm, at least for violent and professional crime, and non-custodial penalties were to be 'alternatives' in the sense that they would be alternative means of securing the same measure of punishment of offenders, protection of the public and deterrence of potential criminals.

Looking back, it seems to have been very much an era of reactive innovation, with penal policy responding to the demands of public/political panics about rising levels of predatory crime, and to fiscal constraints imposed by recession. These stimuli were often, of course, conflicting, and it is only when reformers saw ways of making the two work together that simultaneous progress towards reduced incarceration and reduced crime could occur. The most noteworthy example of such congruence was in the field of juvenile justice, when reformers began to see that increased criminal justice and social work activity had contributed not only to heightened state interventiveness in the lives of young people and their families (Cohen, 1985), but was also contributing to increased levels of juvenile crime by reducing opportunities for maturing out of delinquency, and by occasioning crime associated with situations such as absconding from welfare institutions, or with 'learning opportunities' in penal institutions (Rutherford, 1986; Tutt, 1978).

Up to the beginning of the 1980s, however, the response had been almost frenzied levels of innovation, of new penalties and procedures, and new ways of administering old penalties. Much was added to the penal repertoire with little or anything ever being removed. The reactive, unthought out nature of developments up to the early 1980s are well illustrated by the two phrases which, above all others, characterised the problems and pitfalls of criminal justice, at least Anglo-Saxon style: 'unintended consequences' and 'nothing works' (Austin and Krisberg, 1981; Martinson, 1974).

Whilst the innovative momentum continued through the 1980s the departure was that new powers and new sanctions have gradually become anchored in policy. At the start of the decade one could discern several competing policy and theory strands; in the 1990s some at least of the arguments have been or look like being resolved.

Some emergent themes

The trends which had emerged strongly by the end of the 1980s can be considered as dichotomies, and although, of course, they are more clearly dichotomised in theory than in practice, thinking of them in such a way is useful as an aid to conceptual clarity. To some extent the dichotomies have a continental Europe/Anglo-Saxon divide, but their resolutions are increasingly shared internationally.

1.   Continuum/bifurcation

Contemporary criminal policies are based on the notion of a graduated response to criminality. (Bishop, 1988, p. 142)

The proliferation of sentencing options, legislation or guidelines to prescribe different prison terms for different offences is a reflection of this notion of a graduated response to crime. Even where standardisation or the reduction of disparity is held to be the overriding object-ive, this means that the very definition of disparity is unlike treatment for like offences. Whatever different punishment rationales may be espoused, no serious penologist since the science of penology began has advocated a uniform response to crime of whatever nature. Criti-cisms of indeterminate sentencing and the treatment/rehabilitation ap-proach are in the main criticisms of the distortion to the graduated response to crime, entailed by response to the needs of offenders.

There have emerged, however, two versions of the graduated re-sponse: continuum of sanctions, and bifurcation. Like most dichotomies, this one is not absolute, but there are some opposing tendencies evident in the design of sanctions and in the penal code revisions that have been enacted during the 1980s and early 1990s.

There is nothing very new in the idea of continuums of punishment: prison sentences vary in length according to the severity of the offence, fines vary in amount, probation orders may be for six, twelve or eighteen months, community service can be for varying numbers of hours: the notions of graduation and continuum are almost synonymous. Recently, a new connotation has emerged – the idea of a continuum of the nature of penality across ostensibly different disposals. Wilson's influential book *Thinking About Crime*, for example, asserts that deprivation of liberty should be a common element to punishment for crime, forming a continuum from penalties leaving the offender almost entirely at liberty, to total incarceration (Wilson, 1975). Some of the more apolcalyptic or pessimistic criminological literature has warned for a decade and more about 'blurring the boundaries' between prison and the community (Cohen, 1979; Hudson, 1984), and it is depressing to see these visions not only coming to pass in practice but also endorsed in theory. The continuum principle can be seen at work in many of the innovations of the 1970s and 1980s: weekend or part-time prison in continental European countries; the more rigorous day-centre requirements in England, as well as residential blocks in intermediate treatment programmes for juveniles; the short-term custody which is part of many so-called non-custodial sanctions in the USA (Lerman, 1975; Scull, 1983).

Cohen, following Foucault, has ascribed this blurring of the distinction between incarceration and non-custodial penalties to the ongoing dissemination of the mode of punishment characteristic of modern society – the disciplinary mode – from the archetypal institutional laboratory, the post-eighteenth century prison, through all the other locations of punishment in the developing 'carceral archipelago' (Cohen, 1979, 1985; Foucault, 1977). Looking at contemporary punishments, one can see a common character to those that have been introduced especially since the 1960s. New forms of serving prison sentences have been devised, and many purportedly non-custodial sanctions embody essential characteristics of incarceration: coerced presence in a designated space for a specified time, loss of voluntary choice in associates and activities; loss of freedom to be present in certain locations (Hudson, 1984). Not only do penalties such as probation incorporate periods in custody, but the home-based portions of sentences come more and more to resemble custody with the introduction of curfews and electronic tagging.

Foucault's vision of a carceral society is thus becoming increasingly persuasive, with no longer any absolute distinction between imprisonment and community corrections, but a continuum of gradations between total freedom and total incarceration based on the idea of restriction of liberty as the unifying component of modern punishments.

Even commentators who were formerly sceptical of this dark scenario of an Orwellian society with the distinction between private space and state institutions, liberty and imprisonment further and further eroded, commentators who have supported new sanctions in the belief that their use would genuinely reduce the use of imprisonment rather than insinuate it into previously non-custodial penalties, are becoming more persuaded by the vision. Early advocates of electronic tagging (Ball

and Lilley, 1985) later admitted to having become 'increasingly im-
pressed by theoretical arguments such as those of Foucault' (ibid., 1988,
p. 160) and allow that what they revealingly term 'home incarceration'
gives little hope for those who have tried to resist the view that we
are headed for a totally disciplined 'carceral society' (ibid., p. 163). One
state where electronic tagging is emerging as 'the largest and most
rapidly emerging alternative to prison incarceration' (Esteves, 1990,
p. 77) is Massachusetts, where it was introduced in 1988. This is an
ironic development, since Massachusetts was much vaunted during the
1980s as the pioneer of decarceration. Esteves' review of the use of
electronic incarceration there notes its attractiveness in view of problems of prison overcrowding, and designates it not as an alternative
to imprisonment but as an option among venues for imprisonment.

An opposite trend to punishment as continuum can, however, be
demonstrated. In a much quoted article discussing renewed interest in
separating the punishment of dangerous criminals from the sanctioning
of normal, run-of-the-mill offenders, Anthony Bottoms described the
development in Britain of 'bifurcation': the split in modern penal policy
between tougher measures for the really serious or dangerous offender
and a more lenient line towards the 'ordinary' offender (Bottoms, 1977).
This phenomena of 'bifurcation' was also remarked by Matthews (1979),
and has been noted as a general tendency of Western penology during
the modernist era:

> Throughout the twentieth century [therefore] depending on the par-
> ticular political-economic situation, struggles for reform have as-
> sumed a typically bifurcated trend in terms of a relative diminution
> (on both an individual and a mass level) of prison sentences on the
> one hand, and the growth of repression for certain categories of
> crimes and offenders (above all in moments of political crisis) on
> the other. (Melossi and Pavarini, 1981, pp. 6–7)

This tendency is apparent in the increasing sentence lengths for
crimes considered very serious, and the ineligibility of their perpetrators
for parole. According to some commentators, this trend accounts for
nearly all the rise in prison populations in some countries, particularly
those which have been least affected by factors such as rising unemployment, often held by sociologists to be associated with rising
imprisonment (Box and Hale, 1985). The prison population in The
Netherlands, for example, rose by 105 per cent in the ten years from

1975 to 1985, but this is apparently not due to more prison sentences being given. On the contrary, the proportionate use of imprisonment continued to decline, but the bifurcated criminal justice policy adopted by the Dutch has meant that average prison terms have risen to the degree that this has affected prison numbers:

> On the one hand, the number of short-term prison sentences decreases as a result of their being replaced by non-custodial sentences. At the same time, fines are increasingly being given for misdemeanours . . . On the other hand, both the number of convictions and the average -duration of the sentences for serious crimes involving hard drugs or violence have been increasing as a result of priorities both in detection and prosecution. (De Haan, 1990, p. 63)

Bifurcation has engendered some controversy (Ericson, 1987), although in general most penal reformers would subscribe to a policy which might ensure that prison was reserved for serious offenders. There has been some concern about consequent rises in sentence lengths, but the major controversy with regard to bifurcation has concerned not so much the actual length of sentences served by those selected for the prison track, but the mode of selection, and the legitimacy of enhancing sentence lengths for certain offenders.

Most advocates of sentencing which follows the proportionality of sentence severity to offence gravity rationale stress the importance of the current offence. It is argued that the main difference between the new retributionist, deserts approach and the rehabilitationist approach is that sentencing should be based on the harm the offender has presently perpetrated, not what she/he may have done in the past, still less what she/he may do in the future. Against this are those who, whilst agreeing that serious crimes in general deserve serious punishments and minor crimes in general deserve minor punishments, would argue that the public deserves protection from persistent offenders, and from offenders who might repeat their crimes in future, over and above protection offered by proportional punishment.

Persistent offender legislation has existed in most countries at some time, and whilst it causes little problem where the social defence approach to crime and punishment is paramount (Ancel, 1987), it has always occasioned some discomfort in those jurisdictions which take a more retributivist, classicist perspective. It is held that on retributivist grounds the offender has a right not to be punished more than the present offence warrants (Bottoms and Brownsword, 1983), and the argument advocated by and to sentencers is usually 'previous good character' as mitigation rather than previous bad character as aggravation. In England and Wales and the USA, previous (bad) history is more often used in discussions about parole or remission, where likelihood of reoffending is one of the most important criteria for continued detention, than in pronouncements of the initial sentence.

A new form of preventive detention has emerged, however, in the guise of 'selective incapacitation', and this has proved irresistibly attractive to politicians and judiciaries. Selective incapacitation is based on the belief that a relatively small number of criminals are responsible for a large amount of crime, and if these people can be identified and given long sentences, the crime rate could be reduced without the impact on prison populations that would result from prolonged imprisonment of all offenders committing the crimes concerned. Obviously this idea seems like the answer to many a prayer for politicians anxious to be seen to be cracking down on crime, without incurring greatly increased public expenditure (Greenwood, 1983).

There are two major problems with the idea in practice. The first is that the offenders who would receive lengthy incarceration on likelihood of reoffending grounds might not have committed offences thought to warrant long (or any) imprisonment on seriousness grounds; and the second is that prediction of reoffending might not be accurate, either generally or for any individual offender. These two problems come together in the 'rights' objection to incapacitative sentencing: the right of offenders not to be punished more than their offence deserves, whether because of faulty prediction about recidivism or because of desires to deter others from similar offences (Gottfredson and Gottfredson, 1985, pp. 141–2). The difficulty with prediction of dangerousness or propensity to recidivism is primarily that of avoiding 'false positives' – people who are wrongly categorised as dangerous or recidivist and therefore suffer unjust periods of detention – and 'false negatives' – people who are released because of negative predictions but then reoffend. False positives by definition are almost impossible to identify, but there are some instances where offenders have been released after classification as dangerous and follow-up studies have been made (Bottoms, 1977; Gordon, 1977; Kozol, 1972; Walker, 1985). Although such studies are methodologically controversial and none of the results individually has been in any way conclusive, taken together they do not give any grounds

for confidence in the abilities of criminal justice pe.
dangerousness or recidivism.

The rights argument has been addressed by Bottoms and .
(1983), who apply the view of the American philosopher Dv.   .((
any curtailment of individual rights in the cause of general w.   .re is
a 'compromise with principle' (Dworkin, 1977, p. 11). Bottoms and
Brownsword explain that in general this entails the right of criminals
not to be punished for public good rather than individual desert, but
that this right may be curtailed by rights of potential victims to protection against attack.

Nigel Walker has summarised the main arguments for and against
what he calls 'precautionary sentencing' (Walker, 1985, chapter 22) and
seems to suggest that although the evidence in favour of prediction is at
best equivocal, in fact the rights argument deserves more attention than
the fallibility of prediction argument: 'Whatever the statistics tell us
about the relative probabilities of inflicting unnecessary detention on an
offender and avoidable harm on members of the public, is it not policy
rather than arithmetic which should settle the choice?' (ibid., p. 371).

These dilemmas have led to two developments: first came attempts
to specify a more precise meaning for dangerousness, and then secondly
there has developed the sentencing rationale referred to above as 'selective incapacitation'. The Canadian Criminal Code (Section 687), for
example, specifies the kind of harm to be avoided by preventive detention as a 'threat to life, safety or physical well-being of other persons',
with 'threat' demonstrated by being convicted of offences occasioning
those harms, realised or potential. Selective incapacitation derives
from claims that for offences such as robbery and burglary, which have
been shown to be more amenable to successful prediction of recidivism
than some other offence types (Phillpotts and Lanucki,1979), instruments can be developed that will spot people with high probabilities
of future offending. Studies funded by the RAND Corporation claimed
that use of these predictive instruments could reduce the robbery rate
considerably, but giving shorter or even non-custodial sentences to
those assessed as low risk would mean that crime control could be
combined with rationing of prison use (Greenwood, 1983). A further
refinement is the idea of 'categorial incapacitation', which would compromise between desert and incapacitation theory by confining preventive incarceration within categories of crimes which would in any
case merit severe penalties on deserts ground (Von Hirsch, 1985, part

V). There is certainly a demand from many quarters for such a reconciliation, and many theorists and practitioners would subscribe to the view that incapacitation is:

> the only legitimate primary basis for imprisonment. Rather than trying to reimport it into a defining desert philosophy, it seems far preferable to acknowledge its central place, confront its possible risks, and see whether these cannot be addressed using desert as a limiting principle to ensure the humane and just treatment of those who are incapacitated. (Sherman and Hawkins, 1981, p. 206)

2. *Informalism/formalism*

Many of the innovations of the 1970s and early 1980s can be included under the general heading 'informalism'. One of the most recurrent themes of those who felt that the criminal justice system was in crisis was simply that there was too much of it. Whatever aspect of criminal justice one looked at, there seemed to be more of it than ever before: more crime, more convictions, more people imprisoned, more people employed in criminal justice and law enforcement agencies. As has often been remarked, however modern crime policies may have failed, they have certainly succeeded in recruiting vast numbers of people into the crime/crime control 'industry' (Rothman, 1980). All this criminal justice was demonstrably ineffective at reducing crime, and the insights of labelling theory, as well as the common-sense observations of those working with people who had been in prisons, reformatories, etc., told us that becoming involved in official responses to crime could actually make continued, career criminality more rather than less probable (Becker, 1966; Lemert, 1970).

The call to 'leave kids alone wherever possible' (Schur, 1973) became a rallying cry of the juvenile justice movement, and diversion from court as well as diversions from prison became a dominant theme of reform during the 1970s. Although strongest in juvenile justice, diversion was also advocated to some extent for adults. Where diversion for juveniles usually meant giving all young offenders, except those who had committed very serious offences, a chance of non-prosecution for at least the first offence, with adults diversion has generally meant adopting policies of non-prosecution – *de facto* and sometimes *de jure* decriminalisation – for certain, usually trivial, or non-victimising, offences. For example, it is now common for people apprehended for public drunkenness to be referred to detoxification centres rather than prosecuted. Cautioning schemes, reparation and mediation, and more recently policies to discontinue prosecutions for public interest reasons – usually meaning that the offence is too trivial to justify the expense of court proceedings – long common practice in the USA and Scotland, has spread to England and Wales with the introduction of the Crown Prosecution Service.

In Britain, diversion has been very much the project of criminal justice professionals (probation officers, social workers, police) and involves diversion from one sort of formal process, such as a court hearing, to another, a panel or tribunal of some kind. Examples include juvenile liaison schemes in England where young people who come to police notice are discussed by a group of designated professionals, the family tribunals attended by social workers, prosecutors and others in Scotland. Elsewhere decisions not to prosecute may be taken by police alone, but the point remains that whatever the local format of this kind of diversion scheme, they are controlled by law enforcement/criminal justice professionals, and still operate within existing definitions of illegal or deviant activities.

Whilst the goal of what has been termed 'true diversion' (Rutherford and McDermott, 1976) was to secure the exit of offenders from official processing without penalty other than a formal record of apprehension, many schemes in practice involved some sort of unadjudicated penalty such as making recompense to the victim or the community, or under-going some sort of treatment or social work involvement. In the USA particularly, 'programme-free diversion' was comparatively rare, so that what was happening was a switching of track from one social control apparatus to another, rather than an exit (Lemert, 1981). Even without programmes or penalties, the documentation of an individual's involvement with a diversion forum could be seen to constitute the state's putting up a marker that the person is a candidate for future state intervention.

These schemes proliferated in the 1970s, but in a fragmentary manner without any underlying philosophy (Marshall, 1988). Although gener-ally subsumed under the term 'informalism', informal is the one thing they certainly were not. They were planned and implemented by offi-cials, they often entailed the creation of new bureaucracies, they fol-lowed policies and guidelines. Far from introducing informality, they in many instances converted the traditionally informal into the newly for-mal: the most obvious example being the conversion of informal telling-off into formal cautioning. This characteristic gave rise to the frequently marked effect of these new schemes: 'net widening'. By bringing people who would otherwise have been dealt with either not at all, or genuinely informally, into official processing, the diversion projects expanded and intensified, rather than narrowed and weakened, the grasp of social control (Austin and Krisberg, 1981; Lemert, 1981).

Diversion schemes also formalised the informal by giving quasi-official powers to new people – parents, social workers, colleagues became parties to contracts, treatment, reporting. Rather than a reduction of formal social control, informalism on this reading becomes its dispersal (Cohen, 1979), with the real effects being that powers of adjudication, treatment and punishment are transferred from an overpressed judicial system to the (in the 1970s) expanding social work agencies.

The critics of these diversion projects (Austin and Krisberg, 1981; Cohen, 1985) emphasised the near inevitability of their contributing to an increase rather than decrease of social control: the projects necessitated, after all, an increase in personnel, an increase in funds, an increase in the agencies involved in the administration of social control and criminal justice. No judge was ever made redundant, no police force or prison service reduced because of the success of diversion projects; rather, the law enforcement, judicial and penal establishments were expanded at their margins through the recruitment of social workers, ancillary workers and volunteers to criminal justice functions.

What cautioning, reparation, mediation, etc. did, then, was to complement the formal legal apparatus in an *ad hoc*, untheorised manner. There were, however, proponents of other variants of informal justice, variants which sought to replace the existing criminal justice machinery altogether (Matthews, 1988). What came to be known as the alternative disputes movement sought not only the negative goals of diversion from penalty and from entrapment within the criminal justice system, but more positive goals such as greater participation of victims, and of other parties to disputes such as friends, parents and neighbours. (Christie, 1977, 1982), and greater access to justice, especially for those who find the legal system pays little attention to their troubles. The models for these advocates of informalism were not the panels and case conferences of Western social work approaches to deviance, but the neighbourhood dispute forums in Tanzania (ibid.) or Brazil (Santos, 1979). Neighbourhood justice centres and disputes centres did spring up in the USA, but evaluations of these have been almost unanimously critical. In her review of the Kansas City Neighborhood Justice Center, for example, Harrington found that the result was the expansion rather than contraction of the formal legal apparatus, the confirmation rather than challenging of the legitimacy of the adversarial approach to dispute settlement (Harrington, 1985). As with cautioning, non-continuance and other such diversion ideas, the problem was that the power to define which cases were suitable for 'alternative settlement' always remained with the state. Cain, in reviewing the studies of the neighbourhood justice centres, concluded that the courts tended to offload 'trivia' – domestic matters – and that the clients offloaded tended to be black and female (Cain, 1985). Referrals were nearly always from other social control agencies, so that the impression one gains is of delegation of functions resulting in a second-class justice system for those troubles and those complainants not taken seriously by the state – a form of bifurcation which is accompanied by the expansion noted by those who highlight the net-widening consequences of informalism (Galanter, 1985). The more radical advocates of alternative forms of dispute settlement seek not just not to augment, but also not to replace one sort of tribunal with another, one group of personnel with another, one set of procedures with another. What they seek to replace is one set of values with another. They wish justice to become restorative rather than retributive (Christie, 1982; Mathiesen, 1980), and to uphold intra-class (working-class) values rather than the dominance of the ruling class (Cain, 1985).

Sceptics would claim that these ideals are impossible because the 'community' which would generate ideals of reparation, collective ownership of disputes and solidarity no longer exists in Western society, and that the state commands dominance of values as well as of resources. The most comprehensive critical study of informalism, the two-volumes of evaluations collected by Abel, begins by arguing that informalism is aimed at 'dominated categories' of capitalism: the poor, ethnic minorities and women (Abel, 1982, introduction). Whilst Cain, Santos and others might wish informal justice to be aimed for them, the argument of Abel and other critics is that in the event it is aimed (either advertently or inadvertently) against them, increasing the range of possibilities for their control.

Whether the informal justice movement is regarded as well intentioned but misguided or too easily subverted, or as sinister, the contradictory trend towards formalism emerged as a very dominant theme of the 1970s and 1980s.

In the theoretical domain, the sociological critique of expansion and dispersal of control associated with the proliferation of informal justice innovations coincided with the jurisprudential critique of disparity and disregard of proportionality in sentencing (Cohen, 1979, 1985; Frankel, 1973 *inter alia*). More politically, those concerned with penal affairs amongst humanitarian and civil liberties lobbyists questioned the coercive nature of rehabilitation projects in total institutions (American Friends Service Committee, 1972); Hood, 1978; Mitford, 1974 for example) whilst more right-wing commentators deplored the ineffectiveness of 'soft option' responses to criminals, and called for tough, certain and inescapable punishments for crimes (Van den Haag, 1975; Wilson, 1975). The consensus among all these disparate critics of rehabilitative penology was that doing good was either unachievable or perhaps even undesirable, doing justice offered better prospects of underscoring society's intolerance of predatory crime whilst respecting the moral integrity and civil rights of offenders (Fogel, 1975; Gaylin *et al.*, 1978; Von Hirsch, 1976).

Although the most influential formulations and the most admired implementations of the return to formal justice or neo-classicism (Minnesota Sentencing Guidelines Commission, 1980; Von Hirsch, 1976) either advocated or were based on the principle of desert, the so-called justice model of corrections can adapt itself to differing philosophies about the purposes of punishment in general and the use of imprisonment in particular (Hudson, 1987, chapter 2) and is also of itself non-prescriptive of the overall scale of penalties. There is no necessary connection between justice model penal policies and longer prison sentences (Von Hirsch, 1990a), just as conversely there was no reason to suppose that their introduction would lead to the very moderate tariffs advocated by their more liberal proponents such as Von Hirsch and Fogel. The essence of the model then, is not its advocacy of relating sentence to offence gravity, offender dangerousness or anything else: its essence is its formalism.

At the core of the justice model in whatever formulation, is a desire to curb professional discretion (Christie, 1982; Cohen, 1983). In the USA, the main target was the discretion of judges, whose abuse of their professional discretion was sometimes criticised even from within their own ranks (Frankel, 1973), and prison administrators who under indeterminate sentencing provisions had the power to say when a prisoner was ready for release. It was this power of governors and parole boards to determine the effective length of sentences which was the main complaint of prisoners themselves and which encouraged prisoner's rights activists to ally themselves with calls for determinate sentencing legislation. In jurisdictions such as California where indeterminacy had been taken to its furthest extremes, this indeterminacy was the main cause of sentencing disparity, in other words, the key disparity was in time served rather than sentences pronounced, and so the twin strategies of formalism were sentencing tariffs with determinate terms and either parole guidelines or the abolition of parole altogether. California in 1976 thus introduced a statutory scale of determinate penalties, and also abolished the Adult Authority, the body responsible for parole decisions. In place of parole, many states introduced a system of good time remission, with a clear, formalised linkage of inmate behaviour and days' freedom to be won or lost.

Determinate sentencing need involve no extensive debate about the proper goals of punishment, or the proper basis for decisions to imprison or leave offenders in the community. In California and elsewhere, determinate terms were derived for various offences by averaging the duration of recent and current prison sentences, and thus were aimed much more overtly at eliminating sentencing and parole-induced disparity rather than reorienting penal purposes. In other states and other countries, however, sentencing councils and commissions have produced guidelines which seek to anchor penalties to some distinct rationale, for example, desert in Minnesota and Sweden, incapacitation in New York. In the United Kingdom, too, concern with disparity preceded any attempt to prioritise particular goals in penal policy and practice. Indeterminacy has not been a very pronounced feature of British criminal justice, and the targets for formalism here have been to curb the discretion of judges and magistrates, and also of social workers, probation officers and others. Although there have been and continue to be advocates of a sentencing council, most of whom urge the drafting of a schedule of penalties based on desert principles (Ashworth, 1983, 1989; Wasik and Pease, 1987), the main tactic in England has been to use the Court of Appeal to try to secure consistency of approach in sentencing through the issuing of guideline judgments dealing with classes of cases rather than with just a particular instance (Hudson, 1987; Thomas, 1979). These activities have been backed up by government policy documents and by the issuing of various circulars and handbooks to magistrates to promote consistency in the lower courts as well as in the Crown Courts. Emerging from these various strategies can be seen a clear official attempt to move sentencing more firmly to a desert basis, and it has been a shared concern of officials, politicians, reformers and criminal justice personnel that less serious, non-violent offences should not lead to imprisonment except in unusual circumstances.

Parole as well as the original sentencing has been formalised, and here again the common feature of parole guidelines is that they should be based on formal criteria and procedures, rather than that they should embody any particular penal purpose. With parole guidelines generally resting on a mixture of considerations of behaviour in the institution, community ties and likelihood of reoffending, most parole guidelines seem to incorporate their own form of bifurcation – for example, the English guidelines now deny the possibility of parole for serious and violent offenders, while for those convicted of lesser offences the main criterion is risk of reoffending. Predicting reoffending for parole purposes uses many of the same factors as the various instruments proposed for identifying individuals for incapacitative sentencing, and is open to the same ethical and methodological objections. Although it is claimed that the level of reconviction of parole prisoners has fallen with the introduction of formal risk assessment (Ward, 1987), success in terms of aggregates does not mean that there are not some individuals who remain in prison because of prediction of likelihood to reoffend if paroled, who might well be false positives.

Formalism has been embraced most ardently by those engaged in the ostensibly least formal or less coercive aspects of criminal justice. In social work, probation and juvenile justice, the 1980s saw the adoption of strategies which, though generally aimed at avoidance of net-widening and of increasing the interventiveness of control, have for good or ill certainly had the effect of 'formalising the informal'. Three examples which illustrate this tendency are cautioning, juvenile justice gatekeeping, and probation targeting. A response to early studies of cautioning which reported net-widening, in that many of the offenders dealt with by way of official caution seemed to be those who would formerly have been 'no actioned' (Ditchfield, 1976), was to promote official guidelines for cautioning, and to reduce the discretion of arresting officers and juvenile panels to application of these guidelines. During the early 1980s in England and Wales there was widespread adoption of 'instant caution' schemes, where the apprehending officer could hand out a formal caution on the basis of strict criteria without reference to panels and bureaux, or, on the other hand, to restrict decision-making powers to caution or prosecute a small group of centrally based officers in order to avoid intra-area disparities (Hudson, 1984).

Another widely adopted example of formalism is the introduction of gatekeeping procedures to make the entry of juveniles on to delinquency programmes available only to those who had been formally adjudicated as offenders by courts of law. Designed to stop young people who had not committed offences from being subject to 'predelinquency' control and stigmatisation (Morris and Giller, 1983; Thorpe *et al.*, 1980), one effect was the further penetration of the 'assistancial' social work domain by the judicial domain (Donzelot, 1980), and it became somewhat difficult to provide services for adolescents and young people without them having been judged delinquent. Designed to avoid the 'unintended consequences' of informalism and doing good, one of the consequences of the formalism of 1980s work with juveniles may well have been the denial of support and facilities to many non-offending young people and their families who might need them for reasons other than crime.

Although the move to due process formalism penetrated first and most thoroughly in the domain of juvenile justice and was eagerly embraced by social workers, police and others specialising in juvenile work, probation officers during the 1980s gradually adopted similar strategies. They, too, acknowledged the need for formal criteria for recommending to courts that an offender should be placed on probation, as well as introducing more formally stated specifications of the work that should be done within probation orders. Most probation areas now operate some sort of gatekeeping and monitoring system for reports to courts, and many use devices such as the 'risk of custody' scale to assess the appropriateness of probation recommendations in individual cases. Along with greater use of contracts and of court-imposed conditions such as day centres or specified activities in probation orders, the effect has been to make both strategies to obtain orders and post-sentence contacts with probationers more formalised.

The 1982 Criminal Justice Act gave statutory enactment to many of these trends: passing power to make care orders institutional or home based from social workers to magistrates; imposing criteria for making first custodial sentences and any custodial sentences on offenders under the age of 21; making all youth and juvenile custodial sentences determinate; legislating conditions for probation orders. In the mid-1980s, the trends to greater formalism continued in England and Wales and in the USA, in adult and juvenile jurisdictions, in diversion from prosecution and in diversion from custody. The innovations of informalism have been maintained, but have been incorporated in the formal justice system. They have been subjected to more and more control by the state, to more formal procedures and criteria, so that the combined effect of the seemingly contradictory impulses to formalism and informalism has been aggregative rather than counter-balancing.

3. *Corporatism/individualism*

A third pair of apparently contradictory tendencies which can be discerned in criminal justice policy and practice is that of individualising and collectivising responses to crime. Since the demise of the post-war view of crime as a result of some sort of deprivation – be it material, social or emotional – with the decline at least in England and the USA of social democratic, consensus politics (Taylor, 1981), crime has increasingly been seen as the outcome of individuals' reasoned decision-making (Cornish and Clarke, 1986). Crime, like all other action, is thought on this view to be the result not of determining or even pre-disposing factors, but of fully rational individuals making choices on the basis of their attitudes to moral issues, to the desirability of property, excitement or 'aggravation', and on the basis of their beliefs about opportunities for crime, likelihood of apprehension, probable punishment, etc. (Riley and Tuck, 1986). Criminal behaviour, at least run-of-the-mill criminal behaviour, is something we all may do, those who actually do, do so on the basis of perfectly ordinary reasoning processes.

Deserts sentencing, the justice model, fits this idea of crime as reasoned action perfectly, since it is based on the notion of individual culpability. In its insistence on due process and determinacy, it is also safeguarding the rights of the offender as an individual: the individual's right to be treated as morally competent, to know the nature and duration of punishment, and also the right to be able to take anticipation of penalties for contemplated offences into account when choosing whether or not to go ahead and commit a crime. Individualism is at the very core of desert models. Proponents of the justice model also advocate desert rather than utilitarian, or deterrence, rationales on the grounds that it is wrong to punish an individual more than the particular offence warrants because of any hoped for effects on other people, or society as a whole (Von Hirsch, 1976).

Although indeterminacy and coerced treatment have long become discredited aspects of rehabilitative penal policies, and although the aim of reducing disparity has made for a greater uniformity in sentencing, there has also been a move towards individualising penalties, particularly community penalties, the 'designer alternatives' through specification of individually tailored treatment or rehabilitative components. Most proponents of tariff sentencing, however much importance they give to proportionality and consistency, still allow for individualised sentences, either where imprisonment is not appropriate on desert or public protection grounds, or because of certain offender characteristics. David Thomas, for example, has argued that:

> Cases in which the primary decision is likely to be in favour of an individualized measure can be identified by the characteristics of the offender. While individualized measures are used in a wide range of cases where the claims of the tariff are not strong and there is reason to suppose that an individualized measure will provide the treatment, guidance or supervision needed to enable the offender to make the necessary adjustments to social demands, four types of offenders are normally considered particularly suitable for individualized measures. These are young offenders (predominantly those under 21), offenders in need of psychiatric treatment, recidivists who appear to have reached a critical point in their life and persistent recidivists who are in danger of becoming completely institutionalized as a result of repeated sentences of imprisonment. (Thomas, 1979, p. 17)

Where non-custodial sentences are being sought, the ways in which they are proposed to courts has, as mentioned above, become much more individualised. As well as the largely presentational intent of putting more specification of work to be done with the offender into court reports, there is now a mix of measures such as alcohol education, programmes to change beliefs about offending, and intensive probation courses. This 'pick and mix' approach has been carried furthest in the USA, where community service, financial recompense and probation may be combined. Such sentencing packages have been used since 1979 in Washington, DC (Rutherford, 1984), and became widespread through the states in the 1980s. They are provided for England and Wales in the 1991 Criminal Justice Act.

This greater differentiation and individualisation which can be demonstrated in criminal justice policy and practice, is largely, however, a tactic in a strategy which is anything but individualistic. A clear tendency discernible in most Western jurisdictions has been that the abandonment of post-war optimism of eliminating crime through increased prosperity has been paralleled by abandonment of hope of reforming individual criminals, twin pessimisms which have allied themselves with the critiques of coercion, stigmatisation and labelling associated with criminal justice measures targeted at individuals. Thus policy goals are now expressed in terms of rates and aggregates: concerns with prisons are with overcrowding and the maintenance of order rather than the effects of confinement on individuals; crime control policies aim not to eliminate or even reduce crime but to keep rates at politically acceptable levels, to prevent fear of crime leading to questioning of government competence.

Looking at policies throughout Europe, one commentator has highlighted an 'administrative approach', which he characterises as the 'social control' approach which is the dominant contemporary penal modality, the successor to classicism with its attention mainly on criminal codes themselves and the modernist approach whose concern was with the treatment of offenders and the prevention of crime. The preoccupations of this new social control school are policy, planning and organisation:

> Emphasis has shifted from the maintenance of criminal codes and the other crime statutes to more general control of volume of delinquent activity. Criminal policy is no longer occupied primarily with concrete offenders, nor with problems of doing justice, but with the management of aggregate phenomena of social activity, with criteria for selective law enforcement, with quantitative regulation in the organizational processing of offenders. (Peters, 1986, p. 32)

This corporatist approach has been evident in juvenile justice, where the claims of individualistic approaches might have been thought to be particularly strong (Pratt, 1989) in approaches to crime prevention in several European countries (Van Dijk, 1990), in approaches to reduction of the use of custody in Germany (Feest, 1991) and is enthusiastically promoted as the way forward for criminal justice in the future (Locke, 1990).

Summary: penal policy fin de siècle

In retrospect, the last two decades seem characterised first of all by ill thought out innovation and expansionism in criminal justice, with practice preceding not just theory but also policy. 'Nothing works, everything will inevitably have (malign) unintended consequences, so we may as well try anything', emerges as the flavour of the times. Further, whilst the two decades from the mid-1950s to the mid-1970s have been characterised as an era of decarceration and deinstitutionalisation (Cohen, 1977; Hudson, 1984), it is difficult to deduce any overall goal or ethos for the decade 1975 to 1985. Bifurcation appears to have 'happened', but seemingly without any clear or conscious articulation by policy-makers.

As we progress towards the millenium, however, we can look back over the most recent years and see an emerging clarification of penal policy, with themes shared throughout the Western world. Bifurcation is now clearly espoused in policy as well as practice, with countries with such diverse penal traditions as The Netherlands, France, Scandinavia, as well as the Anglo-Saxon countries, basing their projections of prison populations on the expectation of fewer admissions but longer average sentences as serious, violent offences, offences concerning drugs trafficking and so on receive consistently heavy prison sentences, but more less serious offenders are diverted on to the non-custody track. (Whether this is likely to happen in reality will be very much open to question in the chapters that follow.)

Whilst at the very top end of the crime range a mixture of motives of retribution, incapacitation and deterrence is almost always involved, desert/proportionality has emerged from competing theories as the most widely acceptable principle for the more usual range of offences, and many countries have now introduced penal code reforms which whether by statutory penalties, guidelines or principles, confirm the centrality of desert. There has been some resistance to desert as the only or dominant sentencing principle, particularly from sentencers who wish to retain powers to 'give the public a rest' from persistent, though minor, offenders. Insertion of incapacitating elements into non-custodial penalties through electronic tagging, curfews and such like is also a noteworthy, albeit unwelcome, development.

Desert as a limiting principle to punishment is a common theme of reformers, jurisprudes and criminologists now. As we shall see later, even those who urge the restoration of other penal aims such as rehabilitation would agree that the location and duration of programmes should be limited by desert considerations. The areas of dispute that remain are less about the principle of proportionality than about how it might be achieved. There remain problems of 'transmission mechanisms',

whether sentencing laws, sentencing guidelines, training of and proselytising to judges are necessary or sufficient to achieve proportional
sentencing.

Problems of equality of impact, of equal justice in an unequal society
remain, and are increasingly being admitted by advocates of desert
penality (Von Hirsch, 1990a). Also still in dispute are the factors
relevant to calculations of desert: questions of ranking of offence seriousness, whether the present offence alone is to be considered, the
circumstances that should be allowed as mitigatory. More fundamental
perhaps, the problem of cardinality is still unresolved. Adopting proportionality does nothing to resolve questions about the overall severity
of penalty scales (Ashworth, 1989a), so that apart from a few offences
where international agreements are in force, countries with traditions
of leniency such as Sweden are likely to introduce moderate guidelines, compared with the USA and the United Kingdom which maintain
their traditions of severity (Von Hirsch, 1990a).

The other trend which has very clearly emerged as entrenched is the
'formalisation of the informal'. Concern with equity has demanded that
diversion, alternative dispute processing, be subject to clear criteria and
formal adjudication. Reconciliation between the formalism of deserts
approaches and the objective of side-stepping formal judicial systems
that motivated the early diversion schemes seems to have been achieved
by incorporation of diversion at the margins of formal justice:

> Formal cautioning and many other forms of diversion may be re-
> garded as condemnatory to a degree and they can be incorporated
> into a 'just deserts' approach by regarding them as proportionate
> responses to minor forms of lawbreaking or to offences of certain
> kinds by persons of low culpability. This requires clear and prin-
> cipled criteria for diversion, no less than for sentencing decisions.
> So long as they form part of a system which reflects ordinal pro-
> portionality diversion schemes can be regarded as a manifestation
> of a lowering (or at least a bifurcation) of cardinal proportion-
> ality. (Ashworth,1989a, p. 348)

These principles and trends can clearly be seen in the 1991 Criminal
Justice Act. The Act rests on two main principles: first, that punishment
should be proportionate to the seriousness of the offence, and secondly,
that although there is a commitment to the twin-track, bifurcated approach, the unifying element of restriction of liberty is common to

community sentences as well as imprisonment: the more serious the offence, the greater the restriction on the offender's liberty. Like the new Swedish penal code, but with much less force and clarity, the Act relies on the enunciation of principles on which sentencing is to be based to secure consistency and the use of custody for only serious offences. It retains the English tradition of making sentences available to courts rather than prescribing their use in detail, and continues to specify maximum rather than mandatory or presumptive sentences (except for the life sentence for murder). Although the specification of criteria for custody introduced in the 1982 Criminal Justice Act has, as mentioned above, been retained and extended, what is new is a somewhat similar 'threshold' idea for community as well as custodial sentences. A community sentence – probation, community service, probation, probation with various conditions, the new 'combined order' of probation plus community service, supervision and attendance centres for young offenders – is to be used if the offence is 'serious enough to warrant such a sentence' (section 6.(1)), and community sentences are seen as sentences in their own right, rather than non-sentences (probation was previously regarded as a disposal rather than a sentence, in other words assumed a rhetoric of assistance rather than punishment) or alternatives to custody. A further seriousness threshold must be crossed if a custodial rather than a community sentence is to be passed. Community sentences are, therefore, 'graduated restrictions on liberty, proportionate to the seriousness of the offence' (Ashworth, 1992, p. 243).

Custodial sentences are to be reserved for the most serious offences, and are especially recommended for violent and sexual offences. Apart from violent and sexual offences being urged as more serious than property offences, seriousness is not specified in the Act, and interpretation of seriousness is therefore left to judicial discretion, with guidance from the Court of Appeal. It remains to be seen, therefore, whether the Act will make any real impact on the use of imprisonment, and whether consistency between regions will be achieved. One apparent difference is the clause that requires sentencers to take into account the offence under consideration and only one 'associated' offence, rather than the total number of charges or the number of previous convictions. An offence is defined as associated with another if it is dealt with at the same proceedings, or if the offender asks for it to be taken into consideration (section 33(2)(a)). Another apparent innovation is the greater delineation of circumstances under which a court may pass a longer than normal sentence because of previous offending or likelihood of reoffending. In its approach, the Act is here like the Canadian guidelines, in that it tries to define 'serious harm' or 'danger' in the Canadian terminology, with some precision. A custodial sentence, or a longer than normal custodial sentence, is justified if it is thought neces- sary to prevent the public from 'serious harm', which is defined in section 31 of the Act as 'death or serious personal injury, whether physical or psychological'. Some commentators have pointed out that the inclusion of the words 'from him' in the protection of the public criterion for custody marks the intention of the Act to allow only for selective incapacitation, rather than general or categorical deterrence (NACRO, 1992).

The intention of the Act that sentence should be related to present offence and present or future danger to the public, and that there should not be ascendancy up a punishment ladder on account of successive offences of the same degree of seriousness, appears to be new if one has in mind courts which have sentenced in this 'progressive' way pre- viously. However, one leading authority says that the principle that previous convictions should not count as aggravating factors in sen- tencing considerations is not new, but consistent with Court of Appeal judgments (Thomas, 1992). An offender loses mitigation of former good character, and would find it difficult to argue that an act was out of character, a never-to-be-repeated aberration, an act of desperation associated with some unusual trauma, but this forfeiture of mitigation rather than addition of aggravation has been practice in the higher courts at least for many years. Perhaps the innovation is in seeking to persuade the lower courts – where the sentencing ladder does seem more in evidence – to apply the same principle of not sen- tencing the petty persistent offender more harshly than the current offence indicates.

Another important innovation of the 1991 Act which is in line with trends seen elsewhere and already under way here, is the abolition of the distinction between parole and remission, and their replacement with the provision for 'early release' (Wasik, 1992). The determinate sen- tencing laws in the USA sought to restrict the discretion of parole authorities, and make the time actually served in prison dependent on the sentences actually passed by the courts. Under the provisions of the Act, for prisoners serving sentences of less than twelve months release will be automatic after half of the sentence has been served, and the innovation here is that there will be no supervision under licence after release. For offenders sentenced to terms of more than one year but less than three years, release will also be automatic after half the sentence has been served, but there will be supervision on licence until the date three-quarters of the way through the original sentence. Discretionary release is available for long-term (more than four years) prisoners between half- and three quarters-way through the sentence. These cases will be decided by the Parole Board and the criteria remain, as previously, concerned with danger to the public, and likelihood of reoffending. The main difference, then, is the reduction in the range of cases with which the Parole Board will be concerned, but this continues a trend that was already under way to make the release of short-sentence prisoners routine, and to place more restrictions on parole of long-term and violent offenders. Wasik also notes that the criteria for release continue the shift in emphasis towards protection of the public and away from rehabilitation of the offender (ibid., p. 255).

The 1991 Criminal Justice Act, then, however much it may be promoted by the Home Office as a radical new framework for dealing with offenders, is a culmination of tendencies becoming more and more apparent during the 1980s. It is also consistent with the development of clarification of sentencing principles; articulation of proportionality of penalty to offence seriousness as the main principle to be achieved in sentencing; restriction of the discretion of criminal justice administrators; bifurcation and formalisation:

> it can be claimed that the 1991 Act differs from its predecessors in one significant respect: its sentencing provisions have some fairly coherent themes. This is not to overlook the problems of the 1991 Act, one of which is that its themes do not emerge clearly from the wording of the legislation. The Act does not begin with a clear enunciation of principles: that is not the English way, although on this occasion it would have helped immensely with interpretation. Instead the principles have to be inferred from the legislation, supplemented by reference to other documents. The leading principle is proportionality. Sentences should be calculated on the basis of what the person deserves for the offence committed, and not lengthened for any supposed deterrent or rehabilitative reasons, although there is a limited exception for 'public protection' sentences. The notion of proportionality promoted by the Government is the 'twin-track' approach, which involves less resort to custody for non-serious offences but longer custodial sentences for serious crimes. (*Criminal Law Review* editorial, 1992, p. 229)

Such clarification as has been achieved on sentencing policy has not been matched by equal attention to other criminal justice processes. Focusing on problems like disparity in sentencing and achieving a politically adequate response to crime has not been accompanied by equal concern with the nature of regimes, or by concern with the fate of offenders after sentences, still less by concern for the relationship of penal policy to social justice: the 1991 Act, for example, contains merely what the editorial quoted above describes as 'oblique recognition' of a duty not to discriminate on the ground of race, sex or other 'improper' characteristic.

2 Penal Policy and Social Structure

The preceding chapter suggested a range of differences within and between countries with respect to penal philosophies, penal policies and penal practices. As well as differences in the overall organisation of criminal justice (for example, common law or code; adversarial or investigative), there are differences in such things as the amounts of discretion given to various stages and various personnel such as arrest, prosecution, sentencing, as well as differences in the range of penalties available. Whilst all Western countries provide for discharge, fine and imprisonment, some but not all have probation, some but not all have community service, and whilst in most advanced Western countries today imprisonment is the most severe sanction, some countries, including of course the USA, retain the death penalty. Greater variation is introduced through differences in the way sentences can be served, for example, some countries (The Netherlands, Belgium, Germany, for instance) have part-time imprisonment but others do not, and there are variations in whether or which sentences can be combined, and so on. Still greater differences occur in the actual usage of particular sentences, for example the high use made of suspended imprisonment in Greece and some other European countries; the low use of fines in the USA compared to Western Europe, and conversely the much higher use of probation in the USA. In its relative use of fines and probation England and Wales is, as often seems to be the case, somewhere between the American and Western European patterns.

It was suggested, furthermore, that on top of this existing diversity, amongst the reforms and innovations of the last two decades, some transatlantic differences in both goals and strategies can be discerned. In general terms, the most striking continuing difference is in tendencies to respond to crime in individualised or social ways. The policies which emerged in the USA, and which were often subsequently taken up in England and Wales, have concentrated almost exclusively on individual responsibility and on the threat posed to potential victims by dangerous or predatory individuals. Both the liberal deserts lobby and the right-wing 'get tough' lobby concern themselves with punishments calibrated to degrees of individual culpability or wickedness, or else

55

they are based on selective incapacitation of individuals predicted to be probable recidivists. Crime prevention strategies, too, have in the main been focused on persuading individual property owners to take action to reduce their chances of personally becoming victims (burglar alarms, car locks and so on), and to take actions to spot suspicious individuals through neighbourhood watch and similar schemes. Where 'community' crime prevention schemes have been carried out on housing estates, these have very often meant the individuation of territory through dividing up communal gardens, pathways, etc. into privatised 'defensible space' (Hudson, 1990). On the other hand, Western Europe has continued to place more emphasis on goals of general deterrence in both crime prevention strategies and in penal policies, for instance through the French *étés-jeunes* summer activities programmes, Danish schemes to strengthen the role of primary socialisation agencies such as schools, community groups, youth groups and the like.

In some ways, however, the differences between countries are reducing. The introduction of the Crown Prosecution Service in England brought in an institution similar to that of the prosecutor in continental systems (as well as in Scotland). At the time of writing, the Royal Commission on the Criminal Justice System, set up in the wake of a series of spectacular miscarriages of justice cases, is considering a much more decisive move away from the traditional Anglo-Saxon adversarial system towards the continental investigative system.

What has generally and most significantly been shared, is the move towards bifurcation discussed in the previous chapter, the move in principle at least to reserve imprisonment for the more serious offences, and the move to encourage the use of community penalties for lesser offences (Muncie and Sparks, 1991), the kind of twin-tracking made central to policy in England and Wales with the 1991 Criminal Justice Act. There has been internationally shared concern about sentencing disparities, and there has been an internationally shared impetus towards more inter-agency initiatives to bring about shifts of penal practice in states and regions to achieve twin-tracking, and to reduce disparities within states and regions, and between them and neighbouring areas (Pfeiffer, 1991, for example). Also, there has been near simultaneous similar endeavour in the clearer articulation of penal aims. There has been widespread acceptance of the idea that however much importance different countries may attach to judicial independence, discretion should not remain so unfettered in the name of independence that the penal goals of legislatures can be obstructed or undermined. Whether by leg-

islation, by guidelines or merely by exhortation and training, governments, having (at last) interested themselves in the principles as well as
the practicalities of crimes and punishments, have taken steps to see
that their policies are properly implemented.

What can be noted as a general characteristic of all these policies and
strategies, is a near universal tendency for them to be formulated in
terms of acts rather than actors: contemporary penal policy is concerned
with crimes, not criminals. In proposals for international cooperation, in
sentencing guidelines, in many different facets of criminal justice, this
tendency is apparent. It is incorporated in juvenile programmes where
admission criteria refer to offences rather than to the circumstances
of young people; diversion programmes, whether they are directed at
the stage of arrest/no action, caution/prosecute, continue/discontinue,
recommend probation/not recommend probation, imprison/punish in the
community, have all been formalised mainly on offence rather than
offender criteria. All the developments so far referred to – twin-tracking;
the formalisation and incorporation of 'informal' procedures; the clarification of sentencing policies; attempts to reconcile competing philosophies such as desert and incapacitation – demonstrate the shift
from the offender discourses of the rehabilitating the criminal era to
the offence discourses of the present 'make the punishment fit the
crime' era.

This offence focus can be seen in its most developed form in the
common law (the English speaking countries) and Scandinavian penal
code revisions. In their aim to tie penalty to seriousness of the current
offences, these new penal codes and policies also make most of the
circumstances allowable as aggravating or mitigating refer to the act as
well, rather than to offender characteristics such as whether the person
being dealt with was a ringleader or a minor player, whether the crime
occurred at a time of personal difficulty, and the like. A good example
of this is the 'aggravated car crime' issue in England at the time of
writing, when the Home Secretary has announced that prison sentences will be given to people involved in so-called joyriding, whether
or not the person concerned was the driver or not, was the instigator
or not. Whilst age and mental capacity are still allowed as having
relevance in assessing culpability in most jurisdictions, moves such as
the extension of capital punishment to mentally retarded offenders in
some American states (for example, New York) indicate the strength
of the shift towards minimising concern with offender characteristics
in the drive to achieve more consistent, crime-proportional sentencing.

Cross-national comparisons of criminal justice practices are notoriously difficult (Fitzmaurice and Pease, 1982; Franke, 1990; Lynch, 1988) and it is probably unwise to make any claims in general terms such as 'punitiveness'. Breakdowns of prison statistics, however, while they may not be able to answer questions such as whether imprisoning a lot of people for short terms is more or less punitive than imprisoning fewer people for longer periods, can show some clear variations in the offences most commonly resulting in imprisonment in different countries. Lynch's comparison of prison use in England, Canada, West Germany and the USA, whilst hedged about with caveats about using imprisonment rates to compare punitiveness or even 'propensity to imprison', suggests that the probability of incarceration following arrest is lower for homicide in England than in the USA or Canada, but similar for other offences of violence against persons. The incarceration rates for both violent crime and property crime, he finds, are lower in West Germany. For robbery, the West German rate was approximately one-half of that in the United States, Canada and England; for larceny/ thefts, the incarceration rate in the Federal Republic was approximately one-third of the USA rate and one-half of the rate for England and Canada (Lynch, 1988, p. 194). Differences in the imprisonment rate for robbery and burglary and for rape between England and Wales and The Netherlands have also been noted by Downes. He shows imprisonment rates in The Netherlands in 1981 of 18 per cent of convictions, 41 per cent and 39 per cent respectively for burglary, rape and robbery, compared to 31 per cent, 88 per cent and 78 per cent of convictions respectively in England and Wales, and he tells us that except for rape, these differences persisted further into the 1980s (Downes, 1988, pp. 36–40).

It is well known, on the other hand, that the countries generally regarded as most lenient have high propensities to imprison for drunken driving. Thus in 1981 in The Netherlands almost one-third of prison sentences were for driving offences; this high proportion being also found in Norway and Sweden. In 1984, one-third of all Swedish prison sentences came under the Road Traffic Offences Act; drunken driving occasioned almost as many prison sentences as crimes against property and twice as many as crimes against persons (Svensson, 1986, p. 264). This high use of short prison sentences for drunken driving, as well as the shortness of sentences generally compared to England and Wales and some other countries, explains why although The Netherlands and Scandinavia have comparatively low per capita imprisonment rates, they have high rates of imprisonments. The per capita detention rate (the number of people in prison proportionate to the population – usually given as per 100 000 of population – on the day the prison population is counted, usually an annual census) is lower in The Netherlands than in Germany because average sentences are much shorter, even though the rate of imprisonments (the ratio of prison sentences passed proportionate to the population over a year) is higher in The Netherlands (Heinz, 1989). Similarly, the per capita detention rate is very much lower in The Netherlands than in England and Wales (40 per 100 000 in The Netherlands in 1988 as compared with 84.9 in Federal Germany, 96.7 in England and Wales), even though terms of immediate imprisonment are a much higher proportion of all sentences passed by the courts in The Netherlands: 11.0 per cent in 1990 compared with 3.6 per cent in England and Wales (Muncie and Sparks, 1991, p. 30).

Whilst these national differences in ordinal responses to crime remain alongside cardinal variations in the penalty scales of the various countries and states, an observable general trend which is congruent with the declining importance accorded to offender variables, is that judgments about which offences are the most serious are becoming somewhat more consequentialist, less strictly intentionalist. Until the 1980s this was not a general trend, with Western Europe in particular, with its commitment to rehabilitation making the motivations of offenders all important, strengthening rather than weakening the centrality of intentionality in calculations of seriousness. So, writing in 1986, it was reasonable to claim that in Scandinavia at least, a shift over two decades from 'a consequence orientation to a guilt orientation has resulted in more lenient punishments, for example for "assault resulting in death", where murder was not intended' (Antilla, 1986, p. 39).

On the other hand, the general rise in punitiveness towards reckless driving which is apparent in England and Wales, would seem to imply a greater importance beginning to be attached to consequences, actual or potential. We can note the increasing use here of the imprisonment for driving with excess alcohol that has long been customary in Europe, and where imprisonment is not imposed, there is greater use of probation orders with conditions of treatment, and a corresponding decrease in response to these offences by fines or other minimum-intervention penalties.

Similarly, the increasing use of imprisonment and the increasing length of sentences for rape in many countries, with accompanying changes in police and court procedures, greater protection from publicity for rape victims (although many would argue not enough changes, not enough protection), seem to reflect the realisation that rape is an act of violence with extreme consequences for any woman. The declining emphasis on consent or perceptions of consent fits this shift in attention from the antecedents to the consequences of criminal events.

Burglary, traditionally an offence which produces much higher rates of imprisonment in England and Wales, where intent has always been of prime importance because of the neo-classicist/retributive stance of criminal justice compared to the continental social defence rationale, is now beginning to result in more non-custodial penalties. Again, this fits the more consequentialist mode, for although it is taken seriously, it is possibly seen as not quite so damaging now that more people and organisations are adequately covered by insurance. The general practice – supported by Court of Appeal guideline judgments – of punishing house burglary more harshly than burglary of commercial or other premises might also be interpreted as indicating the elevation of consequences over intent. House burglary is usually seen as more opportunistic than burglary of commercial or industrial premises which is characteristically more 'professional', involves more preplanning, but burglary is a more distressing event for a private householder than for a commercial occupant (Maguire, 1980). The recent exercises of some deserts theorists to link offence seriousness to notions of harm confirms that this is a well-established trend (Von Hirsch and Jareborg, 1991). If punishments are to be proportional to crimes, if disparity in sentencing is to be avoided, then tying calculations of seriousness to some notion such as harm produced by the offence is clearly crucial. Giving precedence to intention brings back the individualised, offender-based sentencing which has produced the disparity that has so worried contemporary criminal justice personnel. Schemes such as that of Von Hirsch and Jareborg accommodate differences in intentionality through the idea of 'culpability'. Seriousness is a compound of the harm produced by the crime and the degree of responsibility that can be attributed to the offender. This kind of idea of seriousness can clearly be seen in the 1991 Criminal Justice Act, where factors such as previous offences are allowable as considerations in sentencing only when they can throw some light on the current offence – a previous offence of a similar nature might indicate that the offender could foresee the consequences of the crime.

Whilst this focus almost exclusively on offences rather than offenders might not have been so overtly articulated in most European countries as it is in the new penal codes and sentencing guidelines of the USA,

Canada, Australia, England and Wales and Scandinavia, the same effect
has been brought about by the shift from an individual rehabilitation
to a management of aggregates mode of criminal justice, apparent in
Germany, France, Italy among other countries, and in juvenile justice
jurisdictions in the United Kingdom and elsewhere (Muncie and
Sparks, 1991; Peters, 1986; Pratt, 1989).

Evaluations of the various laws, guidelines and initiatives have similarly been in terms of their impact on systems, rates, aggregates. Discussion has centred on whether deserts and determinate sentencing
schemes in the USA have led to or been associated with rising rates of
imprisonment (Hudson, 1987; Von Hirsch, 1990a); whether changes in
prosecution policy together with judicial education and wider publication of sentencing information in Germany has reduced incarceration
rates (Feest, 1991); whether there is an increase in imprisonment for
the type of offences deemed deserving of custody and a decrease in
imprisonment for other offences (Knapp, 1984). Whether the reductions
in the use of imprisonment for some offences that have been achieved
in some countries since the early 1980s are really attributable to these
policies, codes, guidelines and initiatives or whether to other factors
(such as the ageing of the population) is not the issue here: what matters
for the moment is to note that the new penal policies have been formulated in modest, impersonal terms and are therefore subject to evaluation in modest, impersonal terms.

The clarification of penal policy that has taken place during the late
1980s and early 1990s can justifiably be claimed to have replaced crisis
with purposiveness, to have substituted modest, rational expression of
goals for chaos and confusion. In the countries I have referred to,
criminal justice has lately become more predictable, with less disparity,
and with discretion much more evenly distributed through the various
stages of the system. It has also become very much more impersonal.

Contemporary neo-classicism's almost exclusive concern with acts
rather than with actors could well be seen as penology's embrace of
postmodernism. Certainly, the modernist criminological enterprise seems
to be at an end. The recruitment of positivist social science to the
diagnosis, classification, reform and rehabilitation of offenders which
has constituted the criminological project since the end of the last century (Garland, 1985) is most certainly in decline. Whilst forensic psychiatry and sociological concern with criminals and their control do
of course continue, it is remarkable how much the attention of theory as
well as policy and practice has turned to events and away from persons.

Thus, crime surveys have been remarkably popular amongst criminological researchers in the late 1980s (Young, A., 1991). The same people who alerted us to the 'aetiological crisis' in criminology (Young, J., 1987) have themselves not given us aetiology, but rather have given us epidemiology. The so-called new realism, of left as well as right, has devoted more attention to demonstrating the reality of criminal acts than to the reality of people's experiences of criminal justice. Such theorising as they have undertaken about the causes of crime has had to be extrapolated from the mapping of acts rather than through entering into the life-worlds of their agents.

The theories of crime which have been most influential on policy – especially in England and the USA – have been based on a negation of any essential difference between criminals and others, seeing criminal behaviour as a simple, rational calculation of costs and benefits, the so-called 'reasoning criminal' (Cornish and Clarke, 1986). This *homo economicus* is the criminal in mind when deterrent punishments, target hardening in crime prevention, and offence-focused probation groups are advocated. Whilst by no means wishing to argue for a revival of determinist, positivist approaches to criminality, this theoretical absence of the offender gives us a criminology which, whilst it may have lost some of the naive romanticism of its sociology of deviancy phase as well as the oversimplified, overpredictive mythology of its positivist phase (Taylor, Walton and Young, 1977), is in some danger of losing its humanity. For 'crime' is not a unitary phenomenon (Hogg, 1988) and whilst earlier new deviancy writers may have subsumed too wide a range of predatory wrongdoing under the vague heading of harmless delinquency or youthful rebellion, so the new criminology risks subsuming a wide range of pain, frustration and relational complexities under the equally vague heading of predatory street crime. It also risks solidifying immaturity, 'drift' into and out of crime (Matza, 1964) into underclass or marginalised survival strategies. In other words, whereas it is eminently sensible to discard the psychoanalytic overinterpretation of 'affectionless thieves' (Bowlby, 1946) for the common-sense situationalism of 'how young burglars choose targets' (Wright and Logie, 1988), the rendering invisible of the impact of absolute poverty and powerlessness under such concepts as 'relative deprivation' and 'the reasoning criminal', betoken an impoverished criminology as well as a dehumanised criminal justice. If criminology merely counts rather than reflexively recounts, then the difference between administrative and theoretical criminology (Young, J., 1988) becomes very hard to spot.

Penal problems as social problems

This loss of interest in people in both theoretical and policy domains is surprising as well as disturbing. Surprising, because much of the motivation for progressive penal reform has been concern with injustices to people; disturbing because the problems of criminal injustice to certain social groups persist.

Among the original proponents of determinate sentencing and desert sentencing, anxiety over the 'cruel and unusual' element in punishment, the not knowing when it would end that was entailed in indeterminate sentencing, was prominent (Mitford, 1974). In the sphere of juvenile justice, evidence that young people were being subjected to state interference because of undesirable associates, residence in high-delinquency neighbourhoods, belonging to young families and, for young females, being sexually active, rather than because they had committed any, or any but the most trivial, offences, led many professionals to join the back-to-justice movement (Hudson, A., 1989; Thorpe *et al.*, 1980 *inter alia*). In adult jurisdictions, belief that sentencing depended as much on the demeanour, economic status and above all the race of defendants was a mainspring of the move to make punishment arise from what people have done rather than from who they are (Frankel, 1973): this motivation was one of the most persuasive arguments of the reform advocates. If we assume that these various lobbyists were genuine in their concerns, it is indeed surprising that there has been almost no evaluation of the new penal codes in terms of their effects on the penal treatment of the poor and unemployed, the minorities and migrants, the unconventional. Assessment of reform has concentrated almost entirely, however, on the size and criminal composition of the penal population, particularly the prison population, and has scarcely mentioned any impact on its social composition (Kramer and Lubitz, 1985).

Theorists of the new penal directions have generally disclaimed responsibility for the social justice outcomes of criminal justice practices, saying – rightly – that penal policy is but one minor plank of social policy and cannot be expected to be a palliative for the social injustices of the wider society (Von Hirsch, 1976). Arguments about the relationship between penality and social justice have usually been rather abstract, concentrating in the main on the question of whether there can be equality of moral obligation to uphold the law, and therefore equal liability to punishment, in a socially and materially unequal society (for example, Paternoster and Bynum, 1982). For the most part, the literature concerned with criminal justice and disadvantage and the literature concerning penal policy and practice – sentencing, prison crowding, etc. – have kept apart from each other. Whilst some deserts theorists are now acknowledging the need to pay more attention to problems of social justice (Von Hirsch, 1990a), and whilst there has been some attempt to establish the potential of penal reforms for bringing about more equitable outcomes for the unemployed, black offenders and female offenders (Hudson, 1987, chapter 4), those involved in formulating and implementing the various codes, laws and guidelines in the main show little evidence of having sustained their original concerns by the time they have come to evaluate the impact of policy changes on penal practice.

The widely commended Minnesota Sentencing Guidelines, for example, have as their first principle that 'sentencing should be neutral with respect to the race, gender, social and economic status of convicted felons' (Minnesota Sentencing Guidelines Commission, 1980, p. 1). According to at least one study, Minnesota was the state with the highest black:white incarceration rate up to introduction of the guidelines in 1981, with a black:white ratio of male prisoners per 100 000 residents of 21.2:1, against the state with the second highest ratio, Wisconsin, with 16.2:1 (Hawkins and Hardy, 1989, p. 88). Whilst the authors of this study concede that this racial disparity reduces if percentage arrests and percentages of serious crimes are controlled for, one would none the less expect that awareness of these kinds of figures would mean that all evaluations of the guidelines in Minnesota and other states with high black:white prisoner ratios would prioritise assessment of their progress in relation to racial imbalances in imprisonment rates. Although some assessments of sentencing guidelines have considered their impact on black:white disparities in incarceration, for example the evaluation of the Pennsylvania guidelines, this is, however, by no means common practice (Kramer and Lubitz, 1985).

In England and Wales, similarly, it has been commonplace amongst juvenile justice workers for many years that youth custodial institutions have disproportionate numbers of black inmates. One author who asks why – despite the efforts of innovative probation and intermediate treatment projects – penal establishments are 'filling up' with black young people, tells us that in one of the country's largest young people's remand and assessment centres, the population at the time of his investigation consisted of 60 per cent of black inmates (Pitts, 1986, pp. 132–4). He supports evidence of apparently discriminatory decision-making in juvenile justice that has been claimed by researchers (Fludger, 1981; Taylor, 1982); practitioners individually and through organisations such as the Association for Juvenile Justice and the National Intermediate Treatment Federation have expressed concern. A NITFED working party on race and juvenile justice, for instance, concluded that 'racism is institutionalised within the juvenile justice system which routinely rather than inadvertently produces racist outcomes' (NITFED, 1986, p. 1).

Policies and practices such as gatekeeping entry to intermediate treatment projects, monitoring social enquiry reports and so forth were adopted precisely to minimalise discriminatory justice outcomes associated with race, unemployment or educational status, family situation and the like, and yet these factors have only been very patchily included in evaluation of projects and monitoring of sentencing. One study of juvenile justice provision for black offenders found that although most agencies approached undertook systematic monitoring of juvenile justice processes (91 per cent of the social services departments surveyed), most of these monitoring systems did not include ethnic data. Just over half the voluntary agencies, but only one quarter of the probation services and one third of the social services departments which had juvenile justice information systems, included ethnic data. This despite the results of the National Association for the Care and Resettlement of Offenders (NACRO) review of the DHSS alternatives to custody initiative, started in 1983 and the impetus for much of the 'second generation' of alternative-to-custody intermediate treatment projects, which found that 15 per cent of young offenders receiving custodial or residential care orders were black, but only 1 per cent of those receiving community-based, alternative to custody disposals (Rogers, 1989).

Given the concerns expressed by proponents of both policy and practice reforms, this lack of follow-up on their impact in relation to personal-social characteristics of offenders is, then, surprising. It is disturbing, because the evidence of discriminatory decision-making at all stages of the criminal justice system is widespread, and it seems to be worsening. The disparities we see between states, regions and countries when we look at the overall severity of penalty scales, per capita imprisonment rates, or imprisonment rates for specific offences, disappear when we look at penal practices in relation to demographic and social factors. Thus, data produced by the US Department of Justice show a variation in the number of state and federal prisoners confined at the end of 1981 ranging from 33 per 100 000 residents in North Dakota to 251 in South Carolina, continuing a pattern of regional differences which has persisted since the first prisoner censuses were taken in the 1920s and 1930s. On the other hand, all states have higher black than white incarceration rates. Although the black:white prisoner ratio ranges from 3.3:1 in South Carolina to 21.2:1 in Minnesota (Hawkins and Hardy, 1989), there is no state which does not have substantially higher black than white imprisonment rates.

Similar data can be quoted for Australia, where state variations in the use of imprisonment contrast with continuities in overrepresentation of impoverished black minorities in prison populations:

> in Western Australia Aborigines comprise 32 per cent of the prisoners compared with 2.5 per cent of the general population. In South Australia the 0.8 per cent of Aborigines in the general population comprise nearly 16 per cent of the prisoners. Even in New South Wales where Aborigines comprise only 0.7 per cent of the general population they represent 7.2 per cent of the prisoners. (Biles, 1986, p. 247)

Biles continues that this 'alarming degree of overrepresentation has been much publicised and widely discussed but shows no signs of decreasing'; overrepresentation of black people in prisoner populations is similarly much discussed but not decreasing, and on the contrary increasing elsewhere. In France, for example, the percentage of African prisoners in mainland France increased from 8.1 in 1970 to 18.6 in 1985. Moreover, this represents an increase in the per capita detention rate amongst north African immigrants and other non-French citizens that is not only much higher than that of the French population, but also shows considerable increase against a stable French per capita detention rate (Table 2.1).

Overrepresentation of black people in prisoner populations is also evident in England and Wales. In June 1989, just over 15.5 of the male prison population and 24 per cent of the female prison populations were from minority ethnic populations. This is an increase from 1985, when the ethnic census of prison department establishments was first conducted, when the proportions found were 12 per cent of males and 17 per cent of females (Home Office, 1990b, p. 13). In the USA, in 1991 the overall incarceration rate was 426 out of every 100 000 residents, but for black American men the rate was 3109 per 100 000, far higher even than the rate of 729 per 100 000 for black males in South Africa

Table 2.1 French detention rate per 10 000

	French	*Others*
1970	5.2	16.0
1975	4.8	10.3
1978	4.4	11.5
1981	5.4	13.4
1982	6.2	18.8
1985	5.7	22.6

SOURCE: Carr-Hill, 1987, p. 296

(*Social Justice*, 1990, p. 3). A projection of prison populations in the USA up to the year 2000 suggests that even with the sentencing reforms of the 1980s, the non-white proportion of prison inmates can be expected to increase from 48 per cent in 1976 to 55 per cent in 2000 (Blumstein *et al.*, 1980).

The reverse side of the coin of offence disparity in criminal justice decision-making, then, is consistency of person-discrimination. It is surely, therefore, important to investigate the impact of evolving penal strategies on these discriminatory outcomes and to be ready to change strategies if criminal justice does not make progress towards greater social justice. The 1991 Criminal Justice Act includes a clause to the effect that race, gender or other inappropriate factors should not bias decision-making, but as we have seen, the Minnesota Sentencing Guidelines and many of the other new penal codes, guidelines and sentencing schedules have included similar clauses. The inclusion of these intentions has not been backed up by evaluation, or by preparedness to look more radically at the sources of overrepresentation of minority ethnic groups in the arrested, sentenced and imprisoned populations. To say that penal policy cannot make amends for discrimination and injustice in society as a whole is by no means the same as saying that it need not be concerned with whether it is itself – within its own sphere – discriminatory and unjust.

Explaining discrimination

Overrepresentation of the poor and of minority ethnic groups among the arrested and the imprisoned has been documented not just for the USA,

England, France and Australia, but also for countries such as Germany
and The Netherlands which generally achieve more penological appro-
bation (Albrecht, 1987; Junger, 1988; Petersilia, 1985 for a review of
US findings). In the United Kingdom, it is Afro-Caribbeans who seem
to be most overrepresented in arrest and prison populations; in the
USA, it is blacks and hispanics. Indigenous groups such as the Ab-
originals in Australia, Maoris in New Zealand and North American
Indians in Canada are heavily prosecuted and imprisoned, as are gypsies
in southern European countries such as Spain and Italy (Cipollini, Faccioli
and Pitch, 1989). In the countries of northern Europe, as well as former
colonials such as the Surinamese and Moluccans in The Netherlands and
north Africans in France, it is guest workers from southern Europe and
Asia, as well as groups from less economically advantaged neighbouring
countries, such as Finns in Sweden, who are prominent in penal
populations. Most European countries, rather than breaking their prison
populations down into ethnic categories, present data in the form of
'nationals' and 'foreigners', and the category 'foreigners', in this context, although it may include some visitors and short-term residents,
consists predominantly of 'guestworkers' and long-term residents. Most
European countries (Table 2.2) record substantial percentages of foreign
prisoners.

Indigenous or migrant, foreigner or citizen, what all these overimprisoned groups have in common, of course, is that they are dis-

Table 2.2   **Prison populations in 1987**

Countries	Percentage of foreign prisoners
Austria	7.0
Belgium	28.0
France	27.0
Fed. Rep. Germany	14.5
Italy	10.8
Netherlands	18.5
Norway	7.9
Portugal	7.2
Spain	14.8
Sweden	19.4
Switzerland	34.6

Source: Council of Europe, 1987, p. 23

approved and disadvantaged in the countries where they find themselves.

Unemployment is another social–structural variable which appears to affect the size and composition of prison populations in most countries. As with the race variable, research has been preoccupied with whether or not the unemployed are so strongly represented in prison populations because they are disproportionately involved in crime, or whether there is a direct bias that can be detected in criminal justice processes. Evidence for higher crime rates for different ethnic groups is equivocal. Much US research (summarised by Petersilia, 1985) claims higher crime rates among black and hispanic than among white Americans, and the consensus of various studies seems to be that there are higher crime rates among Afro-Americans and hispanics, especially for violent and serious crimes (Flowers, 1988). The most exhaustive reviews of studies of discrimination in sentencing suggest that, apart from one or two exceptional states, there is no convincing evidence of discrimination in sentencing (i.e. more severe sentencing that cannot be accounted for by nature of the offence, criminal record, etc.), except possibly for rape and homicide cases (Kleck, 1981, 1985).

European research is much more guarded. Junger argues that because of the number of studies which report no finding of discrimination against minority ethnic groups in arrest decisions, official police statistics can be used with some confidence to show that groups such as Moluccan, Turkish and Surinamese youth have higher delinquency rates than comparable Dutch young people (Junger, 1989, p. 165). In commenting on her review of comparative crime rates, Albrecht emphasises the methodological difficulties involved in such studies, and also argues that inter-ethnic differences often reduce or disappear if economic status is controlled for (Albrecht, 1989, p. 176). None the less, however carefully the evidence must be interpreted, however much we must bear in mind questions about the kinds of offences being counted, reporting rates, and factors such as homelessness, the balance of recent research has seemed to favour disproportionate involvement in crime accounting for at least some of the overrepresentation of black and migrant peoples in prison populations in relation to their proportionate presence in general populations (Sabol, 1989).

Most studies of unemployment, crime and imprisonment, on the other hand, assert a definite relationship between rising unemployment and rising use of imprisonment, but a 'consensus of doubt' about the relationship between rising unemployment and rising crime rates (Chiricos,

1987). The evidence for correlations between crime and imprisonment is principally time series analysis which shows that a general trend to reduce the use of imprisonment, to 'decentre' the prison and make fines and other non-custodial sentences the normal response to run-of-the-mill crimes which can be discerned at least in Western European countries (Bottoms, 1983), is interrupted by short-term rises in imprisonment rates which correspond to periods of economic recession characterised by rising unemployment (Box and Hale, 1982, 1985 for English and American data; Laffargue and Godefroy, 1989 for data referring to France and to continental Europe generally). No consistent correlation of equal strength and consistency can be demonstrated for rising crime in periods of rising unemployment. Fairly typical of reviews of evidence of links between unemployment, crime and imprisonment is a study carried out by the Council of Europe on correlations between economic recession, crime and crime control in England and Wales, France and the Federal Republic of Germany, which concluded that 'there is no confirmation of a correlation between unemployment and recorded crime; . . . on the other hand . . . In England and Wales and in the Federal Republic of Germany, there are indications of rises in crime being connected with the growth of an affluent society' (Council of Europe, 1985, p. 82).

This lack of sustainable correlation between rising unemployment and rising crime, but consistency of correlation between rising crime and rising imprisonment, had until fairly recently become accepted almost as conventional wisdom. In other words, notwithstanding figures such as those covering the late 1970s recession in England and Wales (Table 2.3), the difficulties in discerning whether such increases in crime are real increases, increases in reporting, or the result of increases in crime control activities, make linkages between crime rates and unemployment rates extremely problematic, whereas links between

Table 2.3

	1972	1982
No. of unemployed	800 000	3.5 million
Recorded serious offences per 100 000 population	3448	6226

SOURCE: Box and Hale, 1986, p. 72

unemployment and crime control, especially unemployment and imprisonment, seem clear and unequivocal.

This has been accepted in policy and political circles as well as in academic circles, for instance, the Council of Europe study referred to above quotes the then French Minister of Justice, Badinter, at a conference of European Ministers of Justice, as saying clearly that 'there exists a relationship between the economic crises and crime policy. The correlation is between the economic crises and the functioning of criminal justice rather than between the economic crises and crime' (Badinter, 1982 quoted in Council of Europe, 1985, p. 19).

This climb in imprisonment rates at times of rising unemployment has traditionally been theorised in fairly orthodox Marxist terms, posing prison and criminal justice as a regulator of the labour supply. Following Rusche and Kirchheimer's seminal analysis of the relationship between punishment and social structure (Rusche and Kirchheimer, 1939), it is argued that in periods of rising demand for labour, social control in general becomes more tolerant. In the sphere of criminal justice, this means a swing to punishments that either leave people at liberty and so able to remain within the labour market (fines, etc.) or which equip them with skills, the lack of which precluded their participation previously (vocational training, social skills training, etc. in prisons). In times of oversupply of labour, penalties become harsher, so that not only is there greater use of imprisonment, but prison regimes become more oppressive – longer sentences, less provision of work, education and therapy within the prison (Melossi and Pavarini, 1981). This has certainly seemed a persuasive analysis in the 1980s, as we have seen longer terms, official tolerance of overcrowding, fewer rehabilitative programmes, and more emphasis on punishment, security and control within the prison. On this reading, the move from rehabilitation to desert and incapacitation is a reflection of a change in the discourse of penality, of which a considerable part is a change in the vocabulary of motives for punishment (Melossi, 1985). In other words, since there is no economic need to reclaim lost souls to the labour supply, prisoners become designated as the unproductive, unwanted elements in society (Mathiesen, 1974). A result of the shift from a vocabulary of rehabilitation to a vocabulary of punishment is that the negative impact of imprisonment on people's lives and personalities need not arouse undue concern if the motive for imprisonment is punishment pure and simple, rather than reform, re-education or the reclamation of souls.

Theorists not content with the economic reductionism of this analysis have developed a framework which recognises the ideological as well as the economic functions of punishment in general, and imprisonment in particular. On this analysis, harsher penalties result from the transition from a welfare to a law and order political discourse which seeks to shift public blame for social problems from the capitalist system and its rulers to the victims of recession themselves, the unemployed and the disaffected (Box, 1987; Hale, 1989 *inter alia*). Instead of anger being directed towards the workings of the market economy in failing to deliver jobs, homes, educational and recreational opportunities to the whole population, we are induced to blame the poor – especially the unemployed, the undeserving poor, or any who raise their voices in protest – for failing to better themselves. Crime and punishment do not merely regulate the labour supply, they act to ensure that the failure of the economic system to deliver economic well-being to all its citizens does not threaten the legitimacy of the ruling élite.

Explanations of rising aggregate rates of imprisonment in conditions of rising unemployment, whatever merits they may have, largely miss the point that at every stage of the economic cycle, it is mainly the poor, the unemployed and the minority populations who are the most heavily penalised. It has always been and it remains true that the rich are overprotected and undercontrolled, whilst the poor are overcontrolled and underprotected; in short, now, as ever, the rich get richer and the poor get prison (Reiman, 1979). It continues to be the case that in North America, in Europe and in the Antipodes, and probably everywhere, 'prisoners are not drawn randomly from a population. On the contrary, the character of the prisoner population reflects the stratification system of the larger society.' (Jacobs, 1977, p. 89), and that 'those who populate the [Italian] prisons come from the poorest strata – the pockets of poverty in the south and the ghettoes of the industrial cities' (Invernizzi, 1975, p. 131). The new penal strategies should be evaluated on whether this remains true, or becomes less so.

Prisoners, then, and recipients of the most severe alternatives to custody, are predominantly poor, undereducated and from ethnic minority and migrant communities. They are unemployed or tenuously employed, casual workers, illegal immigrants, those who risk being deported as well as being punished. In Germany, even a fine may lead to loss of residence permit (Albrecht, 1989). Amongst women prisoners, these factors are even more evident. Studies of women prisoners have found overwhelming incidence of poverty, and very often poverty in the present is compounded upon histories of physical and sexual abuse, institutional care and addictions (Carlen, 1983). A Canadian author similarly claims that a large majority of female offenders are poor, undereducated, unskilled and drug- or alcohol-dependent, and quotes one survey of women prison inmates that found 52 per cent of the women reporting being sexually abused as children, whilst other estimates have suggested that the proportion is probably as high as 80 or 95 per cent (Moffat, 1991, p. 185).

Black women are even more overrepresented among prison populations than are black males (see Table 2.4).

Table 2.4   Prison populations in England and Wales, 1989

	% of population
Sentenced prisoners	
Adult males	15
Male young offenders	14
Females	26
Remand prisoners	
Adult males	20
Male young offenders	14
Females	23

SOURCE: Home Office, 1990b

The overall percentage of ethnic minority female prisoners of 24 per cent (as against just over 15.5 per cent male prisoners), is an increase from 17 per cent in 1985. The Canadian author quoted above says that 'native' women comprise 20 per cent of federal female prisoners, although they are only 3 per cent of the total female population. Black women are locked firmly into a 'criminal justice double bind', being both non-white and female they are 'the most powerless of the powerless' (Richey Mann, 1989 p. 107), suffering from institutional racism and also from non-conformity with the white, middle-class stereotypes of conventional femininity which have been shown to produce lenient criminal justice outcomes for some women (Hudson, 1987).

Poverty seems to be the key factor in the penal treatment of all women, as well as being a key precipitating factor in their criminality. In spite of such efforts as have occurred to make prostitution and other minor, usually economically motivated, offences punishable by non-custodial sanctions, poor women, and especially poor black women, continue to go to prison in excess numbers because of their inability to pay fines, to afford good defence lawyers, or to find non-criminal means of supporting themselves and their children. Women in countries with wide repertoires of penal sanctions continue to be imprisoned for minor offences. Abortion, infanticide and writing bad cheques were the main causes beside prostitution for which women were imprisoned in France in the early 1970s (Donzelot, 1975). Whilst the abortion laws have generally been liberalised and infanticide is often more sympathetically dealt with, cheque forgery, theft and prostitution remain the main sources of female imprisonment, and these offences are all clearly related to poverty. Also clearly related to poverty is the latest offence to be filling up the female prisons of Europe: drug carrying by third world women (of which there is more discussion in Chapter 5). These are all offences stimulated by poverty.

Eliminating discrimination in criminal justice

With all these social factors associated with crime and imprisonment – race, unemployment, poverty – a two-part question needs to be asked. First, are the new penal policies and the efforts of governments to secure their implementation beginning to bring about less imprisonment, less crime-inappropriate use of the most interventive non-custodial sentences, less denial of bail and less arrest and prosecution of trivial offenders (apparently) because of race, class, demeanour or other factors not related to offending behaviour? In other words, is formal, equitable criminal justice within the meanings of those words espoused by policy-makers being achieved? But secondly, even if such formal lack of discrimination is achieved, is this sufficient? Would the criminal justice system then be acting in harmony with social justice – if not actively creating a more just society, at least not making social injustice any worse?

There is some foundation for claims that reformed and invigorated penal policy is achieving at least some success in reducing imprisonment rates for minor offences, and that we will therefore see less imprisonment and other discriminatory sentencing which cannot be accounted for by differential involvement in criminality. Although, as argued above, there is too little evaluation of penal developments in terms of characteristics of offenders, there are one or two encouraging straws in the wind. For example, numbers of prison sentences in many European countries dropped in the latter half of the 1980s, despite rising levels of unemployment: of the countries covered by Council of Europe statistics, in 1980 only three countries were reporting an annual decrease in prisoner numbers, but by 1986 this had risen to six. Moreover, increased sentence lengths in many countries means that reductions in numbers of sentences do not always show up as reductions in prison populations (The Netherlands is such a case). Despite efforts in many countries to 'ration' prison sentences to the more serious offences, Council of Europe statistics suggest a 12 per cent increase in the detention rate amongst its member states during the mid-1980s (Muncie and Sparks, 1991, p. 98). The most spectacular cases of reduced use of imprisonment were the Federal Republic of Germany and Italy, where annual increases of the order of 6.9 and 18.8 per cent between 1981 and 1982 were replaced by annual decreases of 9.1 and 22.6 per cent respectively between 1985 and 1986 (Council of Europe, 1987). In England and Wales, with its marked profligacy with incarceration, reductions came later, but came none the less: the proportionate use of imprisonment fell between 1987 and 1988, and again between 1988 and 1989 (Home Office, 1990a). This cannot be attributed simply to falling crime rates, but marks a decline in the use of imprisonment for property offences. Use of custody for theft, for non-systematic benefit fraud, and for less serious offences such as criminal damage, declined.

But if all apparent criminal justice discrimination against the poor, blacks, gypsies and guestworkers could be explained away by the disproportionate extent of their involvement in crime, or the disproportionate extent of their involvement in the types of crime most likely to lead to imprisonment (B. Hudson, 1989), this still would not necessarily mean an equitable criminal justice system. Such evidence would not 'explain away' discrimination, it would, or should, beg the question of whether the so-called legally relevant variables (offence type, previous convictions, criminal justice involvement) systematically favour the white and the rich (Jankovic, 1977).

I have argued elsewhere that limiting sentencing considerations to questions of offence type and previous convictions 'freezes in' all the discrimination which we know takes place at earlier stages of the criminal justice system (Hudson, 1987, chapter 4). Decisions about whether to arrest, what to charge, how seriously to regard the offence, whether to grant bail, have all been shown to discriminate against the powerless, the impoverished and the unconventional, so that whether they actually are perpetrating more criminal behaviour or not (which is undiscoverable, criminologists do have to accept that they can never know how much crime there really is), members of disadvantaged groups are certainly more vulnerable than the socially advantaged to finding themselves in court charged with a serious offence, with several previous convictions. If it were possible to prove that no discrimination in the sense of punishing black or poor people more harshly than their more privileged counterparts for similar offences any longer takes place, this would undoubtedly be a considerable achievement for contemporary penal strategies. It would, however, do very little to change the social–demographic composition of prisons and penalised populations. Offence-focused sentencing, whether based on desert or incapacitation, privileges the items most closely correlated with social structural characteristics.

In considering the impact of sentencing reform in the USA, Sabol points out that in many states guidelines and laws were derived from existing practices. The sentence lengths for various offences, the predictors for parole or remission, were cemented into the new procedures and thereby institutionalised race and class discrimination. If the kinds of offences which characteristically have high black rates of involvement were resulting in high rates of imprisonment, these would be the offences scheduled as imprisonable in the new guidelines; if poor employment record, involvement with drugs, lack of strong family ties were used as indicators of recidivism in existing parole decision-making, these factors would be formalised into the new guidelines. Where the aim of reform is to reduce discretion and disparity rather than to introduce new penological thinking, guidelines and sentencing laws formalised existing practice. The innovation of these new policies was in this formalisation, not in examining practice to look for race or class bias. Speaking of race, but with equal relevance to economic status, Sabol explains: 'In other words, race may no longer be a directly important indicator of sentencing outcomes, but decisions based on factors that are racially neutral but which are highly correlated with race will perpetuate and perhaps exacerbate existing disparities' (Sabol, 1989, p. 427).

Even where guidelines or laws are developed not by standardisation from averages of existing sentences but by *tabula rasa* estimates of rank order of seriousness, the question arises of whose estimates of seriousness should count. Since the founding of criminology, there have been arguments over what counts as crime, still more over what counts as serious crime or as imprisonable crime. Unprovoked, premeditated murder, serious assault, torture and kidnap would probably feature on the list of most people, in most places, of crimes which should lead to imprisonment. Rape would probably be on such a list now, in many places, but it has taken decades of vigorous feminist campaigning to broaden the definition of rape, to make mostly male sentencers and legislators appreciate how seriously violated rape victims feel, and to accept that the victim's appearance, behaviour and previous sexual behaviour is irrelevant: acceptance of the irrelevance of these circumstances is still by no means universal. In the United Kingdom and the USA child sexual abuse is not only taken very seriously, but the expression of taking such behaviour seriously is to prosecute and punish the perpetrator. In much of Western Europe this individualising and punishing approach is thought to be inappropriate and counter-productive. There, sexual abuse is looked upon as a family relationship problem, requiring help not punishment, and the criminalisation and likelihood of imprisonment that is standard here is thought to be a deterrent to disclosure, rather than a deterrent to such behaviour itself.

Sentencing patterns, then, reveal a vast difference between serious crimes and crimes taken seriously (Hudson, 1987, chapter 4). Crimes taken seriously are the street crimes of the urban poor, especially when the offenders are black and the victims are white. Burglary, robbery and assault are taken seriously, but racial harassment is not. (Racial assaults are another example of how definitions of crime can change, subject to political campaigning. For years police forces, the Home Office and others concerned have denied that racial harassment and racial assaults are a significant part of life in Britain, but in the last few years the existence of the problems has been admitted. New methods of classifying racial assaults have been embraced by police forces, at Home Office instigation (Home Office, 1991a). Assertion by anyone who is party to an assault – including, most importantly, the victim – that an incident was racially motivated will now lead to categorisation, rather than an arresting officer's judgment being the only opinion that has counted. The 1991 Criminal Justice Act contains a clause to the effect that racial motivation will count as an aggravating factor in assaults. This is a welcome departure, but illustrates the fact that crimes are not taken seriously until they are taken seriously by those in power.) Assessments of seriousness are formulated by establishment figures: judges, lawyers, politicians, sometimes criminologists and establishment-approved community leaders. Very rarely are seriousness rankings based on surveys of the populations of inner city ghettoes, casual workers and the like.

Such people's views may be solicited by left-realist criminologists, but they are not attended to by those with power in penological discourse.

With the decline of interest in motivation, definitions of seriousness cannot be said to be based on moral qualities such as wickedness, and equally rarely are they based on any rational notion of harm, either to persons or to the economy, despite the efforts of the deserts theorists mentioned above:

> In Australia, the types of crime that cause the greatest harm to persons are domestic violence, occupational health and safety and other corporate crimes of violence such as those of the pharmaceutical industry and drink driving. The property offenders that cause the overwhelming majority of criminal losses are white collar criminals. (Braithwaite, 1991, p. 10)

A list of most harmful crimes would be similar for most advanced industrial countries, but such a list by no means corresponds to a list of offences producing most prison sentences (except, as previously discussed, drink driving in Scandinavia and The Netherlands, and even then, sentences for drink driving are very much shorter than sentences for most other offences provoking imprisonment). It is important to keep in mind that Braithwaite's list is not composed of acts that are not already criminalised. Lists such as his are not suggesting alternative social moralities from that expressed by the criminal law, they are not appealing to politically charged notions of human rights, but they highlight the acts within existing schedules of crimes which cause most harm to persons or most damage to society, and yet which are not taken seriously if prosecution and punishment are indicators of taking behaviour seriously.

Yet it is these very notions – harm to persons, damage to society – that are appealed to when it is urged that street crime is that which should be most assiduously policed and most severely punished (Van Den Haag, 1975; Wilson, 1975). Street crime is, as the realists of left and right insist, damaging to the everyday quality of citizens' lives. The stranger striking out in the street and the burglar invading the home are indeed menacing figures, yet in selecting these crimes for enforcement we must be sure of the basis on which we are prioritising them. Is it really because they are more dangerous than other crimes, or is it because of the characteristics of the people who commit them, or more surely, the characteristics of the people who are apprehended, because of course we cannot know how many of the unsolved or unrecorded crimes fit or do not fit the stereotypes of the marginalised, underclass predator. Whatever the real crime rates of the various social groups, the iconography of crime which is taken seriously is overwhelmingly unemployed, uneducated, disrespectful, and disproportionately black or migrant.

Evidence about the differential enforcement of penalties against ostensibly similar forms of wrongdoing would indicate that it is the social status of the perpetrators rather than the inherent harmfulness of the acts which determines which will be prosecuted and penalised and which will be dealt with either leniently, or even purely administratively. It has been well established, for instance, that the difference in sentencing between the essentially similar offences of larceny and embezzlement is due to the different socio-economic backgrounds of typical offenders (Kittrie, 1980). An analysis of the disparate processing of benefit fraud and tax evasion – both theft from the state – shows that such disparity is a result not only of the different characteristics of the offenders, but also of ideologies of the state which promote a view of taxation as a (maybe necessary) evil, which should be levied at the lowest possible level, and which any reasonable person would pay as little of as possible. Conservative politicians during the 1980s promoted the idea of taxation as a disincentive to initiative, so that there is a cultural tolerance of people who step somewhat beyond the bounds of legality in their attempts to avoid it. Tax evasion is seen as something that any enterprising person might indulge in if they could, and it is only tax fraud on a very large scale that attracts any significant public opprobrium. Welfare payments, however, are given ever more grudgingly, and it is widely held to be the state's duty to ensure that no one gets anything to which they are not beyond doubt entitled. The natural corollary of this imagery is that the state should penalise those who take from it benefits to which they are not entitled, but that there should be equal support for the procedure of securing compliance with tax regulations rather than prosecuting in cases of non-payment of tax (Cook, 1989).

Penal policy based on desert, then, may make criminal justice appear more equitable. It may mean that even more research will be able to demonstrate that race, unemployment, female poverty or unconventionality of lifestyle are less and less directly influential on sentencing or prosecution decisions, but it will do little for social justice if it is not accompanied by radical thinking about what is meant by serious crime, and unless the crimes of the powerful are pursued as vigorously as the crimes of the powerless. And while deserts theorists may be quite rea-

sonable in their claims that penal policy cannot be expected to compen-
sate for social injustice in other spheres, we can at least demand that
penal policy should be cognisant of other injustices, and should not
institutionalise or further compound them in its own practices.

Tailoring sentencing guidelines to accommodate both desert and incapacitation must surely be expected to compound and institutionalise
social injustice still further. As well as building in the existing practices
of sentencing the crimes of the disadvantaged more harshly than the
crimes of the advantaged, proposals for categorial incapacitation would
allow for even harsher penalties for those with a poor prognosis for
avoiding trouble in the future. The RAND Corporation research, which
has frequently been drawn upon by those suggesting both selective and
categorial incapacitation, generated a seven-factor scale to identify likely
reoffenders: including recent incarceration, a similar prior conviction,
juvenile conviction or incarceration, heroin or barbiturate use, and recent
unemployment (Chaiken and Chaiken, 1982; Cohen, 1983; Greenwood
and Abrahamse, 1982). Prediction scales can only be derived by looking
at aggregate factors of general populations which correlate with offending, or by examining, as with the RAND Corporation surveys, characteristics of convicted criminals (Farrington, 1987; Gottfredson, 1987). In
either case, the predictions are built on existing race- and class-biased
patterns of defining, recording, prosecuting and sentencing crime. Minnesota's experience, then, becomes very readily understandable. After
sentencing guidelines were established, the use of imprisonment for
'serious' offences increased, the use of imprisonment for 'lesser' offences decreased (Knapp, 1984) – and the ethnic minority prison
population has increased substantially, as elsewhere, resulting in the
horrific national per capita black imprisonment rate of 3109 per 100 000
quoted earlier in this chapter.

The limited vision of contemporary criminal justice policy indicates
the extent of any improvement in the penal treatment of the racially,
socially and economically disadvantaged that we may expect: discrimination, in the sense of decisions based purely and directly on personal
and social factors, may be held to be unacceptable and may be eliminated or at least reduced considerably, but disparities in the sense of
imposing formalised criteria relating only to criminality and thus possibly treating unlike offenders in like manner, and even more, using
criteria which are weighted against the disadvantaged, will continue to
be tolerated (Petersilia and Turner, 1987). Petersilia and Turner's review
of the correlation of race with various predictive factors highlights

clearly the dilemma for penal policy which contemporary theorists and reformers often seem to ignore or deny; namely, that decisions about which factors to include in criteria for imprisonment or community sanctions, for sentence lengths, for parole or remission, cannot be derived from abstract principles such as 'justice', 'desert' or 'culpability'. Neither can sentencing or other penal processes remain abstracted from criminal justice policy overall or, ultimately, from social policy overall. As these authors maintain, there are inescapable conflicts between trying to treat people fairly (which might suggest allowing for reduced punishment for some classes of offence because of correlations with race, poverty or addictions and, therefore, arguably diminished culpability because of reduced opportunity or incentive to refrain from criminal involvement), and treating acts consistently. There are still further tensions between trying to treat offenders equitably and other objectives such as crime control and public safety.

Deserts theorists claim that

> the principle of proportionality is defended on grounds of its fairness to those punished. Substantial prison terms are to be limited to those convicted of serious crimes. Desert-based sentencing is not offered as a means of reducing crime rates; indeed, most desert advocates have been sceptical about how much crime rates can be made to respond to changes in sentencing policy. (Von Hirsch, 1990a, p. 398)

'Fairness' has been taken to mean lack of discrimination in the sense described above, 'serious crimes' to mean those presently taken seriously by the criminal justice system. Reducing disparity in the form of punishing like crimes dissimilarly has been prioritised at the expense of risking greater disparity in the sense of punishing unlike criminals similarly, with the result that sentencing comes more to resemble a strategy of general deterrence (where priority is given to discouragement of certain acts), to which deserts theory claims to be opposed. Without giving much greater consideration to the motivation and life opportunities of offenders, how could we claim to be putting fairness to them at the heart of the system?

There is, for example, some evidence of differences in typical motivations of black and white, employed and unemployed offenders. Petersilia's review of the literature on racial correlations with crime found that in self-report studies black people more often mentioned economic motives for offending, whereas white offenders more often referred to high jinks, excitement, doing it for kicks (Petersilia, 1985). Surely criminal justice should allow for some leniency to those driven by economic need? This would raise a question for penal policy parallel to that in the desert/incapacitation debate, namely, should leniency, like incapacitation, be on a selective, case-by-case basis, which would mean reintroducing substantial judicial discretion, reintroducing the disparity-producing offender focus; or should we provide for categorial leniency, in other words should there be lower tariffs for those offences which typically have high rates of participation by the poor and socially disadvantaged?

Could it be that there is a *de facto* categorial leniency which produces the much lower rates of incarceration for burglary in Germany and The Netherlands than in the English-speaking countries, or could it be that the greater retention of an offender orientation allows for greater mitigation when personal circumstances of individual offenders are considered? The alternative explanation, however, is that this lower incarceration rate for property offences in 'progressive' mainland Europe comes about because deportation of migrant workers exists as an alternative to their incarceration. The function of regulating the reserve army of labour which is often ascribed to the penal system can be even more effectively achieved when penal policy is linked to migration controls (Lynch, 1988). In any case, whether differences in the use of imprisonment for particular offences come about because of leniency or because of the use of alternative means of exclusion, the point remains that we cannot understand penal strategies without looking at the social–structural context in which they are embedded.

The criminal justice system and the management of crisis

Sentencing policy may well have little impact on crime control, but the criminal justice system as a whole is very much in the business of controlling the criminal classes. In England and elsewhere this has been theorised as regulating the labour supply, and also as managing the 'legitimation crisis' of post-industrial capitalism in decline (Box, 1983, 1987; Hall *et al.*, 1978) and in the USA as managing the underclass (Irwin, 1985).

The essentials of the scenario are the existence of a large subgroup in the population, concentrated in run-down inner cities, where a sizeable minority of those under 30 have dropped out of education, have endured long-term unemployment and have maybe never known proper employment, where a high percentage of births are illegitimate, a high percentage of families are single-parent, where drug addiction is rife, and where hustling and crime are the normal means of getting by. Variants of the theory emphasise the 'culture of poverty', which is supposedly crime-tolerant; the persistence of unemployment, which is crime-provoking; the lack of 'respectable' role models as the more successful inhabitants move out, which is crime-prolonging for youth; and some variants of the theory hint at the importance of white racism, which is criminal-record propelling (Inniss and Feagin, 1989). This underclass also comprises high concentrations of blacks and migrants, although there are white and indigenous areas of urban poverty which are described as underclass. Whatever the varying weight given to factors such as dependency on welfare, family breakdown, chronic unemployment, declining influence of facilities such as schools, churches and community associations, the concept of an underclass *per se* is open to objection because of the ease with which crime becomes uncritically ascribed as a feature of life among the underclass, thus focusing attention on its own pathology rather than on the social policies and law enforcement strategies which neglect, criminalise, contain and punish. Underclass theory accepts that crime rates are the product of real (albeit understandable) involvement in crime, rather than being the product of processes of penalisation.

Analyses which have moved beyond uncritical cultural or sometimes even biological accounts of underclass crime, seek explanation in relative deprivation and marginalisation, explanations which appear acceptably liberal in that they locate the base causes of high race- and class-crime rates in white racism and in the failure of the market economy to afford legitimate opportunities for decent living standards to all citizens and 'guests'. Relative deprivation is favoured rather than absolute poverty as an explanation – because there are many individuals who endure poverty without resorting to crime; because crime rates appear to rise in times of boom as well as slump; and because crime rates in the most affluent nations are at least as high as crime rates in the poorer countries. Being poor in a society where images of wealth are constantly paraded; feeling valueless if without money; living on a run-down estate cheek by jowl with a glitzy docklands development, are plausible sources of disaffection. Relative deprivation connects with control theory, which posits that since human beings (presumably) seek gratification of their own wants before all else, what has to be explained

is not criminality but conformity. According to this theory, people refrain from crime because (or if) they have too much to lose – house, job,
family, reputation – if they were to be convicted of crime (Box, 1981,
1987). Deprivation, even relative deprivation, may not of itself lead
to crime, if people feel they have a chance of improving things. But if
they feel they are marginalised, that there is no chance of things changing, that the more fortunate groups in society do not care about their
plight, then there is a high potential for deviant behaviour (Lea and
Young, 1984; Stack, 1984).

Relative deprivation and marginalisation theories have common-
sense appeal as well as according with earlier sociological explanations
of crime such as anomie and differential association. They only have any
explanatory power, however, if we accept that the have-nots really do
commit more crime than the haves and, as argued above, we have no
evidence of this. What we do know is that the crimes of the poor are
more heavily penalised than the crimes of the rich. Relative deprivation
or marginalisation theory does not, of course, set itself to understand
why this excessive penalisation of the urban poor should be, it merely
colludes with it. After all, most crime is intra-class and intra-racial.
The urban poor form a class of the superexploited: they are exploited
by each other as victims of crime, and they are exploited by the state
through excessive punishment (Platt, 1981). What needs explanation is
why the powerful should, as evidence of law enforcement and penal
policies would suggest, care so much about the troubles of the powerless, when in other respects they exhibit so little concern? Why, in
other words, does the state spend so much money policing and imprisoning the urban poor when it spends so little on housing, educating and
employing them?

There is overwhelming evidence that the powerful do not care greatly
about the troubles of the powerless, especially in the law and order
societies of late twentieth-century Britain and North America. Whilst
homelessness, unemployment, decaying schools and declining health
care provision attest to this lack of concern, criminal justice priorities
also show little regard for the problems of the powerless. The struggle
that has been needed to get violence against women taken seriously;
the difficulties of establishing the extent of racial harassment; the evidence that sentencing is more lenient when the victim of crime is black
(evidence which accounts for the finding of some research of greater
severity of sentencing for white offenders (Petersilia, 1985)), would

make us suspect that excessive policing of deprived urban areas (Lea and Young, 1984) is not the result of concern for their inhabitants.

When residents of areas like the Meadow Well and Scotswood in Newcastle, Toxteth in Liverpool, Brixton, Tottenham, Brent and Newham in London and similar areas in many cities, complain both about police not responding to emergency calls and at the same time about oppressive, mob-handed policing, they are not being contradictory. It is the policing that is inconsistent: police tactics vacillate between swamp and no-go. This inconsistency can be understood in terms of the (establishment) necessity to create and sustain a public mythology of black and poor crime, to justify neglect in social policy and provision. There is a necessity for a received ideology of fecklessness and instability, rather than recognition of structural unemployment, flight of capital as the reason for worklessness, and the necessity for an ideology of lawlessness rather than racism as the problem of the ghetto. Mythologising poor, and especially poor black, criminality is revealed as a necessity not just of contemporary racism, but as a necessity for the survival of contemporary *laissez-faire* conservatism (Gilroy, 1987). Periodic police crackdowns provide an image of concerned state response to the troubles of the inner city; they provide an image of the state doing something vigorous about crime, whilst at the time they provide a dramatic imagery of criminality as a characteristic of the urban ghetto.

A perspective which potentially reconciles the models of the mythologising of black crime and of marginalisation/relative deprivation is that which sees selective enforcement against the crimes of the urban poor as a response to the degree of anticipated threat to the establishment posed by the deprived and marginalised. Such a perspective is notably found in the works of Steven Box (Box, 1983, 1987). If it is unreasonable to expect people, particularly young people with time and energy to expend, passively to accept a no-hope way of life, then rising long-term youth unemployment in particular comes to seem a near certain catalyst of violent protest and predatory crime. As this threat is perceived, increased powers of enforcement which predominantly affect the young, such as the invention of 'new crimes' (for example, affray, aggravated taking and driving away), accompany tendencies to more coercive styles of policing, law-and-order politics and get-tough sentencing campaigns. This power-threat hypothesis can explain such things as regional differences in levels of policing, and regional differences in black:white sentencing disparities. According to this hypothesis, the more a dominant group perceives a potential threat to its power or well-being from subordinated groups, the more likely are three forms of discrimination (Hawkins and Hardy, 1989):

1. restriction of political rights;
2. symbolic forms of segregation;
3. threat-oriented ideology.

All three of these elements can be seen in contemporary social and criminal justice policies towards the young unemployed, towards the poor, towards the black and the migrant. Restrictions on welfare benefits such as young people's eligibility to housing benefit, deportations as well as coercive policing and disproportionate imprisonment work cumulatively to restrict rights, to segregate and to threaten.

The rising differential imprisonment of the 1980s, then, can best be explained not by direct reference to unemployment, peak numbers of the most crime-prone age groups in the population, or high black crime rates. Although these factors may all have some impact individually or together, the key factor is the perception by the powerful of an increased potential threat from the powerless, which makes repression of the powerless a priority for maintenance of the status quo. Urban disorder, strikes and protests would thus be expected to be followed by increased ideological promotion of the powerless as criminal, and of their crimes as especially dangerous to individual potential victims and damaging to their communities, and consequently by increasingly robust policing, prosecution and sentencing. The crimes of the urban poor are thus singled out as more serious than the crimes of the powerful, with the expected consequences for enforcement and sentencing.

Conclusion: penal policy and social structure

It remains true, therefore, that 'the character of the prisoner population reflects the stratification system of the larger society' (Jacobs, 1983, p. 17). However much penal policy may have developed during the 1970s and 1980s, the criminal law still seems to operate in exactly the same way the conflict theorists would have us believe, as a means whereby the white, middle-aged, middle-class repress the young, black and migrant poor (Chambliss, 1969; Quinney, 1977). Desert or incapa-

citation, sentencing guidelines, interagency initiatives, unit fines, alternatives to custody, anti-racism training for police and sentencers, seem
to be having little impact on the class- and race-bias of criminal
justice. We can readily understand why this should be so if we think
of criminal justice not as a system for controlling crime or dispensing
fairness to offenders, but as a system for sifting and classifying harms.
The various stages of criminal justice systems successively filter all
sorts of individuals accused of committing all sorts of social harms, the
effect of this filtering being to homogenise what started off as a hetero-
geneous population perpetrating a heterogeneity of acts into a homo-
geneous population suffering a homogeniety of penalties (Headley,
1989). Of all the wrongdoings committed,

> very few of these acts come to the attention of the police . . . only a
> small percentage (less than 20 per cent) results in an arrest. Even of
> those arrested, many are never charged with a crime . . . As we
> proceed through the stages of the system, we see that the number
> of people involved as defendants is further reduced. Also, and
> more importantly, the kinds of people involved become more and
> more homogeneous. For instance, they become more alike in terms
> of age (younger), sex (more are males), race (increasingly non-white,
> social class (increasing numbers of lower- and working-class people),
> offense (more and more 'index' offenses) . . . When we arrive at the
> last stage, the prison population, we have the most homogeneous
> grouping in which the vast majority are poor, unskilled, uneducated,
> and have had much more contact with the criminal (and juvenile)
> justice system. (Shelden, 1982, pp. 1–2)

This homogenisation process obviously involves definitions of crimes,
perceptions of which crimes are serious and which are to be taken
seriously, as well as which factors should be used for decisions about
arrest, prosecution, remand, sentence and parole. Reducing the discretion of professionals in the system could only ever have a marginal
effect (and this effect might be in the direction of either more or less
social justice) on the social composition of the penalised population,
because the partiality of criminal justice is much less the result of
the actions of its individual agents than it is the reflection of inbuilt
structural bias of the social role allocated to criminal justice (Laffargue
and Godefroy, 1989).

The criminal justice system is but one institution for the regulation of infractions and disputes. Breaches of regulation such as tax evasion, labour, environmental and consumer protection laws are dealt with by specialist agencies and do not normally fall within the ambit of criminal justice. Similarly, family matters, neighbourhood disputes and the like are dealt with in most countries by separate jurisdictions – the civil law which does not have the same penalising powers as the criminal law. Some of these infractions and disputes may be transferred to criminal jurisdictions if they seem to be becoming increasingly threatening for the state. Activities associated with industrial disputes and anti-nuclear protests have in recent years been transferred to criminal processing. Even some crimes, such as traffic act violations, may be dealt with quasi-administratively by spot fines, automatic disqualifications, etc., whilst other behaviours may remain on the statute book but be dealt with more and more by non-prosecution.

Thus the criminal justice system is a 'penal-penalising circuit' (ibid., p. 379) dealing mainly with the street crimes of the urban lower classes. Penal and social criteria are inextricably intertwined in determining which behaviours, which persons, are dealt with by the penal-penalising circuit and which are dealt with by the administrative circuits. To imagine that penal policy can be formulated or implemented according to abstract, legalistic notions of justice, fairness or seriousness is therefore a nonsense. It is, after all, impossible to punish crimes, we can only punish people (Mohr, 1980).

We have seen that there are many intra- and international differences in penal policies and provisions, but that the populations who are penalised and, above all, the populations who are imprisoned, are similar everywhere. As Matthews has pointed out in discussing the phenomenon of 'net-widening' in relation to informal justice processes: 'To visualize the operation of social control as some sort of trawling operation is to present a picture of a unified, co-ordinated and structured offensive aimed at a random population. But it is precisely the population which is predictable, whereas the strategies are variable' (Matthews, 1988, p. 19). Exactly. This is and remains true not just of informal justice but of penal processes in general, and not just of net-widening but of penal outcomes in general.

3 Penal Policy and Social Policy

The previous chapter was concerned with the demographic–social structure of the penalised population, pointing out that it is made up predominantly of the poor, minorities and migrants. This composition of the penal population was discussed purely within the framework of crime and criminal justice: the correlation of personal–social characteristics such as race and unemployment with crime, arrest and sentencing; the dilemmas for penal policy posed by differential representation of blacks, the unemployed – members of what is commonly referred to in sociological discourse as the underclass – in offence commission and offence processing. In this chapter I wish to look at the interaction of penal policy with other aspects of public policy. Questions such as the differences and similarities between penal policy and policy in other areas, of overlap between them, of the impact of wider social policy on penal policy, will be examined.

Social policy is commonly understood as being something different from other aspects of public policy, such as economic policy or defence policy, but there is no single, clear-cut definition of social policy which is agreed on by analysts in this field. Hill and Bramley offer a useful review of various definitions which are associated with the different schools and perspectives within which social policy is studied (Hill and Bramley, 1986, chapter 1). By *public* policy they mean 'the actions and positions taken by the *state* as the overriding authoritative collective entity in society' (ibid., p. 2). In defining 'policy' they refer to a definition by Jenkins (1978, p. 15): ' a set of interrelated decisions taken by a political actor or group of actors concerning the selection of goals and the means of achieving them within a specified situation where these decisions should, in principle, be within the power of these actors to achieve' (quoted by Hill and Bramley, 1986, p. 3). These authors explain that this definition of policy is helpful because it stresses a pattern, or cluster of decisions rather than a single decision; because the term 'political actors' could include officials as well as ministers; because ends and means are both involved in policy; because policies are formulated with reference to contingencies such as the state of the economy, and are therefore different because of their specificity from more universal or enduring statements of values; and because policy implies decisions of those with authority to implement those decisions. They then review the three dominant traditions of social policy analysis, and discuss the key elements which each ascribes to *soeial* policy as opposed to other kinds of public policy.

First, the social administration perspective defines social policy as concerned with the provision of welfare goods and services to individuals, and takes an institutional approach to social policy analysis. It sees its subject matter as being those decisions, practices and institutions involved in delivering the services of the welfare state – housing, personal social services, health, education, social security benefits – and sees defining characteristics as being that provision is organised collectively but delivered to individuals. The second tradition, that of welfare economics, again sees social policy as being welfare goods and services provided to individuals, but the emphasis in this perspective is that of redistribution – the services and institutions concerned are those which are made necessary because of malfunctions of the market economy, or which cannot sensibly be provided on a market basis. The third perspective they describe is that of political economy, the critical or neo-Marxist approach. This perspective sees social policy and its resultant services being essential for the maintenance of the capitalist economy, and sees social policy as essentially concerned with reproduction of the labour force. Social policies such as health, housing, child benefit and family income support are concerned with the physical reproduction and maintenance of the labour force, whilst services such as education are concerned with its ideological reproduction. This task of reproduction of the productive elements of the labour force is combined with repression or neutralisation of unproductive elements: through legitimation (the securing of consent) and control (overcoming dissent). Although the 'core' social services and policies would be included by all these traditions, the boundaries of what would be considered social policy would differ. The element that is common to all three approaches is those policies, practices and institutions concerned with support for groups dependent on the state.

Hill and Bramley themselves conclude that there is no one satisfactory, intellectually coherent definition of social policy, and they therefore adopt a pragmatic approach. In their own analysis, they concern themselves with what are 'conventionally' included as social policy areas – social security, health, personal social services, education and housing (ibid., p. 18). By conventionally, they seem to mean within the social administration tradition; they then draw considerably on the political economy tradition in their actual analyses.

The way in which I wish to consider social policy is consistent with that of Hill and Bramley. It is not usual to include penal policy and the criminal justice system as social policy, although there are aspects of the criminal justice system that are concerned with the welfare of offenders and victims. Probation officers share the same qualification as social workers in local authority social services departments, and endeavour to provide welfare services for offenders under their supervision; some staff in prisons carry out welfare functions; providers of drug, alcohol and mental health services have offender clients; local authority social workers and probation officers often work together in juvenile justice projects. One could also argue that the whole purpose of penal policy is the redistribution of rights and benefits (from offenders back to victims or society), and under the rehabilitation rationale, criminal justice often assumed at least a rhetoric of welfare. To claim penal policy as a branch of social policy is not my purpose, however. What I wish to show is, first, that the same ideological movements and social-economic contexts that influence social policy also influence penal policy; and secondly, that because social and penal policy deal with the same client groups (the poor, the addicted, the disturbed) there is necessarily a close relationship between the two domains.

The social policies with which I am primarily concerned are housing and social security payments, mental health policy, and the general movement away from institutional forms of welfare which received their formal expression in the community care White Paper *Caring for People: Community Care in the Next Decade and Beyond*, presented to Parliament in November 1989 and in the early 1990s becoming the main policy direction for central government and local authorities in Britain. This White Paper incorporated the recommendations of the 1988 report *Community Care: An Agenda for Action* (Griffiths, 1988) and the Audit Commission report *Making a Reality of Community Care* (Audit Commission, 1980), and between them these three documents mark firm commitment to the principles that welfare services should be provided in the community rather than in institutions, that the voluntary and private sector are to be used, and the role of local authorities to become that of 'care enabler' and 'care coordinator' rather than care provider.

The White Paper reaffirms commitment evident in the earlier reports, and in official reports on provision for the mentally ill and mentally handicapped throughout the 1970s, to

> promoting care for the older people, people with mental illness, disabilities or learning difficulties in the community, preferably in their family home or in a 'homely environment'. It recommends a transformation in the role of local authority social services depart- ments from that of service providers to that of 'enabling agencies', concerned with assessing need, planning services and promoting con- sumer choice among a range of public, private and voluntary organ- isations. It proposes a new funding structure which removes the financial incentive towards residential care. (Langan, 1990, p. 59)

Some of these themes are already familiar from mental health policy of the mid-1950s to mid-1970s, and from penal policy of the same era.

Deinstitutionalisation and decarceration

During the 1960s and 1970s, penal policy seemed to be developing along exactly the same lines as policy in other spheres. Deinstitutionalisation, or the destructuring impulse (Cohen, 1985), appeared to be the dominant tendency in responses not only to crime, but also to other forms of deviancy and problems posed by difficult populations. The search for alternatives to custody, innovations such as community service and intermediate treatment, as well as expansion of the use of established alternatives such as probation and suspended sentences, seemed to par- allel exactly the shift away from in-patient treatment for illness – espe- cially mental illness – towards out-patient and day hospital treatment. Developments such as specialist fostering schemes, provision of warden-controlled and other sheltered accommodation for the elderly and handicapped, all seemed part of a general move away from depend- ence on segregative institutions as the normal way of coping with problem populations. The moves towards diversion, informalism, and reduction of custody described in the first chapter can readily be fitted in with this deinstitutionalising scenario, which at the time seemed entrenched, widespread, progressive and wholly desirable. At the begin- ning of the 1980s, the United Nations secretariat was able to report:

The main difference between current trends and the recent past is that while alternative approaches once consisted of sporadic and scattered experiments, especially on the part of charitable organizations, today they are planned and implemented as part of a differentiated strategy intended to deal with the problem of criminality in a global perspective, where the various sectors of criminal justice are viewed as an integrated system. Governmental efforts and resources are increasingly being devoted to the development of new or the redevelopment of old alternatives in the wake of a growing realization of the prison's inability to rehabilitate and as part of the overall trend to deinstitutionalization, which also characterizes the mental health field. Society, in fact, does not remove all the mentally disturbed and retarded to asylums, exile the poor or send the aged to workhouses. The care and support of such people has gone back to the community. (United Nations Secretariat, 1983, p. 9)

In the eagerness with which deinstitutionalisation was embraced, the therapeutic optimism which was – at least at the time – seen as one of the main bases for decarceration of the mentally ill, could also be seen in the projects which sprang up to deal with the criminal and delinquent. Offenders may never have had the same claims on public sympathy as psychiatric patients, so that Scull in his autocritique of his earlier work, which had looked at the decarceration of the mad and the bad as aspects of the same phenomenon, is right to point out that arguments that prisons are degrading and unpleasant are no automatic spur to their abolition (Scull, 1983, 1984). At the time, the argument that they were ineffective in reforming offenders, further that they actually increased the criminality of inmates, seemed persuasive in that reformist, therapeutic zeitgeist. The 'decarceration era' of the mid-1950s to mid-1970s (Hudson, 1984) was also the era when there was still faith that crime rates could be reduced, that individuals could be reformed, that offending was linked with some form of deprivation and/or pathology which had its roots in offenders' lives in their communities, and so could only be 'cured' by treatment in the community.

Just as psychiatry could place its faith in psychotropic drugs to control the symptoms of chronic mental illness and in various forms of therapy to cure most neuroses, similarly the community corrections movement came up with a variety of prophylactics for offending. Drop-in centres, motor projects, canoeing and climbing, social skills training, literacy training, addictions therapy, self-awareness and self-encounter groups of all kinds – the point is not simply that these responses to crime were thought to be more humane than imprisonment; at the time they were championed as being more effective. In the era of social-democratic optimism crime was indeed perceived as 'a challenge to us all' (Taylor, 1981), a challenge that could be met and overcome by the application first and foremost of the knowledge and skills of social work and psychotherapy.

The critiques of deinstitutionalisation that developed in the later 1970s and gained force in the 1980s asserted that community corrections were not necessarily more humane, more effective, or cheaper than institutional corrections (Greenberg, 1975), and that some of the myths of community care facilities as self-governing communities masked a more authoritarian reality (Beck, 1979). The most substantial caveat was that the overall effect of the deinstitutionalisation movement was not just to widen the social control net, but also to extend the segregative principle from the institution into the community (Hudson, 1984). The 'dispersal of discipline' thesis has urged that the development of community corrections represents not the restriction of the mode of penality that has its paradigmatic case in the modern prison, but its dispersal throughout a multiplicity of locations, agencies and persons (Cohen, 1977, 1979). According to these critics, the most important point about community corrections is that they have supplemented and replicated, rather than replaced, institutional corrections.

It is the persistence of prisons and juvenile custodial institutions which, it is argued, reveals the differences between policy towards offenders and other policy domains. At least in England and Wales and the USA, community corrections have generally (except in the celebrated and isolated case of juvenile institutions in Massachusetts) been put in place before institutions have been closed, whereas with psychiatric patients, the elderly and other problem populations, institutional closure has preceded the development of the community care network that was supposed to replace the large mental hospitals. The alleged failure to develop community care facilities has led to the conclusion that:

1. deinstitutionalisation of the mentally ill cannot be explained by therapeutic alternatives or increased humanitarianism; and
2. policy in respect of the criminal and the mentally ill is essentially dissimilar.

The best known statement of the first proposition is that by Scull (1977) who contended that the main impetus to deinstitutionalisation is states' desire to contain welfare spending. He argued that a combination of burgeoning sector claims on the public purse because of factors like increased unionisation and professionalisation of care personnel, and higher spending to revenue ratios as economies moved into recession, in the context of the existence of a safety net of 'outdoor relief' welfare payments (unemployment benefit, etc.) encouraged the state to divest itself of its responsibilities to the aged and insane. Closing the institutions did not, he claimed, in reality mean a shift from segregation to integration, but meant a shift from public to private finance, with care for those who could afford it and a neglect that is often far from benign for those who are without sufficient means to pay for residence in the mushrooming privately owned care facilities. Far from being a caring community, welcoming back those who have been decanted from institutions, well-to-do neighbourhoods have used zoning laws and planning procedures, sometimes even vigilante groups, to repel even those facilities states have sought to provide (Dear and Wolch, 1987). The NIMBY (Not In My Back Yard) philosophy is much more entrenched than the community care network. By the time of the second edition of his seminal work, Scull had accepted that the trajectories of mental health policy and criminal justice were very different (Scull, 1984). In the earlier edition, he had anticipated that prison populations would fall as had mental hospital populations, but he was later persuaded by events that this had been an incorrect expectation. Critics of the first edition had also objected that not only had prisoner numbers failed to fall (Chan and Ericson, 1981), but that the incarcerated populations which showed the greatest rise were those for whom community corrections had expanded most, namely juveniles and first offenders (Matthews, 1979).

There are, perhaps one could say with hindsight, fewer similarities than Scull first thought but more than he or others later allowed in policies towards the mentally ill and towards offenders. It is undoubtedly true that the humanity or leniency of community disposals does not necessarily recommend them to those making decisions in criminal justice processes – police, sentencers – as one might expect such claims to weigh with those making decisions in the psychiatric realm, such as doctors and social workers. Humanity might not be quite the Achilles heel of community corrections (Scull, 1983, 1984), but it is certainly not a sufficient reason for their use in preference to custody. On the other hand, humanity is presumably a very strong recommendation in the sphere of mental illness. The general view would probably be that humane solutions are acceptable for offenders if they are at least as effective in preventing crime as imprisonment (although they might still have to satisfy the demands of punishment), whereas with the mentally ill community care might be expected to be preferred so long as it is not significantly less effective than institutionalisation.

Empirically, Scull is undoubtedly correct that the spectacle of large numbers of the mentally ill and handicapped roaming our city centres, sleeping rough, plainly uncared for by either community or institution, calls into question the benevolence of the mental hospital closures that took place in England, the USA and elsewhere in the 1960s and 1970s. He also points out that the large scale of the closures of mental hospitals which took place in the USA in the 1950s and 1960s, and which started in England after the 1959 Mental Health Act, was not repeated throughout Europe, although psychotropic drugs and psycho-therapeutic techniques were equally available there.

The decline in state mental hospital populations in the USA and in England was indeed phenomenal. In California, for example, the in-patient population fell from 50 000 in 1955 to 22 000 in 1967 and to only 7000 in 1973 (Scull, 1984, p. 69). Although the pace and extent of deinstitutionalisation varied from state to state, between 1955 and 1980 the resident population of state mental hospitals over the USA as a whole declined by 75 per cent (Steadman and Morrissey, 1987, p. 233). In England, a 1971 Department of Health and Social Security memor-andum, *Hospital Services for the Mentally Ill*, anticipated the complete abolition of the mental hospital system, and although this has not happened, and although the decline in inmate populations was not quite as dramatic in England and Wales as in the USA (Table 3.1), it was nevertheless substantial.

Although similar trends have been noted for Canada (Richman and Harris, 1983) and elsewhere in western Europe (World Health Organ-isation, 1980), the timing and the rate of decline of psychiatric in-patient populations has differed markedly from country to country, and region to region. These variations have been cited by those who have ques-tioned the idea that it was availability of out-patient treatments that was the prime stimulus to psychiatric deinstitutionalisation. Peter Sedgwick, for example, in his impassioned indictment of the misery that has been occasioned by the abandonment of so many mentally ill people, informs us that the drug marketed here as largactyl, the most

Table 3.1   Resident population of mental hospitals, 1951–80

Year	Number resident USA	Number resident England and Wales
1951	529 300	143 200
1955	558 000	146 900
1960	535 000	136 200
1965	475 200	123 600
1970	339 000	103 300
1975	191 400	87 000
1980	132 200	75 200

SOURCE: Scull, 1989, pp. 312–13

widely used drug to suppress symptoms of some of the more florid disorders, was synthesised in France in December 1950, but hospital populations in France continued to increase throughout the 1950s and 1960s. He also quotes rises in mental health admissions in Italy throughout the 1970s, with opposition to the use of compulsory admission not being given official recognition until 1978 and 1979 when legislation halted new admissions to psychiatric hospitals and diverted emergency cases to casualty wards of general hospitals. West Germany, the base for several pharmaceutical companies active in the tranquilliser market, also continued to rely on in-patient treatment throughout the period during which deinstitutionalisation was taking place so rapidly and extensively in England and in the USA (Sedgwick, 1982, pp. 198–200).

In both these latter countries, there have been two distinguishable waves in psychiatric hospital population reduction. The first, often referred to as opening of the back doors, concentrated on reintegration of existing residents into the community through review of long-term patients and early release of recently admitted patients; the second wave, the closing of the front doors, aimed at reducing actual admissions (Steadman and Morrissey, 1987, p. 234). During the first wave, population reduction was achieved through shortening the average length of stay; during the second wave, occurring in the 1970s, admission criteria were tightened, involuntary commitments were made more difficult, and screening procedures were introduced to divert potential inmates to out-patient or community facilities.

The parallels with criminal justice here are clear. Parole is the penal system's mechanism for opening the back door, and there is evidence that in the USA at least, it has been used in the same way as the early wave of mental hospital releases, to take the pressure off institutions, rather than necessarily following any therapeutic idea such as an optimum release date for offenders (sufficient time for rehabilitation, not enough time for institutionalisation) (Nagin, 1978). Similar claims have been made about the use of parole in Canada (Ratner, 1987). There have been attempts to make overcrowding result in automatic extension of remission in some US states (Rutherford *et al.*, 1977) and in Europe the use of amnesties and pardons is a familiar response to overcrowding, usually linked to some auspicious public occasion such as the inauguration of a new president. Periodic reviews are also part of the system of parole in the USA and the United Kingdom, where the 1982 Criminal Justice Act also introduced mandatory periodic reviews of residential child care orders. 'Front-door' strategies in mental health also have a familiar ring for those in the criminal justice field: gate-keeping, diversion, criteria for incarceration, increasing emphasis on rights and civil liberties have been marked trends in both policy spheres. One initiative in particular makes the similarity of approach very obvious: in California the 1967 Lanterman–Petris–Short Act gave counties financial incentives not to use state psychiatric hospitals; the California Probation Subsidy made similar incentives available for avoidance of state imprisonment.

The apparent and seemingly enormous difference between deinstitutionalisation of the mentally ill and of the criminal is that in the case of the former, there has been a reduction of inmate facilities without a corresponding expansion of community facilities, whereas with corrections there has occurred the reverse case of expansion of community facilities without the corresponding reduction of inmate facilities. Although comparison of overall statistics of falling hospital populations and rising prisoner populations would seem to suggest that this has been the case as simply as just stated, in fact the real trend has been towards differentiation in both spheres. As Busfield rightly says, Scull and those advancing a similar reading of the deinstitutionalisation of the mentally ill underestimate the development of community facilities that has in fact taken place. What has happened, she explains, is not a neglect of mental health services in toto, but

> a significant reorientation of services away from the chronic, long-stay patients towards those with less serious, shorter-term problems, who were formerly little cared for by public mental health services.

It is not, therefore, that all mental health services have been run down under the guise of community care, rather that resources have largely gone into selected community services, those for acute, less serious mental disorders and not into those dealing with chronic, more serious complaints. (Busfield, 1986, pp. 329–30)

Much the same could be said of provisions for offenders. Most development has taken place in juvenile justice and in methods of working with specific offences which have from time to time become fashionable, or become the subject of moral panics. Thus there has been a proliferation of projects for taking and driving away offenders and lately for sex offenders, although these are hardly the crimes that have been contributing most to prison populations. Just as there has been a neglect of the chronic sick in psychiatric provision, so there has been little development of rehabilitative expertise in dealing with persistent, run-of-the-mill theft, even though it is the petty persistent property offender whom most people involved in criminal justice agree should no longer be imprisoned. Busfield also stresses that the patients whose needs are most neglected are those requiring residential services. Again, the same applies to offenders: although there has been some expansion of bail hostels in the last few years, there has been little general expansion of accommodation facilities for homeless offenders post conviction and post release. Busfield suggests four factors which, in combination, she claims give a more adequate account of de-institutionalisation of the mentally ill than either the discovery of therapeutic drugs or the fiscal crisis of the state taken alone:

1. undermining of beliefs in the therapeutic value of institutions;
2. development of non-institutional forms of welfare;
3. advantages to the psychiatric profession of integration with the community and with general medicine;
4. therapeutic optimism.

These conditions certainly have been present in the context of corrections: for a long time there has been widespread scepticism about the reformative value of prisons; community corrections have been made available; those professionals providing correctional programmes have generally been optimistic about their value, although they have not always been successful in advertising this to the public or to sentencers; and probation officers, juvenile justice workers and the like have achieved higher professional status than have prison officers.

Theoretically, too, the two fields have developed in parallel. In psychiatry, the critique of institutions and institutional therapies such as electro-convulsive treatment has been accompanied by a proselytising faith in out-patient approaches such as psychotherapy and counselling, just as prison-based rehabilitation programmes have been condemned as coercive and ineffective at the same time that extra-institutional cognitive approaches to offending, such as the attitude-change programmes used in much intermediate treatment work, have been vigorously promoted (Blagg and Smith,1989). Goffman's work influenced both mental health and criminal justice workers, and interactionist approaches were developed in both psychiatry and corrections (Goffman, 1968). Wolfensberger, for example, in his proposal of 'normalization' as the key principle for mental health services, echoes labelling theory approaches to delinquency, when he claims that people's appearance and interactions influence their careers as patients, with the result of exacerbating rather than abating their clinical conditions (Burton, 1983; Wolfensberger, 1980). Early interactionist formulations such as Lemert's distinction between primary and secondary deviation, which claims that social reactions to an original deviant act can provoke further delinquency, and may lead to the assumption of a deviant identity and the stabilisation of deviant acts into a delinquent career (Lemert, 1951), were followed by more radical attacks on almost any form of intervention. The anti-psychiatry of Laing and Cooper and the radical non-intervention tendency in criminology clearly have much in common (Cooper, 1967; Laing, 1967; Schur, 1973).

Although, like Scull and Sedgwick, Busfield acknowledges that the availability of psychotropic drugs cannot have been the only or even the prime cause of the deinstitutionalisation of the mentally ill, she claims that pharmacological control of the more florid symptoms of psychiatric disorder made the policy acceptable to the public at large. Herein is probably the main difference between the potential for decarceration in the two spheres, the true Achilles heel of community corrections: there is no equivalent nostrum to control the behaviour of the criminal and delinquent. The mentally ill arouse our pity as they prowl around our cities, homeless, friendless and occupationless. They do not, in general, endanger us, and so if we are disturbed by their plight, our demand is likely to be for better facilities in the community, rather than that they be reinstitutionalised. This is certainly not the case with the criminally deviant, who only come to our notice when they offend and thereby incur our anger rather than our sympathy. When they are not committing crimes, offenders are invisible, they are indistinguishable from the rest of the community. Rising crime rates are, then, truly the Achilles heel of community corrections: benevolence and leniency might well have been politically and popularly acceptable if they had been accompanied by reliable control of offenders, demonstrated by falling crime rates. The failure, then, has not been in regard to the development of provisions for offenders, but in regard to the neglect until very recently of advertising their effectiveness, and of complementing them by general crime prevention strategies. Control of the florid symptoms is as much a prerequisite for decarceration of offenders as for decarceration of the mentally ill. Although some commentators are proclaiming that the 'nothing works' era is over in respect of corrections (Pitts, 1992), the most optimistic view is that some things work, sometimes, for some offenders. We have not developed a community control for offending that has anything like the success rate of largactyl for schizophrenia. Until community corrections programmes start to demonstrate positive impact on reoffending rates, there will remain much support for segregative responses to crime, especially strategies such as selective incapacitation, strategies which offer the hope of isolating those responsible for the most crime. If crime is not an illness that can be cured or at least remitted, it will be dealt with as a plague to be isolated and contained.

From decarceration to transcarceration

Rising prison populations soon led to re-evaluations of the decarceration thesis. On grounds of timing, the thesis proved defective in that expansion of community corrections and community care both took place before the fiscal crisis of the late 1970s and early 1980s, and as the crisis gathered momentum, the pace of mental health deinstitutionalisation slowed, and prison populations rose. There is room for disagreement about whether any measure of decarceration was achieved for offenders, with some observers saying that there was, in that the proportionate use of imprisonment declined (Michalowski and Pearson, 1987), whilst others have argued that there has not been any genuine deinstitutionalisation in the penal realm (Chan and Ericson, 1981). There is, however, sufficient empirical evidence of increase, or at the very least stability, in the overall use of institutional solutions to problems of criminal and delinquent populations, to have occasioned virtual abandonment of any idea that the era of segregative penal institutions was at and end. Between 1957 and 1977 – the so-called decarceration era – in England and Wales, adult male prison populations were comparatively stable, rising from 27 838 in 1957 to 29 564 in 1977. The receptions into custodial institutions of males under 21, however, rose dramatically, from 4901 in 1957 to 22 169 in 1977 (Hudson, 1984, p. 51)

In an important collection of papers published in 1987, Lowman, Menzies and Palys brought together evidence and theorisation to reorder conceptualisation from *de*carceration to *trans*carceration. They argue first, that the effect of fiscal crisis has been to strengthen rather than weaken the role of segregative institutions. In times of restricted public expenditure, they propose, it is community provisions which bear the brunt of cutbacks, leaving the core institutions, the 'segregative nuclei', the hospitals and the prisons, with a revitalised role. Secondly, they point out that in times when all the social control and social care subsystems are suffering constraints, the boundaries between them will shift as they accommodate to circumstances. Deviant populations will therefore be shunted around from one subsystem to another, from one institution to another:

> For delinquents, deviants and dependants, this means that their careers are likely to be characterized by institutional mobility, as they are pushed from one section of the help-control complex to another. For control agents, this means that 'control' will essentially have no locus and the control mandate will increasingly entail the 'fitting together' of subsystems rather than the consolidation of one agency in isolation from its alternatives. (Lowman, Menzies and Palys, 1987, p. 9)

Both of these tendencies are apparent here and now: the 'population shift' believed to have taken place between hospitals and prisons; the interagency approach which is a more and more important feature of the lives of social workers, probation officers, mental health workers and the like. The near simultaneity of falls in mental hospital populations and increases in prison populations has led to revived interest in 'Penrose's law', which proposes an inverse relationship between the size of prison and mental hospital populations:

> Penrose's pre-Second World War research demonstrated that developed countries with large penal populations had small psychiatric populations, and vice versa; additionally the number of prisoners, the

murder rate, the suicide rate and the country's mortality rate had an inverse relationship with the rate of psychiatric hospital admission. (Craft, 1984, p. 21)

Commenting on Penrose's hypothesis, Craft claims that its continuing applicability is demonstrated by contrasting England and California, for example, where psychiatric hospital places have been drastically reduced and prison populations have (consequently?) increased, with more cautious jurisdictions such as Scotland and Queensland, Australia, where large psychiatric hospitals have kept beds available, and where prison numbers have not risen so much.

The phenomenon that has been referred to as the 'criminalization of the mentally disordered' (Abramson, 1972) has three related aspects:

1. mentally disordered people who would formerly have been in hospital are released into the community without adequate support and are committing crimes either as a manifestation of disorder or as a survival strategy;
2. first-line agents such as police and social workers coming into contact with people manifesting disordered or disorderly behaviour are channelling them into the penal rather than the medical-welfare system;
3. within the criminal justice system, psychiatric discourse has lost influence relative to juridical discourse, with the effect that offenders are less likely to be diverted out to the mental health subsystem.

All these three scenarios have common-sense, anecdotal plausibility, but are difficult to substantiate through data. In a study to test the idea of functional interdependence of mental hospitals and prisons in six states during the era of most radical deinstitutionalisation, 1968–78, Steadman and his associates start from the fact that during the decade, the hospital population in the USA fell by 64 per cent, whilst the prison population rose by 65 per cent, so that a straightforward transfer of the mentally ill from one institutional sector to the other seems obvious (Steadman *et al.*, 1984). They look at the proportion of prison inmates with prior contact with mental health services, and mental hospital patients with prior contact with the criminal justice system, and find that while in some states there were marked increases in the prisoners with prior mental hospitalisation, suggestive of direct transinstitutionalisation, in as many states this proportion declined. On the other hand, there was a consistent finding that by 1978 the proportion of mental hospital patients who had prior contact with the criminal justice system was greater than it had been in 1968. They suggest by way of explanation for this consistent finding that deinstitutionalisation has increased levels of deviancy, producing levels which exceed society's tolerance. The transinstitutional path, they suggest, is from hospitals to homes and boarding houses, and thence to local jails rather than to state prisons. Steadman and his coauthors suggest that there are fairly stable levels of institutionalised populations, but that community care facilities and jails act as buffer groups between the state asylums and the state prisons. Such an explanation seems to suit the case in England and Wales where the biggest expansion and overcrowding has been seen in local prisons and remand prisons, rather than in the dispersal prisons and among sentenced prisoners. It also raises the possibility that the continental European tradition of using custodial remand more than has been usual here, together with less drastic psychiatric deinstitutionalisation, could explain why progressive mental health policy has not had so much impact on prison populations there.

The likelihood that someone apprehended for offensive conduct will be processed through the criminal justice system rather than the mental health system appears to have increased substantially through the period of deinstitutionalisation, not merely because of lack of psychiatric facilities but also because of the tightening of admissions criteria and the increasing complexity of admissions procedures to hospitals. The Lanterman–Petris–Short Act did not merely provide inducements to switch from hospital to community care, it also introduced criteria for hospital admission centring on the concept of dangerousness, and also gave patients the right to refuse treatment. These principles have been widely imitated, not merely throughout the USA but also by the Psychiatrica Democratica movement in Italy. 'Dangerousness' has been defined in behavioural rather than psychiatric terms, whilst the concept of 'refusal of treatment' has been defined in ways totally inappropriate to the chronically psychotic, disorganised, homeless and friendless sufferer who is being left to cope unsupported outside the asylum (Whitmer, 1980). Not taking medication, missing clinic appointments and so forth are being interpreted as refusal of treatment, rather than a more positive, competent declaration of a wish to forgo treatment having to be obtained.

The police are the most likely control agents to be summoned if a mentally disordered patient is behaving bizarrely or aggressively, and they are untrained for and culturally unadapted to the role of psychiatric intake worker. Although little research attention has been given to police decision-making in these circumstances, Teplin's review of available evidence suggests that police might be funnelling mentally disordered people into the criminal justice system (Teplin, 1983). Her own research found that police were aware of the limited number of psychiatric placements available and of the stringent admission criteria. She found that arrest rather than hospitalisation or an informal warning or caution was likely in three types of situation:

(1) when hospitalization would have been preferable but the potential patient was thought to be either unacceptable by the hospital or showed symptomatology such that he or she fell into the cracks between the various caretaking systems; (2) in encounters characterized by their 'publicness' and visibility which, at the same time, exceeded the tolerance for deviant behaviour within the community; and (3) in cases in which the police felt that there was a high probability that the person would continue to cause a problem unless something was done. (ibid., 1984, p. 169)

As in the previous chapter, the findings of high arrest rates for mentally disordered persons committing minor offences, and the frequent recourse to the local jail (Schuerman and Kobrin, 1984; Steadman *et al.*, 1984; Steadman and Morrissey, 1987) beg the question of why the police and magistrates should pay so much attention to their behaviour. Although analyses of the situational dynamics remain few, it is easy to imagine that by their demeanour (lack of repentance, aggression) and general appearance, by their characteristic homelessness, unemployment and rootlessness, mentally disordered people fail to meet criteria for cautioning, for bail and for community corrections. Once apprehended, therefore, it is quite consistent with our understanding of the formal processes of the criminal justice system that mentally disordered offenders should have difficulty in negotiating their way towards the various exit routes that now exist. The question remains as to why the police bother at all, if Scull and other deinstitutionalisation sceptics are right when they depict the former or would-be patients drifting round the ghettoes, joining the marginalised, the people whose troubles are frequently thought worth little official attention.

Although the hotels and halfway houses are primarily located in the run-down margins of towns and cities, during the day most close their doors and decant their residents on to the streets. They stray out of the ghettoes, attracted by the town centres, disturbing 'respectable' citizens in shops and cafés, on the streets and on public transport, so that as Teplin describes, behaviour becomes so public that it cannot be ignored. Even inside the ghettoes, the police cannot entirely abandon concern without some loss of legitimacy, and the factors described in the previous chapter come into play. It has been suggested that deinstitutionalisation of the mentally ill, by straining public tolerance, has led to some redefinition of the boundaries of deviance (Steadman and Morrissey, 1987), so that eccentricity becomes indecency, and once redefined as crime, police inattention might correspondingly be redefined as ineffectiveness rather than humanity. Scull summarises the dilemma thus:

> The crazy and the senile can, by and large, be contained and isolated whilst being neglected. Even were we to grant the attractions of unpoliced ghettoes, however, the same result cannot be secured by releasing criminals. The targets they victimize are insufficiently selective and not adequately geographically contained or controllable. Moreover, a strategy of this sort creates serious ideological problems. To allow criminals to violate the law, with something approaching impugnity, significantly weakens the incentives to conform while simultaneously provoking public outrage. It is likely to trigger vigilante responses, thus threatening the state's monopoly of legal violence. In the process, it exhibits an insidious yet powerful tendency to undermine the legitimacy of a social and political order that permits such developments. (Scull, 1984, p. 180)

Scull writes as though the mentally disordered and the criminal are two distinct populations, whereas I am arguing that there is a considerable fluidity between the two categories. Available life chances, behavioural manifestations, personal characteristics, consequences of previous labelling, accessibility of facilities, regulations and procedures, professional cultures of control personnel, and the socio-political ideologies of the day, result in people drifting between statuses such as victim and perpetrator, patient and offender. People will be seen as 'social junk' which may be ignored, or 'social dynamite' which must be controlled according to contingencies such as the extent to which the state monopolises the management of problem populations; the size and level of the threat presented by problem populations; the power and degree of political organisation of deviant populations; the effectiveness of wider, less formal control structures (family, religion, etc.); the availability of alternative modes of control (health, welfare systems, neighbourhood and voluntary organisations, etc). (Spitzer, 1975, pp. 644–5). In the cities and towns of contemporary England and North America, we can see the breakdown or run-down of community facilities, the congregation of large numbers of problematic, dependant populations, and we would therefore expect that the more services for dependant populations and community facilities are cut back, the more likely are people such as the mentally ill, the rootless and the workless to be dealt with as offenders (Dear and Wolch, 1987).

Once caught up in the criminal justice system, there is increased probability of remaining within it, rather than being transferred to the mental health system. Mentally disordered offenders are becoming less likely to receive treatment rather than punishment disposals, they are increasingly likely to be sent to prison rather than hospital, and less likely to be transferred from prison to hospital. A hospital order cannot be made by a court unless there is a hospital willing to accept the offender as a patient (NACRO, 1986), and in both the USA and England and Wales, local mental hospitals since the 1970s have refused more and more potential patients because they are untreatable, difficult to manage or both, whilst the state institutions and special hospitals are only admitting on dangerousness criteria. Thus the mentally disordered who have committed less serious offences have more frequently been given short prison sentences and they are the group who, more than any other, comprise the 'revolving door' population. With the dangerous patients referred to them by local hospitals, special hospitals have become overburdened, with the result that they have not been able to offer places to anything like the number of offenders for whom the courts agree that there is clear evidence of mental illness (Higgins, 1984).

Transfers from prison to hospital in England declined particularly dramatically between 1962–4 and 1972–4, when the average daily prison population rose by 22 per cent but the number of transfers fell by 30 per cent (Parker and Tennent, 1979). This has been attributed mainly to the reluctance of local hospitals to admit chronically disturbed offenders with little prospect of quick improvement (Cheadle and Ditchfield, 1982). Although there was some recovery in the numbers of transfers in the early 1980s, by the mid-1980s the number of transfers was less than two-thirds the number in 1962, despite the rise in the prison population (Robertson, 1984). The number of transfers to local hospitals by the mid-1980s was only about half that of the early 1960s, whereas the number of transfers to special hospitals by 1984 had recovered to about three-quarters of the early 1960s level, after being much lower during most of the 1970s. A problem that remains with special hospitals is late transfer: offenders are being transferred later in their sentence, and then have been released later in relation to estimated date of release (Grounds, 1991). These changes are reflected in sentencing practices. More mentally abnormal men convicted of diminished responsibility homicide received sentences of imprisonment (Dell, 1984), whilst the insanity defence and the plea of diminished responsibility itself has been used less (Wells,1983). Women still continue to be seen by the courts as mad rather than bad, but the use of psychiatric rather than criminal disposals for men is at a very low level. In the introduction to her analysis of gender differences in psychiatric disposals, Hilary Allen comments:

> The conclusions suggest that the importance of the current imbalance lies not so much in the excess of psychiatry in relation to female offenders as its deficiency in relation to males. It is certainly true that many women now receive psychiatric disposals on the most slender of grounds, sometimes without even any diagnosed disorder. But more disturbing is that disordered male offenders are refused a psychiatric disposal, even in the face of obvious need for treatment, and sometimes in the face of a general consensus by all the professionals that a psychiatric disposal would be desirable. (Allen, 1987, introduction)

The declining influence of psychiatric discourse

Allen draws on the idea of discourse to explain the likelihood of psychiatric disposals in juridical decision-making. She identifies first a 'complex of formal and institutional provisions' spanning both medical and legal discourse, which importantly includes the legal statutes and guidelines concerning the role of psychiatric witnesses, the specification of the insanity defence, qualifications for 'diminished responsibility', admissions procedures and the like. Her second discursive modality is 'the set of premises and expectations that are involved in assessing and judging the offender' (ibid., pp. 112–13).

The research (by Steadman *et al.*, 1984) quoted above is addressed to only the first of these discursive elements, and shows the impact of a social policy – the deinstitutionalisation of the mentally disordered – on criminal justice. Thinking in terms of Allen's second discursive component, however, we can readily understand the impact of penal ideologies on the disposal of mentally disordered offenders. The emphasis on rights and the priority of punishment in the new penal orthodoxy combine to downgrade the psychiatric input into judicial decision-making. If we are no longer seeking to use penal policy to rehabilitate offenders, then the offender's mental state logically has little bearing on the outcome except in the extreme case of the defendant being so impaired as to bear no responsibility because of, as the McNaghten rules specify, being unable to understand the nature or quality of the act, or because of some compulsion being unable to resist commission of the act. This is the traditional insanity defence, which is inevitably very limited in application since it is rare for mentally illness completely to deprive sufferers of rationality or control. An impairment of reason, reduction of sensation such as compassion or remorse, deficiency in forethought about the consequences of acts, increased aggressiveness and volatility are more common than total loss of reason, sympathy or restraint, or complete personality change. The insanity defence is difficult to establish, therefore, but anything less still admits responsibility, and therefore points to punishment rather than treatment. Diminished responsibility through addictions, provocation, depression or psychosis would indicate less punishment than for a fully responsible agent, but would still leave the individual in the frame of reference of criminality rather than illness.

The insanity defence is unpopular with defendants, their legal representatives, criminologists and civil libertarians because of its conflict with desert principles, and because of its association with indeterminate sentencing. It is contradictory in desert terms because it absolves from responsibility – and therefore culpability – but because it establishes dangerousness, it makes the offender liable for the most severe punishment, indefinite confinement. If people committing crimes of less than the highest levels of seriousness were to be confined to a secure hospital because of their need for treatment, whilst mentally intact offenders committing similar acts received community penalties on desert grounds, we would be imitating the customs of Erewhon: 'In the land of Erewhon people were punished for their illnesses and treated for their crimes. The value systems operating in most contemporary societies broadly speaking adopt a contrary viewpoint, but then what are we to do when a crime is committed by a mentally ill person?' (Rawnsley, 1984, p. xii). Recognition of rights highlights the dilemma: as an offender, an individual has a right not to be penalised beyond the limits of proportionality of punishment to crime: as a sufferer from mental illness, surely a person also has rights not to be punished in ways that do nothing to alleviate the condition and make reoffending and therefore further penalisation probable? The dilemma is most acute when the choice is between indeterminate confinement in a special hospital and a prison sentence, brutalising but at least determinate, but there is still a problem in the choice between, for example, the instrusiveness and indeterminacy of a psychiatric probation order or the abandonment and burden of a fine.

There is no doubt that the insanity defence, and diagnoses of mental illness more generally, have fallen into disfavour because of their links to excessive periods of confinement, to the use of aggressive therapeutic techniques such as chemical castration and behaviourist techniques such as the aversion therapy depicted in Burgess's *Clockwork Orange*, and even to psychosurgery. Speaking of the insanity defence in particular, but applicable to psychiatric approaches to offending generally, Gostin is undoubtedly right that under the guise of benevolence the real objective is not to relieve mentally ill offenders of their punishment, but to facilitate confinement beyond the limits that straightforward legal considerations would allow (Gostin, 1984). Rather than escaping criminal labelling, mentally disordered offenders are doubly stigmatised as both mad and bad (Morris, 1982). When classification as mad and bad is combined with classification as dangerous, then the offender's chances of being returned quickly to the community are very slight, and psychiatry is an instrument of repression rather than recovery.

Critique of this coercive aspect of psychiatry was at the heart of the back to justice movement, and of course the relationship between psychiatry and the rehabilitative ideology in penality is so strong that the latter is frequently termed 'the treatment model'. One of the rights proclaimed by justice lobbyists is the right to punishment rather than treatment, or in Kittrie's words 'the right to be different' (Kittrie, 1973). The critiques of psychiatric involvement in criminal justice have, therefore, not surprisingly been most thoroughgoing in countries which have most ardently adopted the new retributionism. Even where rehabilitation has been less comprehensively renounced, however, curbs have been placed on the 'medicalisation of crime'. In Denmark, 'special detention' was dropped in 1974; the number of psychiatric reports for courts has declined; the number of mentally ill offenders sent to prison has risen (Higgins, 1984, pp. 8–9). Dutch criminologists including those belonging to the Utrecht School who have been among the foremost advocates of rehabilitative penality, as well as penal reform groups such as the Coornhert League, have criticised the use of t.b.r. (detention at the government's pleasure in order to be treated on its behalf). The number of t.b.r. confinements reduced in the 1970s and early 1980s (Downes, 1988; Koenraadt, 1983) and the measure was replaced by a determinate hospital order in 1988.

Special or preventive detention, whilst abolished in name throughout the Western world, has returned in the guise of incapacitation of the dangerous or those likely to recidivate, and the same considerations which used to justify confinement under special sections in special institutions, are now being built into predictive instruments to justify extra terms under ordinary legislation in ordinary prisons. For everyone who is spared unjustified indeterminate confinement, more are being deprived of treatment whilst serving determinate, but destructive, sentences. The rhetoric of penal policy may use the image of the reasoning criminal, calculating the costs and benefits of offending, may stress rights, choices, agency and responsibility, reducing disparity and making the punishment fit the crime, but correctional professionals continue to speak of the despair, the helplessness and the deterioration of those unable to make effective choices, ill-equipped to survive the rigours of life either in prison or in the community. Whilst indeterminate carceral sentences are certainly not the answer to the problem of mentally disordered offenders, neither is the assumption that all offenders are competent and culpable, and that individual needs of offenders are not important for criminal justice decision-making (Halleck, 1987).

A resolution suggested by some is that the offence should determine the right of the state to confine and for how long, but that the offender's mental condition should determine whether she/he is confined in hospital or prison, whether probation should include treatment, etc. Mental state at the time of sentence (or at any subsequent time during the punishment) would be relevant to deciding need for treatment; mental state at the time of the offence could remain relevant to assessment of culpability. In the USA there is already considerable restriction on courts' abilities to confine beyond the length given by sentencing guidelines for fully competent offenders. Any confinement or treatment beyond the length of time specified on offence criteria has to be by civil procedures, with the same rights of review and cessation as for non-criminal patients. One suggestion is that within these limits set by desert principles, offenders should be placed in prison or in hospital on the

basis of two criteria: their own preference, and the prospect of effectiveness of treatment (Gostin, 1984). This would mean that the offender-
patient would have the same sort of rights as the general patient population, but the state would retain its right to punish transgressors and to
protect itself from the dangerous. The author points out that almost no
country has adopted the principle of good prospect of benefit from
treatment, but that without it, the offender is better off with a tariff
sentence. The principle of choice is also unknown: at present offenders
can refuse therapeutic disposals (they can refuse to participate in therapeutic programmes inside institutions; they must also agree to be made
subject to a probation order and to the conditions of treatment specified
within orders), but they cannot opt for such a disposal if it is not
suggested by the court, the prison administrator or the probation officer.
The idea being put forward is to separate legal concepts such as seriousness, dangerousness, which should be governed by jurisprudential criteria, from medical concepts such as need for treatment, which should
be governed by psychiatric standards (ibid., p. 239).

Separating legal concepts and medical concepts appears to be a sensible idea, but experience in other spheres would counsel some caution.
Juvenile justice has been subject to similar criticisms of mixing welfare
and delinquency matters, with similar concerns over stigmatisation and
indeterminate sentencing. The resulting re-emphasis on due process has
seen increased interventiveness of so-called alternatives to custody, it
has seen the numbers of young adults given custodial sentences rise, and
it has seen a withdrawal of welfare and developmental facilities by
agencies inhibited by the possibility of net-widening and labelling disorderly youth. It has only been when reformers have begun urging
increased awareness of the youthfulness of this group, of the difficulties
posed by large-scale youth unemployment, homelessness and lack of
community facilities that we have seen any move away from punitiveness, any readiness by officials to consider a 'moving frontier' whereby
young adults could be dealt with by a more welfare-oriented juvenile
jurisdiction. The moving frontier in Germany and parts of the USA, the
introduction of the youth court in England and Wales, the raising of
the age for juvenile court jurisdiction in France, are examples of ways
in which a step back from emphasis on due process and a punishment
orientation may be – hesitatingly and tenuously – under way.

Separation of psychiatric/welfare concerns from jurisprudential concerns would be all very well if psychiatric and legal discourses enjoyed
equal authority. This is patently not the case. The demise of rehabilita-

tion following the critique that so comprehensively damaged its credibility in terms of effectiveness, benevolence and fairness; the questioning of the role of experts; the assault on the discretion of criminal justice and allied professions, have all diminished the status of non-legal discourse. As Carol Smart comments in relation to standards of proof and rules of evidence in child sexual abuse cases, legal forums are particularly resistant to recognising other knowledge claims as valid, and even when other discourses are admitted, they have to conform to the parameters of legal discourse with cross-examination, opposing experts, and so on. When their knowledge is invalidated, she says, the 'psy' professions find it so hard that they opt out rather than endure the process (Smart, 1989, p. 58). Smart is describing a particular type of case, but over a whole range of criminal justice circumstances, psy professionals have opted out rather than defend their claims to knowledge and valid professional standpoint. Thus not only psychiatrists but also probation officers and social workers have acquiesced in the jettisoning of their own discourse – writing reports which confine themselves to talking about the offence, adopting tariff-estimating devices to choose sentence recommendations rather than assessing the needs of the defendant, dropping use of words like 'client' in favour of 'offender' and 'defendant'.

This downgrading of psychiatric/social work discourse in court proceedings is, of course, a reflection of its downgrading in the political–social ideology of the post-welfare state, and not surprisingly has gone furthest in the USA and England and Wales. Not only do we doubt the wisdom of the psy professionals, we also doubt their good intentions and seek to protect ourselves against them; we also emasculate our caring professions materially and ideologically. When lack of resources, restrictions or professional reticence prevents them offering welfare assistance in problem situations, we call on the penalising circuit to define an offence, establish a guilty party and apportion a punishment. Child sexual abuse has been the subject of a recent moral panic, although whether there really is a massive increase of this behaviour, or whether some combination of greater victim awareness, greater credence to children's claims, greater professional acceptance of the existence of the problem, plus greater punitiveness towards perpetrators has meant more action being taken, and more publicity being accorded, it is not possible to know. The criminalising approach taken in England is thought by many Europeans to be quite inappropriate. Criminalisation, with the near certainty of a prison sentence if the offence is proved, can make it much harder for victims and other family members to report the behaviour, and for perpetrators to admit it. The punitive approach exposes victims to interrogation and the standards of proof required mean that the risk of a case being dropped, or a perpetrator acquitted, is high. In such instances, the juridical approach provides no protection for victims, and even where a case is proved, the victim may well feel guilt at the consequences for the perpetrator and for the rest of the family. In a comparison of the treatment of serious child sexual abusers in England and Wales and The Netherlands, it is demonstrated that many more cases are dealt with by non-penal means in The Netherlands than in England and Wales, and that even where perpetrators are prosecuted, custodial sentences are avoided where an offender agrees to treatment. The Dutch approach is to facilitate an outcome of support and reconciliation for the whole family, in contrast to the English approach of isolating and punishing the perpetrator (Cornwell and Arendsen, 1991). The fate of such offenders within the prison, where they are often kept in solitary confinement at their own request, isolated for fear of attack by other prisoners, is well known.

Whilst child abuse is a very serious form of sexual misbehaviour, there has been an increase in the use of custodial sentences here for the whole range of sexual offences. A sudden increase occurred in the latter half of the 1970s (Walmsley, 1984). The proportionate use of custody for sexual offences in England and Wales rose from 20 per cent in 1979 to 33 per cent in 1989; despite the overall reduction of the sentenced prison population at the end of the 1980s, the number of sex offenders sentenced to immediate custody rose from 1900 in 1986 to 2400 in 1989 (Home Office, 1990a). Again, we cannot know if this reflects a real increase in sex offenders or not, but it certainly shows that we have become more likely to think in terms of crimes and punishments and less likely to think in terms of problems and help.

The penal and the assistancial

In more general terms, the effect of the fiscal and political policies of the Reagan–Thatcher era has been to reduce welfare spending, to leave the ghettoes to rot, to do nothing about problems such as unemployment, housing shortfall and racism. For example, the incoming Reagan administration cut public expenditure through the Omnibus Budget Reconciliation Act in 1982. This resulted in grants for alcohol, drug abuse and mental health services in 1984 being 25 per cent less than in 1979

(Samson, 1990). Social problems are ignored unless and until they manifest themselves in crime – unemployed youth are ignored unless they riot; the chronic mentally ill are ignored unless they offend the respectable or offend too publicly; family pathology is ignored unless criminal abuse can be proved. Even where people ask for help, staff shortages in social work agencies mean that cases go unallocated. Added to this state imposed withdrawal of welfare, the psy professionals have withdrawn themselves, being drawn into the dominant discourse of rights, labelling and avoiding dependency. The danger is not only of people being 'left to rot with their rights on', but that being left un-labelled as a welfare client means acquiring the even more stigmatising label of criminal, that avoidance of dependency on social workers leads to total loss of self-determination in prison.

As the welfare net has contracted, the penal net has expanded to become the new catch-all. Relative to welfare agencies, all criminal justice agencies have expanded in both resources and influence. Reagan's welfare cuts contrast with Bush's proposal to add one billion dollars to the federal budget to pay for the addition of 24 000 beds to federal prisons, an increase in capacity of 77 per cent (Greenberg, 1990, p. 50). In England and Wales, new prisons are being built at a time when welfare services are experiencing severe expenditure cuts. In mid-1990, eight new prisons had been built since the mid-1980s, and twelve more were under construction (Muncie and Sparks, 1991, p. 99); the police force and the probation service have also increased their establishment during the late 1980s to early 1990s.

Not only has this shift between subsystems and agencies occurred, it has also happened within them. We shall look in the following chapter at how penal policy has affected criminal justice agencies and institutions themselves, but other agencies have been given quasi-judicial functions, and have adopted a quasi-judicial ethos. Benefit officials check for fraud as well as dispensing money, their task is no longer primarily that of assessing need, it is more and more concerned with assessing the 'genu-ineness' of the claimant (Squires, 1990, chapter 7). Social workers are agents of the courts, overseeing supervision orders, taking 'clients' to court for breach of orders, overseeing the payment of fines and other money orders; child welfare charities become involved in juvenile jus-tice programmes. It has become ever more difficult to address social problems directly. With the pre-eminence of crime concerns and law-and-order discourse (Hall, 1980), it is often only by linkage with offend-ing that help can be provided. This is especially true of services for young people. Participation in motor projects, day centre activities, etc. is restricted to young people who have been convicted of offences – even though their neighbourhoods may lack jobs, youth clubs, community education projects; accommodation projects may be funded only if they can demonstrate crime-prevention impact.

The criminalisation of homelessness shows similarities to the criminalisation of mental illness, and the same analytic approach to housing as that used by Scull in relation to mental illness policy has been applied in recent work (Dear and Wolch, 1987). It is once again in England and the USA that the problem of homelessness has risen to crisis levels, and the differentiation or bifurcation of the housing market shows a pattern familiar from the differentiation of psychiatric provision. Until the slump at the very end of the 1980s, those on the home ownership ladder were receiving tax subsidies, had ready access to loans and credit, and were improving their homes and trading up regularly. 'Gentrification' entered the language: 'improving' areas so that accommodation there became out of the financial reach of the original inhabitants. Areas that were not gentrified decayed, and investment in public housing virtually ceased. Housing benefit has been withdrawn from young people and students, and those who are eligible receive it in arrears, whilst landlords demand rent in advance. The response to rising levels of homelessness has not been to step up provision, but to blame the homeless and to deplete the public housing stock still further. Reagan referred to homelessness as a deliberate act, asserting that the homeless 'make their own choice for staying out there' (Samson, 1990, p. 41); after a winter of record numbers of building society repossessions of owner-occupied homes, in July 1992 the British government announced a further phase of the 'rent-into-mortgage' scheme (*The Guardian*, 21 July 1992). As well as being blamed, the homeless have been criminalised. Ancient vagrancy laws have been revived, people sleeping rough have been prosecuted for loitering and trespass, people reduced to begging have been arrested for importuning. One study of different approaches to the problem of homelessness reports:

> In Arizona, the homeless have become objects of law enforcement and subjects for criminalization. In Tucson, for example, where state general assistance is not available to homeless people, where few shelter beds and soup kitchens exist, and where the unofficial policy of the city is to drive the homeless out of town, homeless people have

been verbally harassed and physically abused by the police. The homeless have also been subject to handcuffing, arresting and charging for criminal trespass, squatting and loitering. The police have gone so far as to harass individuals for trying to feed themselves and for constructing shelter by arresting them respectively for the 'crimes' of possessing glass (i.e. a peanut butter jar in the park) and carrying a concealed weapon (i.e. cardboard cutters). (Barak and Bohm, 1989, p. 279)

Similar approaches to the homeless could be cited for England: for example, in the spring of 1991 the shelters in London's 'cardboard city' were demolished and several residents arrested; laws against squatting have been strengthened. Even countries usually more tolerant of squatting and alternative lifestyles have become less so: the respectable residents of Copenhagen have demanded the clearance of Christiania; in Amsterdam squatters have been cleared out of buildings they had occupied for years. Always, the reason given for harassment of the homeless is crime – the homeless solicit, thieve and trespass; squats and settlements are dens of vice and drug-taking. The contemporary obsession with crime is such that homelessness is rarely discussed in terms of the straightforward awfulness of being cold, without shelter and privacy, but in terms of its leading to crime. The homeless, it seems, especially the young homeless, are a cause of concern only because of their vulnerability to taking up theft, prostitution and drug dealing as ways to survive (O'Mahoney, 1988).

This chapter has drawn on work in the field of social policy, especially mental illness, to argue that penal policy cannot maintain its mythology of being totally separate from other public policy subsystems. The same material and ideological forces affect the way policies towards the insane, the poor, the homeless and the criminal are configured. The boundaries of agencies and subsystems overlap; they expand and contract; they interchange functions, professional discourses and personnel, to accommodate to each other. People pass from one institutional sphere to another as their behaviour is deemed to need help, treatment or punishment; as they are labelled disadvantaged, disordered or delinquent according to the contingencies of time and place. Social policies create clients for the criminal justice system by withdrawing legitimate means of survival, by straining public tolerance, by posing dilemmas for state legitimacy, by making it likely that one agency rather than another will be summoned or will have the resources to respond, by making it likely that one label or another will be affixed to problem behaviour, that one sort of disposal rather than another will be preferred.

In England and North America, and to a lesser extent in Europe, we have witnessed an almost complete take-over of the assistancial domain by the judicial domain (Donzelot, 1980). This is surely a much more incontrovertible shift than that from the institution to the community (prisons are overflowing; the community is fairly successful in repelling deviants) or from public to private provision (most 'private' or 'voluntary' facilities are state funded and/or state regulated). Assistance proceeds, if at all, from judicial decisions, and is given on condition not only that recipients accept their deviant status and acknowledge the state's right to give or withhold aid, to allow or remove liberty, but also on condition that intervening agencies accept their role of imposing the judicial labels, administering the judicial conditions, reporting to the judicial overseers.

The market society and the client as consumer

Reduction of the assistancial domain means withdrawal to core functions – the people who unquestionably belong in the welfare subsystem are the disabled without caring families, the indigent elderly and parentless young children. Those outside these categories who cannot survive on their own resources become the dangerous classes, whose difficulties are ignored until they become too visible or too predatory, when they are assigned to the penal realm. Status ascription comes to depend not on the help people ask for, but on their credibility as patients or supplicants, their accordance with our stereotypes of the mad, the needy and the helpless. Thus women retain a much higher probability than men of being diagnosed mentally ill or inadequate, and their chances of being assigned to the health–welfare system, or being given a help or treatment option within the penal system, remain comparatively high (Allen, 1987; Roth and Lerner, 1982). Where people are (all too) readily seen both as insane and as criminals, they are liable to double penalisation as mad and bad, as evidenced by the numbers of black people remanded to prison for psychiatric reports or – especially black females (Chigwada, 1989) – being administered drugs in prison rather than receiving therapy in a community medical centre or help under a probation order (Browne, 1990).

Apart from credibility as belonging to one of the remaining categories for whom state assistance rather than state punishment is still available, the other way to ensure receipt of services is by plausible construction of self as a consumer. As the welfare state gives way to the market society, the 'social construction of the consumer' has been a central ideological project. This notion has been used to illuminate the mystification of coercion in penality and repressive welfare, for example the rhetoric of provision of services, contracts and the like in discussions of prison privatisation, new regimes and the Woolf report masks the fact that people are in prison through the exercise of state power (Jefferson, Sim and Walklate, 1991).

There is another way in which the notion of the social construction of the consumer is useful in understanding contemporary developments in social and penal policies, however. Those who have managed to demonstrate a need for treatment either by payment, sponsorship or by active participation will in all probability be acknowledged as patients or clients, and receive the services they need. Colin Samson illustrates the way mental health services in the USA have developed so that it is the economic rather than the clinical status of potential patients and clients which determines the treatment they will receive. First, there has been the growth of specialised services for those who can pay:

> services can be offered which are targeted at certain higher socio-economic groups, and which are beyond the financial reach of the poor. One such tactic is the development of specialisations in particular, often fashionable types of services, such as chemical dependency, eating difficulties, alcoholism, and adolescent behaviour problems, to attract paying patients. Specialised programmes are advertised in glossy brochures and are designed to attract the attention of middle class professionals, who might be encountering mental, emotional and situational difficulties associated with fast-paced life-styles and high pressure work environments. (Samson, 1990, p. 47)

As well as these programmes for the affluent middle-classes, services are available for those who are covered by insurance, and those who have access to occupational services. It is, of course, the absence of these demand capabilities that characterises the deinstitutionalised mentally ill, the 'dumped' patients as Samson describes them, and the crisis homeless. In the penal subsystem, those who manage to project themselves as credible consumers of addictions programmes, voluntary social work help, debt counselling, etc., by using the correct motivational language may receive help rather than carceral punishment, and ability to pay (financial recompense in some diversion programmes in the USA, substitution of fines for custodial sentences in Europe, perceived likelihood of paying fines in England), sponsorship by employers in the form of supportive statements in court, offers of employment, can lead to non-imprisonment and sometimes non-prosecution. In some European countries private treatment voluntarily undertaken can lead to diversion away from the penal system. Successful construction of oneself as a consumer, then, can help people extricate themselves from the penal system and achieve reassignment to the assistancial agencies.

I have attempted to demonstrate that although the penal system and social policy may not have the simple hydraulic relationship that Penrose suggested and that some more recent commentators have proposed, such that there is a direct negative correlation between populations in one set of institutions and those in the other (Biles and Mulligan, 1973), the two subsystems are closely intertwined: they share material and ideological contexts, they frequently share personnel and 'clients'. Assignment to one or the other subsystems is not so much the result of chance, as has sometimes been suggested (e.g. Craft, 1984), but is more the result of discursive processes. Goals of both social and penal policy, resources, stereotypes and hierarchies of credibility, levels of tolerance, all play their part in assignment to the penal or the assistancial. So, too, do theoretical fashions – the degree of determinacy we see in criminality, the types of behaviour we recognise as mental illness, the degree of blame or compassion we bestow on the homeless – and the relative prestige of juridical, psychiatric and assistancial discourses.

Foucault illustrated these dimensions of the crime/illness debate with his account of the rival claims of psychiatrists and lawyers in the case of Pierre Rivière (Foucault, 1978). We can find similar discursive contests in individual contemporary cases and in generalised debates over the way to deal with drug addiction, child sexual abuse and, at a more mundane level, whether drunks should be sent to detoxification centres or police cells. Sometimes, as Foucault depicts in the case of Pierre Rivière, there is competition between legal and psychiatric reasoning, but sometimes there is withdrawal or collusion. Psychiatry and social work discourses are in demise in relation to penal decision-making in much of the English speaking world; they are in uneasy alliance with jurisprudence in much of Europe. They are used in the service of the judicial (for example, treatment for sex offenders and for psychopathic disorders is more readily available within prisons than within health service facilities); they are used at the instigation of and to the extent conceded by the juridical domain. This is epitomised by the reference to mentally disordered offenders in the 1991 Criminal Justice Act: the legislation requires that a pre-sentence report should be considered before a custodial sentence is passed on mentally disordered offenders, rather than proscribing the imprisonment of mentally disordered offenders.

Penal policy and social policy are inextricably linked. It is right to understand, with Steadman and Morrissey, that it is not a matter of functional interdependence of particular bipolar institutions – prison/hospital, probation/clinic – but of whole subsystems. Transinstitutionalisation does indeed take place mainly in the buffer zones: many deviants have careers which see them move between hostels, halfway houses and treatment programmes sponsored by either subsystem. The relationship between health/welfare and criminal justice, social policy and penal policy, is therefore one of structural coupling. That is to say, the two subsystems are closely connected and are more closely adapted to each other now than previously (Jessop, 1990). Individualised sentencing, professional discretion, increased participation of social workers and probation officers on the one hand, plus involvement of courts to assure due respect for rights in health and welfare settings on the other, as well as the phenomenon of transinstitutionalisation, demonstrate that this structural coupling is a much more accurate understanding of the relationships between penal policy and social policy than are the claims of penal policy to be rooted entirely in the juridical domain, and thus removed from considerations of social policy and social justice, acknowledging only legal concerns, legal concepts, legal processes.

4 Penal Policy and Criminal Justice

The last two chapters have examined the relationship between penal policy and other social configurations: the demographic and socio-economic structure of populations, and other spheres of social policy. In this chapter, the focus will be on the relationship between penal policy and the criminal justice system itself. Questions will be asked about the impact of penal policy developments on various subdivisions of the criminal justice system such as prisons and the probation service, looking at implications for their goals, their personnel, and above all for their 'clients'. Another focus will be the effects of the recent rationalisation of policy on the range of goals and purposes with which the criminal justice system must be concerned as a whole: control of crime, protection of the public, satisfaction of victims, as well as the punishment of offenders. As in the foregoing considerations of the interaction of penality with structural inequalities and social policy, my standpoint is that although penal policy cannot correct all the depradations or deficiences of other social subsystems, it ought at least to be cognisant of its interrelationships with them, it ought to acknowledge their aims, and it ought to endeavour not to undermine the goals set in other domains. In other words, I take seriously the proposition that if penal policy cannot be expected to do very much good, it ought to be organised so as to do the least possible harm (Gaylin *et al.*, 1978).

Aims of penal policy

In the preceding pages, I have argued that the elaboration of penal policy which took place as the 1980s progressed contained the following features:

1. a concern to develop clear principles for the assignment of some offenders to prison, some to community sanctions;
2. a desire to base punishment on the seriousness of the offence and/or likelihood of reoffending rather than on the needs or circumstances of the offender;

3. a concern with rights (formally defined) rather than remedies – rights of offenders to fair punishment; rights of the public to protection from predatory criminals; rights of the state to retribution and of victims to compensation.

However many different penal ideas have been put forward, they have been addressed to some or all of these themes; these have become the paradigmatic terms of contemporary penal discourse. I further argued that these features taken together demonstrate a clear predominance of jurisprudential over competing discourses, particularly those of medicine/psychiatry and social work. From competing ideas about the purposes of punishment – especially custodial or non-custodial penalties– only those formulated within the jurisprudential frame of reference have achieved any significant measure of assent.

Whilst the evolution of penal policy has involved rivalry between alternative theories such as desert and incapacitation, freely chosen reasoned criminality or socially generated crime, there has also been extensive rivalry between legal theorists and legal practitioners. Though it remains true that lawyers make law, there have been shifting degrees of autonomy and influence between lawyers in legislatures, lawyers in academia, and lawyers in courtrooms. Theorists have been enlisted in the campaign to promote consistency of outcome and clarity of guidelines, and the professionals targeted for reduction of discretion include sentencers as well as social workers and psychiatrists. The very idea that there should be articulation and clarification of penal policy signifies a new role for theorists: courtroom lawyers see themselves as in business to enforce and interpret laws, not to design or implement policies.

In the manner of theorists in almost every field, the early forays of jurists into the formulation of penal policy were to urge primacy for one particular principle: desert or incapacitation, reform or deterrence, determinacy or indeterminacy. Basing actual policy and practice, rather than theoretical writings, on unitary principles, however widely those principles might in themselves be accepted, brought forth judicial resistance. Sentencing guidelines based on existing practice or on desert, such as those designed for Illinois and Minnesota, met resistance either in enactment in the legislature (Cullen and Gilbert, 1982) or in enactment in courts by judges wanting the facility to pass incapacitative sentences. Early attempts to base new criminal justice legislation in England and Wales solely on proportionality to current offence, as exemplified in the green paper *Punishment, Custody and the Community* (Home Office

1988), faltered in face of judicial demands for incapacitative sentencing powers for persistent offenders, so that the section dealing with previous convictions in the 1991 Criminal Justice Act is very fuzzily worded (Wasik and Taylor, 1991).

In a second wave of theory, some of those who originally championed a single principle against others, have explored the reconciliation of alternative penal principles. Thus, in the continuing debate between desert and incapacitation, compromises have been suggested. Von Hirsch, one of the most persuasive advocates of desert, has been a frequent and penetrating critic of incapacitative sentencing, and has comprehensively reviewed the claims of the two principles (Von Hirsch, 1985).

He introduces a third possibility, that of 'categorial incapacitation', which proposes preventive prison sentences for offences which are both serious and correlated with high recidivism rates. The essence of categorial incapacitation, as opposed to the selective incapacitation mentioned in Chapter 1, is that all persons convicted of felonies in the designated categories would be subject to precautionary imprisonment, rather than instruments being designed to select out particular individuals within these offender groups. Von Hirsch discusses Jacqueline Cohen's studies of recidivism within selected offence categories, and reports her estimates of an about 8 per cent reduction in robberies being attainable if such a penal strategy were followed (ibid., p. 154). He concludes that categorial incapacitation fairly easily satisfies one of the principles of deserts sentencing, that of similar penalties for similar crimes, but insists that only if desert is given precedence over incapacitation can the objective of commensurability of penalty to crime be achieved. For example, if minor crimes have high recidivism rates, they should not on that account be categorially punished by imprisonment. Von Hirsch does suggest, however, that the idea of categorial incapacitation might prove useful in giving guidance as to where to draw the prison/non-prison line once assessments of seriousness (based on harm, public opinion or whatever) have been used to draw up a ranking of offences.

Other legal theorists regard the principle of desert as almost a truth by definition, holding that to say that a certain behaviour is criminal is the same as to say that it deserves punishment, and further, the same as to say that it deserves proportional punishment, since this is the only way in which announcing punishments can be congruent with one of the essential functions of criminal law, that is, pronouncing on the degree

of reprehensibleness of acts (Jareborg, 1986). The imposition of proportional punishments is thus seen as a structuring component, a justifying or defining aim, of criminal law, and while other aims of penal policy
may be relevant to sentencing decisions in practice, they are essentially
second order aims, which do not have the definitional character that
the apportioning of punishment does (Ashworth, 1991).

On this account, desert/proportionality and denunciation are entailed
in each other, but other theorists see just deserts and the 'expressive
theory' as alternative responses to pessimism about deterrence and reform (Walker and Marsh, 1988). The so-called expressive function of
punishment (Feinberg, 1981) has had many celebrated adherents among
the judiciary as well as among theorists, but in fact it offers little guidance for actual penal policy, as opposed to jurisprudential pronouncements. Suspended sentences apparently fulfil the expressive function,
since they pronounce the gravity of the offence, but on the other hand
denunciation would also justify a draconian sanctioning policy that is not
necessarily anchored by any commitment to deterrence, reform or culpability of the offender (Walker and Marsh, 1988, p. 57).

The main difference between theorists and practitioners, however,
arises not over the correctness of any one principle as compared with
another, but arises over the very idea that there should be any sort of
hierarchy of principles in sentencing, and that the same principle must
be applied in all (or at least most) cases. Thus, whilst the theorists might
argue over the superior justness of alternative principles, whilst legislators or guideline-givers might seek to realise one policy goal on a
consistent basis, most sentencers see it as their task to decide 'what
should be my sentencing aim in this case?' (Cooke, 1987, p. 57). If
sentencers do have a primary penal goal (as opposed to the formal
function of expressing disapproval), they more often see this as the
protection of the public by prevention of further crime rather than as
the meting out of just deserts.

Thus:

> The aim of the criminal law, and hence the first concern of the
> sentencer, is to protect and preserve society, and to promote good
> order and discipline within it, that is, to protect the public by preven-
> tion of crime. Any other objective of the sentencer must take second
> place. (ibid., pp. 57–8)

and a not dissimilar view from a representative of the lower courts:

> The first charge of the magistrates court is to protect society from
> deviants while protecting deviants from over-reaction by society . . .
> we aim to achieve a balance between the welfare of society and the
> good of the individual. In adult courts, the scales of justice have
> mainly to come down on the side of protecting society. (Acres, 1987,
> p. 61)

Both of these fit more easily with an incapacitation rather than a deserts
rationale for sentencing, so it is hardly surprising to note the judicial
opposition to the attempts of policy-makers to give primacy to desert, or
to note that attempts to ration prison use solely on the basis of desert,
such as in the sentencing guidelines in Minnesota and elsewhere, have
been undermined by the incapacitative proclivities of judges and some
legislators (Von Hirsch and Hanrahan, 1981).

The cross-national developments that have taken place in penal policy
have been concentrated in the main on the courtroom: avoidance of court
appearance for some, pronouncement of the appropriate sentence for the
rest. Where at least theory and policy, if not practice, have coincided
has been in the area of sentencing: commitment to the idea that sentencers should be implementing a clearly defined policy. The practical
manifestation of this has been the overriding attention given to the
question of when to imprison. This concentration on sentencing has had
considerable implications for criminal justice agencies other than the
judiciary. Bifurcation at the point of sentencing, plus the dominance of
the idea that all penalties, even if designed to serve other, utilitarian
goals should incorporate an element of deserved punishment, has changed
the nature and content of non-custodial penalties, provoking much controversy among criminal justice practitioners and commentators.

From alternatives to custody to punishment in the community

It was noted in Chapter 1 that the 1970s and early 1980s saw a wave of
expansion of sanctions designed to be alternatives to imprisonment,
especially to the short custodial sentence. In Europe, this primarily
meant increasing the use of suspended sentences and promoting the
success rate of fines. The day fine or unit fine, whereby an offender is
fined a proportion of a number of days' income, rather than the English

system where a flat rate fine has been levied, fixed by the seriousness of the offence, with offenders' means taken into account in the amount of time allowed for payment, is widely used. Scandinavian countries, the Netherlands and Germany among others use day fines, and there the fine is the standard penalty for less serious offences, and is also widely used for offences of intermediate seriousness. Day fines accord with notions of equity more readily than do flat rate fines, although of course they are still inappropriate for offenders entirely without, or very nearly without, means. Because of the high use of fines and comparatively low use of custody in these countries, new penalties such as community service have been developed more as alternatives to the fine for offenders without incomes. To the extent that they are seen as alternatives to custody, this is more as an alternative back-up sanction for fine default-ers than as alternatives to original custodial sentences. Although some commentators have criticised this use of community service, it cannot be said to represent a failure of penal policy objectives as the role of community service as an alternative to fines for the unemployed rather than as an alternative to custodial sentences seems from an English perspective (Junger-Tas, 1986; Vass, 1990).

In England and Wales use of the fine declined steadily from the mid-1970s to the mid-1980s, dropping from about 60 per cent of all sentences for indictable offences to a low of 38 per cent in 1987, its decline corresponding to rising unemployment. At the very end of the 1980s it recovered a little (Home Office, 1990a) and the introduction of the unit fine system will perhaps ensure that this recovery is sustained. The combination of lowering use of fines, judicial dislike of suspended sentences, and high rates of custody indicates that in England and Wales community service has been intended as an alternative to prison sen-tences, as have new forms of probation and enhanced supervision, such as supervision with specified activities or with intermediate treatment requirements, in juvenile criminal justice. In the USA, probation is the principal alternative to imprisonment, and the main impetus for innovatory probation programmes was the correspondence of record high prison populations and a reduced use of probation in the 1970s. In England and Wales and the USA, then, it is probation which is bearing the major impact of the penal crisis and the new directions in penal policy.

Until the 1970s, probation usually meant sporadic contact with of-ficers who saw their major role as counselling in the hope that this would help offenders improve their personal relationships, increase their com-mitment to finding employment and stable accommodation, and provide a non-criminal friend and role model. Size of caseloads meant that this contact was likely to be occasional, that offenders' accounts of change could not be checked up on, and that neither probationer, the sentencer, the public or even the probation officer could see much efficacy in such contact either for reforming the offender, deterring others or delivering a suitable dose of punishment. Probation was generally seen as a slap on the wrist, a soft option, getting away with it. Hardly surprising, therefore, that as the socio-political climate moved towards getting tough, and criminal justice personnel including probation officers lost faith in rehabilitation as the legitimating rationale of penality and as an achievable aim of their dealings with offenders, the use of probation decreased and the use of imprisonment increased.

Probation services in England and Wales and the USA, thus faced the twin tasks of finding a new rationale for their work with offenders, and reviving judicial confidence so as to increase their share of the sentencing market. In the USA, experimental projects in intensive probation and 'sentencing packages' were undertaken, whilst in the UK the response was to introduce day centres and to try to target reports to the court to achieve greater take-up of recommendations for probation orders. Intensive probation and combined sentences are now also being introduced in England and Wales.

The first moves away from the pure counselling model of traditional probation were in the direction of borrowing techniques from other areas of social work, rather than other areas of criminal justice. Task-centred casework became popular, the idea being to have a shared agenda with the probationer so that specific problems could be addressed rather than the contact being vague, unstructured conversations which from the perspectives of both the offender and the officer seemed to achieve little more than conforming to required rituals. The radical social work movement emphasised the importance of clients' own selection of problems to be addressed, moving away from the pyschoanalytic notion of the practicalities with which social work clients seek assistance, being 'presenting' rather than 'real' problems (Walker and Beaumont, 1981) and also anxious to apply labelling theory cautions about pathologising individual deviants (Bottoms and McWilliams, 1979). As the search for renewed credibility with sentencers gained momentum, this task-centredness was increasingly concentrated on problems thought to be connected with the circumstances surrounding the probationer's criminal behaviour (Raynor, 1985).

Parallel to this search for a new rationale and the moves to give more structure to the content of officer–client relationships, was the introduction of day centres and the efforts towards more precise targeting of pre-sentence reports. Voluntary 'drop-in' centres have long been provided by probation services, but during the 1970s day centres with far more rigorous regimes began to appear, with attendance required as a condition of a probation order. Other conditions began to be inserted also, resulting in a court judgment that intensive requirements should not be imposed because of the legal format that the probation order was technically an alternative to a sentence, and therefore should not contain overtly punitive conditions. The 1982 Criminal Justice Act removed this legal restriction and day centres, specified activities conditions, and conditions of treatment began to be frequent embellishments of probation orders. Although day centres and conditions were rationalised by probation officers as having rehabilitative effectiveness, they were promoted to the courts as injecting both incapacitative and retributive elements to probation.

Whilst probation officers may have advertised the new orders to the courts on the basis of their tough and demanding requirements, and of the incapacitative effects of probationers being off the streets all day, within the service the main concern has seemed to be not their efficacy for reforming, punishing or incapacitating offenders, but whether sentencers really would use them instead of imprisonment. Far more research and management attention has been paid to targeting referrals and reports than it has to design of the content of the programmes. Much effort has gone in recent years into devising schemes to ensure that only offenders who would be likely to receive custodial sentences would be dealt with by the new toughened probation orders. Most English probation services now use some sort of gate-keeping procedure to restrict recommendations for probation, especially probation with day centre or similar requirements, to offenders convicted of serious offences and/or with several previous convictions. Sophisticated devices such as the 'risk of custody' matrix which computes a score from factors like the nature of the current offence, previous offences, previous sentences, whether remanded on bail or in custody, and then for offenders with the required score offers a detailed programme of work to be done, conditions to be imposed within the probation order, in the recommendation of the report, are widely used. The problem with this kind of targeting is similar to the argument about false positives in predicting dangerousness: in the absence of presumptive sentencing laws, it can never be certain that a prison sentence really would have been imposed in a particular case, and so there is a danger that the new forms of probation are merely increasing intervention and punishment for defendants who would otherwise have received simple probation or other non-custodial option (Roberts, 1987).

The debate about alternatives to custody in Britain until the late 1980s was dominated by this question of whether or not they could offer a real prospect of eroding the use of custody or whether they were at best alternatives to each other, at worst a way of incorporating the characteristics of imprisonment into supposedly non-custodial sanctions. This debate has been documented extensively enough not to need detailed repetition here (for instance, Vass, 1990, chapter 3 provides a good summary). Suffice it to say that even the more optimistic proponents of the reduction of custody through expansion of alternatives strategy, such as Rutherford, could point to only a few, localised instances of success (Rutherford, 1986), and most commentators have agreed with Bottoms that British experience with innovations has not been encouraging about the prospects of reducing imprisonment by providing an even wider choice of penal measures (Bottoms, 1987). The view that non-custodial sanctions operate mostly as alternatives to each other rather than to custody, so that the most that could be hoped for is a 50:50 diversion from other community penalties and from imprisonment, is widely shared (Bottomley and Pease, 1986). In spite of this general pessimism, day centres and other enhanced probation programmes continue to be evaluated primarily in terms of whether participants satisfy risk of custody criteria, whether their criminality profile is similar to that of offenders sentenced to imprisonment or to that of offenders sentenced to probation without such refinements. Few published evaluations have looked at the benefits offenders might have derived from the programmes, an exception being Raynor's study of a Welsh project which, he claimed, managed to satisfy diversion from custody goals and offer valuable help with probationers' practical, offending-relevant problems (Raynor, 1988).

In general, probation programmes have been reticent to specify goals other than those aimed at affecting sentencing. Reducing local custody rates, having fewer people convicted of minor offences, and fewer first offenders on caseloads feature in management and research evaluations, but goals of work to be achieved once offenders are sentenced to probation are less frequently articulated. This undoubtedly reflects some cynicism or fatalism among probation officers about their own effectiveness in changing offenders' criminal behaviour or helping them achieve improvements in their circumstances, a mood which can also be found among juvenile justice workers, who during the 1980s very definitely adopted system-influencing rather than person-influencing goals. As well as the radical non-intervention value base, that is that the content of probation or supervision is of little concern, what matters is persuading sentencers to forgo custody, this inattention to articulation and monitoring of post-sentence goals demonstrating once again the overemphasis on the sentencing stage of criminal justice and the neglect of other concerns which has been apparent in penal policy. It also demonstrates the management of aggregates approach which, it was suggested in the first chapter, is a prime characteristic of contemporary criminal justice.

To the extent that 'success' of orders post-sentence is monitored at all widely or systematically, this means rates of completion of orders without breach of conditions or reconviction. Although prevention of reoffending is, of course, a perfectly proper goal of penal sanctions, overreliance on it as a measure of success is problematic (Mair, 1991). The difficulties of being certain that convictions properly reflect re-offending has been acknowledged at least since Lerman's re-evaluation of the California Treatment Project (Lerman, 1975). Rates of termination of orders through reconviction or non-compliance with conditions may also reflect differing practices of programme staff, as much as they reflect success in inducing compliance with conditions or restraint from offending.

In the USA, the first wave of intensive probation was promoted to increase usage of probation at the expense of imprisonment, and evaluation was concerned, as in England, with this question of whether enhancement of probation conditions really did divert offenders from prison, or merely increased the stringency and intrusiveness of orders for offenders who would have been placed on probation in any case. The best-known studies seemed to conclude that net-strengthening was more apparent than diversion (Austin and Krisberg, 1981), whilst the evidence for success in reducing recidivism was, at best, equivocal.

Despite this pessimism at the beginning of the decade, during the 1980s intensive probation and other forms of enhanced community penalties were developed in most states. The goals they professed were mixed, but most contained some or all of reduction of imprisonment, cost effectiveness, reduction of reoffending through deterrence and treatment, and increased public protection through greater control (Clear, Flynn and Shapiro, 1987). These are ambitious sets of goals, some more realistic than others, and some in conflict with others. Diversion and cost effectiveness are two sides of the same coin, for although intensive probation is cheaper than prison, it is obviously far more expensive than simple probation or fines. Ensuring properly diversionary use was approached by specifying the programmes as side-door and back-door as well as front-door escapes from prison; namely, whilst most programmes were designed to persuade sentencers to use them instead of prison, some, such as in New Jersey, were made available only for people who had been sentenced to imprisonment, and elsewhere they were linked with early release schemes. Even these strategies do not necessarily guarantee reductions in incarceration, and there is some evidence that prison sentences have been passed in marginal cases, or terms have been longer than normal, because of the expectation that there would be diversion into an intensive probation programme at some later stage (Pearson, 1988).

As the get tough mood grew, and public and political concern with crime levels grew more insistent, intensive probation began to stress its potential for incorporating incapacitation into community penalties more than it drew attention to its potential for diversion from imprisonment. Diversion would only be acceptable if the same levels of protection through control and incapacitation could be achieved in the community as are guaranteed by imprisonment. Through the 1980s, therefore, the surveillance and control features of new forms of probation were developed more than were treatment or rehabilitation features (Byrne, 1990). Public protection came to be seen by many not only as one among several objectives but as the primary one: the only way to save probation from a complete collapse of public and judicial confidence was to deliver on public safety (Clear and Hardyman, 1990). Protection was offered by curfews, house arrest (with or without electronic monitoring), frequent, random urinanalysis to check for drug use, daily reporting, and sometimes volunteer befrienders or supervisors to join the probationer in what little 'free' time remained available. In some places, probation officers themselves have taken on many of these new surveillance functions; elsewhere offenders are assigned both a rehabilitation probation officer and also a surveillance officer.

However the surveillance is organised, there is a contrast between this situation in the USA and that in England where, to date, developments in treatment have been in advance of developments in surveillance. With or without day centres and other restrictive conditions, the packages that probation officers have offered to courts have included alcohol education programmes, drugs counselling, employment and social skills training and so forth, whilst electronic monitoring, curfews and other negative conditions have been more energetically resisted. Although it looks at the time of writing as though these negative conditions are to be made generally available to the English courts, there has been more success here in demonstrating that probation can be both credible and effective through enhanced focus on offenders' problems, in advance of wholesale incorporation of incapacitation principles into community disposals.

In the 1990s, there appears to be some revival of interest in the treatment/rehabilitation potential of probation. The 'nothing works' nihilism of the 1970s and 1980s may, one hopes, be giving way to an appreciation that incapacitation can secure at best only short-term reductions in offending. In the most recent wave of evaluations, results 'suggest what many probation officers probably knew all along: . . . (1) you cannot change these offenders' lifestyles unless you address their (usually long-standing) problems, and (2) individual offender problems must be addressed in the broader contexts of lifestyles and communities' (Byrne, 1990, p. 33).

Probation may, therefore, be coming round something like full circle. Having, albeit reluctantly on the part of many probation officers, acquiesced in demands to become less welfare oriented, to embrace criminal justice language and concerns in place of those of social work – now the necessity of individual rehabilitative programmes and of help with using community resources, and above all the necessity of attention to social–structural conditions conducive to criminality, is beginning to be more keenly appreciated by those involved with criminal justice. The new generation of community corrections seems to be seeking not to overemphasise incapacitation through control and surveillance, but to achieve a balance between surveillance/control and reform/treatment, with the most consistently adopted net-strengthening being deterrence through enforcement of conditions.

Sanction stacking

European, especially English, concerns that new penalties act as alternatives to each other rather than to imprisonment have had somewhat different parallels in the USA. Community service, for example, has appeared to be as much an alternative to fines for the unemployed as an alternative to custody in much of Europe, and day centres also seem to be in competition with community service here, but in the USA community service is a component in enhanced probation rather than a sentence in its own right. As mentioned above, the argument about intensive probation is that it can be an alternative to ordinary probation as much as to prison, but the new problem is not so much competition between community penalties as 'sanction stacking' (Byrne, 1990, p. 30). Probation and sentencing packages in the USA now often combine several elements such as reparation, day fines, community service, reporting/counselling sessions with a probation officer, participation in intensive probation programmes, house arrest and curfew, and may also include periods of 'residential community correction' at intervals during the order, and a short term of 'shock incarceration' at the beginning. Although it is common in Europe for probation or probation-style supervision to be combined with fines, custody or suspended sentence (parallels in England have existed for some time: the money payment supervision order, parole and licence supervision, the suspended sentence supervision order), this new mix-and-match sentencing is imposing levels of penalty on offenders which are arguably more onerous than short prison sentences. With imprisonment as a back-up sanction for non-compliance with conditions as well as for reoffending, it is no wonder that some researchers are reporting offenders as saying that they would prefer to serve a short- to medium-term prison sentence and get it over with (Petersilia, 1989).

The likelihood of these excessively onerous community penalties acting as delays in imprisonment rather than as diversions from imprisonment is obviously great: the more elements and conditions imposed, the greater the likelihood of non-compliance or failure in at least some parts of the package. If these packages are applied, as originally intended, to the more serious and frequently convicted offenders, with greater likelihood of recidivisim than first offenders, then so too the risk of subsequent reconviction is increased to the detriment of success statistics of probation. In addition to net-strengthening, these packages are now – predictably enough – being said to produce adverse consequences for offenders, such as escalating rather than diminishing behavioural difficulties, unwarranted domestic intrusion with marital stress and break-up from some of the family intervention practices being used, and accelerated penetration through the criminal justice system for those unable to comply with requirements (Blomberg, 1987). Whatever the impact on prison numbers, for those of us who have up until now worried about competition between alternatives, this aggregating of alternatives is a truly disturbing phenomenon.

The horror stories of the 'dispersal of discipline' theorists seem to be being fully realised in these amalgamated sanctions. Not only is the disciplinary mode of penality becoming more pervasive, but all its techniques and purposes of punishment are spreading into the community. Through combination, community corrections become less and less differentiated; not only is there a less clear-cut distinction between prison and the community (is 'residential community correction' custody or not?), but there comes to be less distinction between disciplinary penalties, such as probation, and non-disciplinary punishments, such as fines (Bottoms, 1983).

Sanction stacking looks set to succeed 'alternatives to alternatives' as a major phenomenon here, too. The Criminal Justice Act 1991 urges that community penalties should be seen as sentences in their own right rather than as alternatives to custody, and although they are provided for 'imprisonable' offences, this is not the same as saying that they should be used for offences for which the judge thinks imprisonment appropriate. Quite the contrary, the Act clearly prefers the principle of twin-tracking, and community sentences are the provision for the non-prison track. Penal inflation is thus threatened because strengthened community penalties are being made available for people for whom imprisonment would not be justified by the seriousness of their crime. Aggregation of community penalties, rather than differentiation, with penalties being chosen according to the needs and circumstances of individual offenders, is encouraged by the provision for combination of sanctions. Not only is there a 'combination order' *per se*, which combines probation and community service, but apart from these two, any other community orders may be combined (because of the different ages for whom orders such as supervision and attendance centre are envisaged compared to probation, this effectively means that probation may be combined with curfew, as well as any conditions such as residence or treatment specified in the probation order), and any community sentence may be combined with a fine or compensation (Ashworth, 1992). This latter provision may well undermine the distinction between fines/discharges and community penalties. Community penalties are supposed to be for a band of offences more serious than those for whom fines are the appropriate response, but since there is no definitive offence seriousness ranking, there is nothing to stop a court adding community sanctions 'for their own good' to fines given on deserts grounds. One would expect this to be particularly likely in the case of female offenders, where propensity to see sickness or inadequacy already leads to overuse of probation. Probation managers and penal reformers have, with few exceptions, yet to focus on the risk of sanction stacking in any sustained way, still seeing – as Home Office ministers and officials have encouraged them to do – rising prison populations rather than penal inflation or aggregation as the major cause for concern.

Penal aggregation has been facilitated by two aspects of recent penal discourse. First of all, there has been the promotion of the necessity for consistency in sentencing. As I pointed out earlier in this chapter, policy-makers have urged the following of the same penal purposes on sentencers – desert always, incapacitation if they must, deterrence now and then if the public seems to demand it – rather than leaving judges and magistrates the discretion to decide first and foremost which penal purpose is most called for in a particular case. The logic of differentiated sentences is that they will serve different aims; imposing only a single aim as the basis for all or most sentences cannot but lead to lack of content differentiation in dispositions.

Secondly, it has often been pointed out that the promoters of deserts (and the same could be said of the promoters of incapacitation) have paid very little attention to non-custodial penalties, thereby encouraging criminal justice to become ever more custody focused (Hudson, 1987; Wasik and Von Hirsch, 1988). In part, this is because the original advocacy of guidelines based on desert was specifically addressed to questions of when to imprison, and partly it is because it is difficult to see how disposals such as probation, which has long proclaimed itself assistancial rather than punitive, or discharges, fit into a theory explicitly designed to apportion punishment. In looking at the congruence of community corrections with desert principles, probation is discussed among penalties that would 'partially fit' a desert model, and it is clear that it is the stringency of conditions that would determine its place in the severity rankings. Even with conditions, it is seen as an alternative to the 'normally recommended sentence within specific (middle range) penalty bands' (Wasik and Von Hirsch, 1988, pp. 568–9), in other words it is not regarded as an alternative to custody. These authors' argument also suggests that to be reconcilable with desert principles, probation should have some conditions (for example, curfew with electronic monitoring) which are specifically painful, since punishment is by definition the infliction of some pain or deprivation, in order to justify inclusion as a 'punishment in the community'. Satisfaction of desert requirements may conflict with ethical requirements which apply to punishments generally. Electronic monitoring, especially if via a device such as the affixing of·a bracelet, may be deemed humiliating and degrading, and many of the programmes in operation would be questionable if the requirement of avoiding punishing the innocent were taken seriously, since house arrest, home visits, family counselling and the like interfere in the lives of more people than the individual offender (Von Hirsch, 1990b).

If sanction stacking and consequent penal inflation are to be curbed, therefore, it is urgent that penal values are assigned to the various community sanctions, and that combination of purposes is not allowed to result in penalties of a greater total penal value than desert considerations would dictate. As usual, desert is important as a restricting mechanism in the imposition of harsh or overcomplicated penalties in the name of rehabilitation, deterrence, incapacitation or denunciation. Sentencers should be able to choose the penalty which best suits the appropriate purpose for the case in hand, from among sanctions of equivalent penal value.

The other neglected feature of the new community corrections is, of course, their impact not just on the size of prison populations, but on their social composition. Although it is established, for example, that black offenders are underrepresented on probation caseloads (Moxon, 1988), once again we find a striking absence of intensive probation or packaged sentencing evaluations which devote any attention to proportions of black offenders, success rates of black participants, etc. As Vass rightly argues, the present generation of community sanctions seems to be designed for the young adult, male, white offender convicted mainly of burglary or car theft (Vass, 1990, pp. 159–61). Although no day centre or intensive supervision programme would declare itself to be excluding blacks, the mentally confused or the homeless, nevertheless stereotypes of black offenders' characteristic unwillingness to keep appointments, cooperate with white officers or comply with conditions have been found in studies of pre-sentence reports on black defendants (Hudson, 1988). The degree of organisation that would be needed to be at all the required places at all the required times, plus conditions such as curfews and house arrest which depend on residence at a secure and approved address, as well as perceptions shared by most criminal justice personnel from the various agencies that the sorts of activities entailed by community service or on offer at day centres are suitable only for young, able-bodied males, make the predominance of white, male, under-30s in community corrections scarcely surprising.

If community corrections are, as Matthews argues, bringing about not so much a reduction of the prison population but a restructuring of the penal population, then there is clearly a danger that they are assisting in restructuring towards a young, white, hopeful penal population in the community, and a black, mentally disordered, homeless and hopeless population in the prisons. The strengthening of community corrections, then, is in perfect accord with the processes of differentiation within and between the health–welfare and penal subsystems described in the previous chapter, and results in criminal justice agencies such as probation services playing an ever more efficient role in the homogenisation process described in the chapter before that.

Within the prison walls

One facet of the penal crisis has been a 'crisis of containment' (Fitzgerald and Sim, 1982; Sim, 1987). This crisis within the prison has several dimensions: overcrowding, conditions, order, security and purpose. As penal policy has been reshaped along the lines described, the various aspects of the prison crisis have assumed greater or lesser urgency, but there has been some shift of equilibrium in the relationship between prison problems and penal policy. Where it used to be said that the containment crisis arose because of the lack of coherent penal policies, it is now the existence of such policies which is seen to be fuelling the crisis. As so often in criminal justice affairs, it is in Britain and the USA that all the elements of crisis have been persistently present, but other countries are also suffering prison troubles. Overcrowding and control problems have been experienced in France and parts of Germany (Matthews, 1989), and whilst some countries such as The Netherlands inhibit overcrowding through legislation forbidding multiple occupancy of cells, there, too, there are capacity problems as the population of sentenced prisoners increases (Brand-Koolen, 1987).

Overcrowding has been caused by numbers of persons sentenced and by increasing sentence lengths. In the USA and England and Wales, before the latest initiatives in penal policy both factors have been at work, but in the USA especially the main cause of crowding has been assumed to be increases in the number of incarcerations because of increasing crime rates, associated with demographic trends, bulges in the groups most likely to be imprisoned – young adults and blacks (Blumstein, 1987). These demographic influences on prison populations have been exacerbated by unemployment in these groups and by other social policy trends, as discussed above. During the 1980s, to this has been added the impact of criminal justice policies which, though they were propounded originally in the main by liberals anxious to reduce excessive imprisonment, have increasingly been hijacked by the get-tough movement, so that presumptive terms in US determinate sentencing laws have repeatedly been increased, whilst parole restrictions have ensured that increased terms pronounced are increased terms actually served (Austin and Krisberg, 1985).

The same processes are now affecting prison numbers in England and Wales, where a small decrease in prison sentences at the end of the 1980s has not been sustained, making it look like a small blip in a generally upward trend. Strategies for reducing prison crowding have been of three kinds: increasing capacity through prison building programmes; reducing admissions through changes in sentencing policy and development of alternative sanctions; and extension of good time remission, early release, emergency release, etc. All these strategies are in use, although none has had any significant, positive effects. Increased capacity has sucked in increased incarceration (Rutherford, 1984), whilst, as we have seen above, alternative sanctions have not had the reductionist impact their proponents had hoped for. Making remission automatic rather than discretionary could be expected to produce reductions in inmate populations – this was certainly an objective of English legislators in the 1982 Criminal Justice Act and in subsequent directives – but any reductionist effect has been offset by restrictions on parole for certain types of offences, for longer sentence prisoners and for prisoners classified as posing risks of reoffending. Parole prediction scales in the USA link addictions, unemployment and lack of community ties with likelihood of reoffending, and in France candidates for release on licence must produce certificates guaranteeing employment and lodgings to be successful (Gwynne Lloyd, 1991).

With penal reformers in England now pressing for mandatory sentencing guidelines if the combination of enhanced community penalties and official exhortations fail to limit the number of non-violent, non-professional offenders sent to prison, the lesson to be learnt from experience in the USA is that guidelines or sentencing laws will only curb rises in prison populations if they are introduced in jurisdictions which already have established traditions of liberal penal policy, or if they are formulated with an eye to impact on prison capacity. Minnesota, as ever, is frequently cited as a state where guidelines were linked to capacity: if any member of the guidelines commission proposed an increased term for any offence, they had to nominate an offence to be correspondingly reduced. Pennsylvania also considered capacity, subjecting its proposed mandatory minimum sentence bill to a prison impact analysis. When the impact study showed the minimum extra capacity that would be needed if the proposals were implemented, mandatory minimum terms were restricted to a narrow group of offences. These states have suffered far smaller increases in prison populations than have others (Blumstein, 1987).

In England and Wales, the only link between capacity and sentencing policy is the oft-repeated Home Office commitment to provide places for all those whom the courts wish to send to prison. The 1991 Act, whilst it states criteria for custody, does not introduce any notion of quotas or capacity limits to sentencing: that there must be an empty cell in a purpose-built prison is not one of the criteria for custody! Home Office estimates predict a prison population of 62 000 in 1998, compared with 48 610 in 1989 (Sim, 1991a).

Keeping them in and keeping them quiet

Guidelines or policies to reduce imprisonment for minor offences, alternative-to-custody or punishment-in-the-community strategies, emergency release schemes and automatic remission, are all targeted at short-sentence prisoners. If the fundamental problem, however, is really that of longer sentences and increasing proportions of long-sentence prisoners, then these strategies are not likely to have much effect on crowding. Apart from the case of very long sentences, it seems plausible that numbers of receptions may well fluctuate more in accordance with demographic trends and economic cycles, or greater or lesser investment in crime prevention measures, than with penal policies and practices. In any event, the more successful are attempts to reduce use of imprisonment for all but the most serious crimes, the greater are likely to be the discipline and management problems posed by consequent increasing proportions of long-term prisoners, convicted of very serious offences.

The problem of long-term prisoners was first occasioned by the substitution of life imprisonment or long determinate terms for capital punishment (such as the minimum of twenty-five years before parole eligibility for first-degree murder, ten years for second degree murder, in Canada), but even in places where capital punishment still exists, numbers of life- or long-sentence prisoners are increasing (Lowman and MacLean, 1991). In the USA, one writer revealed that a quarter of prisoners in federal institutions are serving sentences of fifteen years or more (Walker, 1991); George Bush's 1991 anti-crime bill proposes increasing mandatory sentences for serious, non-capital violent offences, while extending the death penalty to offences such as large-scale drug trafficking – consideration of capacity dictates that the bill envisages doubling the federal prison capacity by 1996. Whether awaiting execution, serving life sentences or (merely) serving very long sentences, prisons hold more and more people imprisoned for dangerous, violent crimes, including drugs offences, terrorism, as well as robbery, rape and murder. The management of these prisoners poses many problems, and the debates have clustered around two main themes: dispersal versus concentration, and the nature of regimes.

As prisons come to contain more dangerous and/or serious criminals, at least two problems become pressing: the problem of preventing escapes, and the problem of maintaining order amongst inmates with no hope of parole or remission to be forfeited by misbehaviour. In England, a series of escapes in the late 1960s made security seem the most urgent of prison problems, whilst in America control has assumed priority. The two problems are inextricably intertwined, however, in that creating conditions in which security is guaranteed exacerbates control problems, whilst keeping more prisoners in conditions of relaxed regimes and open conditions, whilst it may make control easier, obviously makes escape easier.

The Mountbatten Committee, reporting in 1966, saw security as by far the most pressing problem for the prison service, and recommended the building of a single fortress prison in the Isle of Wight to house maximum security prisoners – the island prison is a time-honoured solution to the problem of very dangerous prisoners, the USA has had Alcatraz, South Africa its Robben Island, etc. Only two years later, the recommendation was contradicted by the Radzinowicz Committee, which was worried about the near inevitability of control problems in a concentrated maximum-security prison, and recommended instead that the most dangerous prisoners should be dispersed among a number of high-security prisons. By the 1980s eight dispersal prisons had been built, and although they seemed to have provided an adequate answer to security needs, the control problem was not avoided, but was dispersed along with the prisoners (Bottoms and Light, 1987). One effect of dispersal has been that high levels of security thought necessary for

maximum security prisoners have meant that many prisoners with lower
security classifications have been subjected to the heightened restrictions appropriate to a concentration prison (King and McDermott,
1989). Although there have been disturbances in the dispersal prisons
(Sim, 1987, 1990, 1991a) these did not receive much official attention
until the Strangeways disturbances of April 1990. Throughout the 1980s,
security remained the main preoccupation of officials in relation to
British prisons. In the USA, after an experimental use of the dispersal
system for a few years following the closure of Alcatraz, there was a
return to concentration with the building of a new maximum-security
prison at Marion, Illinois, the 'electronic Alcatraz'.

The USA has not, however, experienced security problems to the
same extent as Britain, and Marion has functioned more as a control
facility than as a security facility. Marion is usually a temporary assignment, with prisoners transferred there more often because of misbehaviour within the prison than because of the nature of the offences for
which they were originally sentenced (Ward, 1987). Although there are
inmates whose escape would be extremely dangerous to the public, and
who are subject to the greatest imaginable degree of restraint throughout their very long sentences (the regime depicted in the film *Silence
of the Lambs*), most Marion prisoners are 'difficult' within the prison
rather than 'dangerous' outside it.

Marion, then, is effectively a segregation facility for the federal
system. The use of segregation or punishment units has been a principal
response to the problems of keeping order among long-service prisoners.
Solitary confinement, strip cells, regimes based on sensory deprivation,
have been central to the management of difficult or dispruptive prisoners. The 'special handling units' in Canada, the 'electronic coffins' in
England, as well as the total isolation regimes in the USA have been
at various times denied and admitted by states, but consistently referred
to in ex-prisoners' accounts (Sim, 1991a). For prisoners without hope
of remission and with little hope of parole, trangressions against prison
regulations have been punished by removal from the mainstream life of
the prison to blocks where they are kept stripped, in restraints, with no
communication from officers and other prisoners, and where success-
fully completing the punishment earns not remission but transfer back
to the ordinary wing. The cages within cages are supplemented as control resources by medication (the 'liquid cosh'), by loss of privileges, by
the practice of 'ghosting' – that is, shunting from one institution to
another, with the not uncommon result that family and friends do not

know the whereabouts of prisoners and so can not maintain contact – and violence. Not surprisingly, there have been serious and frequent prison disturbances: as Sim puts it, 'when you ain't got nothing to lose', by way of remission or parole, rebellion at least restores some dignity and activism (Sim, 1991b).

Crowding, security and control problems, together with the age of the prison stock and the enormous costs of replacement or refurbishment, have contributed to unconscionable deterioration in prison conditions. Although prison spending has been much higher than other comparable public expenditure, many inmates are still held in institutions built in the nineteenth century, and, furthermore, in old and new prisons are confined to their cells for longer periods than ever out of a combination of control anxieties, cutbacks in staff (especially in educational and recreational staff), and general lack of concern for the rehabilitative or brutalising effects of regimes and conditions. As penal policy becomes more focused generally on rights, and as prisoners, like citizens in general, become more assertive of their rights (Brand-Koolen, 1987), questions of prison standards have perforce received increased – and overdue – attention. In Europe, the question is that of adherence to the 'minimum standards' convention of the Council of Europe, which in spite of a vigorous minimum standards campaign waged by all the penal reform groups has yet to be given any statutory force in United Kingdom legislation (Council of Europe, 1987). Challenges on prison conditions in several states have been made in the USA, on the grounds that the 'totality of conditions' infringes the constitutional guarantee against cruel, unusual or degrading punishment (Ingram and Wellford, 1987).

These issues of security, control and conditions are inextricably bound up with those of penal policy. Loss of confidence in rehabilitation has posed the question of the nature of regimes in very acute form. The question of 'who are prisons for' at the sentencing stage has its post-sentence equivalent of 'what are prisons for?' The answer that has been given by policy-makers is simple – to receive those deserving of deprivation of liberty or posing a danger to the public – but this leaves prison administrators with the problem of what actually to do with prisoners post-sentence. For policy-makers the shift of primary objective from helping prisoners lead a good and useful life, to keeping in custody those whom the courts decree should be confined may be a move towards pragmatism, but it does leave unanswered the important question of what should happen to or for inmates, what should prison be like?

The official solution is the rationale of humane containment, which would emphasise physical standards, accountability, and rights such as recourse to legal rather than administrative tribunals for disciplinary transgressions (King and Morgan, 1980), but this still leaves these 'what' questions largely unresolved. Although the notion of 'normalisation' which informs the policy of humane containment, that is, that standards inside the prison should approximate as far as possible to the standards which govern the lives of offenders in the community (ibid.), is a great improvement on the notion of 'limited eligibility' (that conditions should be worse than any which the offender would be likely to encounter in the community) which it seeks to replace, the formula is still a safeguarding of minimum standards rather than, as its proponents have sometimes claimed, a positive formulation of a programme for a prison regime that would complement just deserts sentencing (Adler and Longhurst, 1989).

The mix of incapacitation and desert, a tension in sentencing, is having adverse consequences inside the prison. Whilst the critique of the rehabilitation goal in prison – that it acted as a coercive rather than a curative ingredient of imprisonment because of its link to parole – is well taken, the incentive of acquiescing to rehabilitative programmes in the hope of early release has now been replaced by the threat of punishment regimes: now that the carrot of parole is no longer available, the stick of punishment has to be wielded. The problems of keeping order in the incapacitative prison-as-punishment ethos make the reality of imprisonment less compatible than ever with the ideal of just deserts. To keep order without the reward of parole, early release for rehabilitative progress, prison administrators must resort to the sanction of administrative punishment – and the punishment blocks of contemporary prisons are very far removed from any idea of normalisation.

In addition to the requirements of discipline, the composition of the prison population is adding to the injustice of life within the walls. More addicted offenders, more professional criminals, more mentally disordered offenders, more people convicted of sexual offences, means that there is ever more differentiation post-sentence. The offender who is not classified as dangerous, but whose offence is deemed to deserve incarceration, may be assigned to an open prison, or to a prison approaching as nearly as imaginable the normalisation ideal, and for this prisoner the punishment may indeed be the deprivation of liberty rather than any depradations of the regime. For those who are segregated because of fear of other inmates, who are held in high security prisons, who suffer sexual or racial abuse in prison, or who are punished for disciplinary transgressions, the 'depth of imprisonment' (Downes, 1988,

p. 166) is profound indeed. Moreover, if progress towards more local prisons, more open prisons, more normalised prisons is achieved, but the Marions and segregation units remain, inequality of impact of imprisonment could become even greater, rather than less: 'between two persons treated equally at the point of sentence, one could end up in "the hole" at a maximum security penitentiary while the other could live where the action is in a downtown, minimum security, community corrections centre' (Ericson, 1987, p. 24).

The more we succeed in realising a bifurcated response to crime, the greater become the problems for the prisons. As the incarcerated become more and more concentrations of the difficult and the dangerous – this time in reality as well as in public mythology – the greater the emphasis is bound to be on security and control. Some faith has been placed in the so-called 'new generation' prisons, where high security on the perimeter is combined with more relaxed regimes within the walls, with the institutions divided into small accommodation and recreation units. These prisons are believed to be easier to manage as well as more tolerable to live in, with flashpoints such as the mass association yard avoided. Disturbances have occurred at new model prisons such as Mecklenburg, Virginia, and even if large-scale disturbances could be avoided, behavioural problems will probably still prompt recourse to punishment and segregation.

Just as Attica provided the impetus for American rethinking on the role and nature of prisons, so the 1990 Strangeways disturbances have led to the most wide-ranging report on prison conditions here, the Woolf enquiry into the disturbances (Woolf and Tumin, 1991). The 1991 Criminal Justice Act provides for early release of short-sentence prisoners through automatic release, and provides for disciplinary offences in prison to be dealt with by imposition of extra days in custody (Wasik, 1992). In this, it is consistent with moves in the USA to substitute automatic remission for discretionary parole for offenders convicted of less serious offences and regarded as non-dangerous, and it continues moves in this direction in England and Wales during the 1980s. The Act reinforces all the trends so far discussed, to restructure the penal population to be more criminal, serving longer sentences, and therefore more difficult to manage.

Woolf addresses prison conditions as a whole as well as the grievances and transgressions of people involved in the disturbances, and in this his report is much to be welcomed. To a large extent, the report breaks with earlier reactions to prison disturbances in that it does address conditions, disciplinary processes and other general prison problems, rather than perpetuating the 'rotten apple' approach to criminal justice difficulties. The report breaks 'the umbilical cord of individualization – identifying and isolating the hard-core of prisoners who, it was argued, were disrupting regimes and subverting good order and discipline' (Sim, 1991a, p. 113). In this respect, the report is more searching than previous reports on prison ills, although to say that it is 'penetrating, profound and went to the heart of the problems of the criminal justice system' (Tuck, 1992, p. 41) is perhaps overstating the case a little.

Lord Justice Woolf makes twelve main recommendations, including:

a compact or contract for each prisoner;
a national system of accredited standards;
Certified Normal Accommodation not to be exceeded after 1992 unless Parliament is informed;
sanitation for all inmates not later than February 1996;
a move towards community prisons near the main centres of population;
a division of prison establishments into smaller and more manageable units;
reforms in justice and grievance procedures. (Woolf and Tumin, 1991, pp. 19–20)

These recommendations accord with the minimum standards movement, and also endorse the 'new model prison' design in advocating prisons being divided into smaller units. As has been insisted upon by Rutherford, among others, and as Woolf recognises, any possible remedy for prison troubles must be sought in regimes as well as in architecture (Rutherford, 1987). The irony here is that just as twenty years ago it was prison disturbances which led to influential reports such as *Struggle for Justice* (American Friends Service Committee, 1972) and the Committee on Incarceration (Von Hirsch, 1976) advocating the abandonment of rehabilitation in favour of the more modest aim of just and humane punishment, so in 1991 it is the Strangeways disturbances which have lead to endorsement in the Woolf report of something that comes close to the 'new rehabilitation' agenda, which will be considered in the next chapter. By advocating contracts for each prisoner, Woolf acknowledges that the state has responsibilities to the inmate – to provide decent standards of accommodation, to provide a constructive regime – as well as the prisoner having obligations to serve the sentence and obey prison regulations.

Whilst Woolf has generally been welcomed by prison reformers because of the commitment to certified normal accommodation, sanitation, local prisons, smaller units and the idea of the constructive sentence, a more critical reading will appreciate that far from being a radical new departure, the Woolf report is consistent with the tendencies that I have been demonstrating as representative of contemporary penal practice. Although the report talks in terms of general conditions, none the less its language of contracts and compacts is firmly within the traditions of individuals having responsibility for problems and their solutions. The word 'contract' conjures up some freely entered into agreement between equals, which is very far from the reality of the relationship between the prisoner and the state; as in other contexts, the use of the terminology of contracts and compacts masks the power relationships involved. It is the state which has power to decide what will and will not mandatorily be offered in the contract – toilets but not education, telephones but not conjugal visits – and it is the state which has the power to decide what the penalties will be for non-performance of the contract. As with privatisation, the language of the market, of services offered and obligations honoured, masks the coercion and repressiveness of the situation of the prisoner (Sim, 1992).

Woolf's recognition of the brutalising effect of lack of sanitation and other degrading conditions does not extend to recognition of the fact of brutality itself as a routine aspect of prison life. In particular, he declines to address the problems in women's prisons, where use of drugs as tools of control rather than therapy, insistence on petty regulations and recourse to disciplinary proceedings are rife.

Another problem which Woolf largely ignores is that of racism in prisons. The findings of Elaine Genders and Elaine Player's study of race relations in prisons (Genders and Player, 1989) contrasts sharply with the complacency of the Director-General of the Prison Service when he claims: 'Race relations is an area of real distinction in the Prison Service' (Pilling, 1992, p. 32).

Unless problems of racism, sexism, brutality, persecution of groups such as sex offenders and mentally disordered prisoners (Lowman and MacLean, 1991) are confronted, and unless long sentences devoid of any constructive activity and possibilities for personal growth are avoided, then the achievement of penal aims will make the problems of prisons and prisoners even more acute. If community prisons are built, if private prisons and open prisons offer better standards, whilst segregation units and punishment blocks continue to exist, then justice and equality of impact of imprisonment will become even more remote.

Summary – the present relationship of penal policy to social justice

Penal policy, then, seeking bifurcation of response to crimes, prioritising punishment and incapacitation over rehabilitation and deterrence, does not seem to be achieving even criminal justice, still less contributing to social justice. In solving or at least ameliorating one set of difficulties – alternatives to alternatives, too many short prison sentences, coerced participation in rehabilitation programmes, too much discretion vested in prison and community corrections administrators – penal policies are creating new problems or exacerbating others. Sanction stacking and prison management are just two that have been highlighted here. The relationship of penal policy to social policy and social structure has been examined in previous chapters and found to be complex, and the outcome of their interrelationship is far from satisfactory on social justice criteria.

Although I grant that penal policy cannot be expected to solve all the dilemmas of criminal justice, let alone social justice, it at least ought to be consistent with the ideal of justice and should not be adding to the sum of social injustice. On the evidence presented so far, the justice case against penal policy is strong; the following chapters will sketch out some possible directions which could take penal policy closer to, rather than yet further away from, the justice ideal.

5 Some Ideas Whose Time Has Come

In spite of so much activity in both penal practice and penal discourse, criminal justice continues to be a disaster. It is a disaster in its own, lately clarified terms: it does not reserve prison for serious offenders, since prisons continue to be full of minor property offenders; it does not apportion punishments fairly, since the rich continue to get fines, suspended sentences or administrative processing, whilst the poor, the mentally disordered, blacks and migrants get penalising processes and prison; it does not protect the public, since crime rates continue to soar; it does not legitimate the system, since prisoners have become more prone to riot and the public has become more prone to criticise the police, the courts, the correctional services and the politicians. By any broader utilitarian or sociological standards – lessening the oppressiveness of the state, increasing citizens' dominion over their own lives, promoting social cohesion and harmony; in other words, contributing to social justice – criminal justice is not only ineffective but also pernicious. On all counts, therefore, criminal justice stands in urgent need of reform. This chapter will put forward some ideas for reform that disenchantment with the outcome of revamping of penal codes has made newly acceptable, or brought to the verge of acceptability. These are ideas generated from within the system itself by sympathetic critics or by commentators who, whilst not exactly sympathetic to current practice, at least accept that the penality characteristic of late capitalism is susceptible to reform, rather than needing total abolition. This, then, is the penal agenda of the reductionists, the realists and the moral pragmatists.

The problems penal systems encounter in attaining their objectives and which they cause for social justice are in large part related to their self-enforced isolation from other domains. They are related to their insistence on abstraction and separation when what they really need is socialisation and integration. Contemporary penality promotes

1. the abstraction of acts from agents, individuals from their collectivities;
2. the abstraction of punishment from other penal purposes;

3. the separation of sentencing from other criminal justice processes;
4. the separation of criminal justice from other areas of public policy.

Description of these abstracting and separating tendencies has been the task of the earlier chapters of this volume; the strategies to be described below all involve to a greater or lesser extent the reuniting of criminal acts with people, their problems and their social groupings. They also involve the reuniting of sentencing and punishment with other criminal justice processes and purposes, and the reuniting of criminal justice agencies with other official and non-official agencies.

Common to these ideas is a desire to control the use of imprisonment, which to some may mean purely and simply a reduction in the numbers of prisoners, while to others it might mean rather bringing the actual use of imprisonment more in line with the principles that have been enunciated for its use. The strategies also have in common the desire to promote a more effective response to crime – they all take crime seriously. Some writers explicitly specify amelioration or at least non-aggravation of socio-economic inequalities as a primary goal, whilst others neglect this objective or (we must assume) take it as self-evident.

Selective abolitionism

Attempts to reduce or ration imprisonment through developing altern-ative sanctions and/or by disseminating principles or guidelines have already been discussed. They have largely been unsuccessful, and most reductionists now urge this positive strategy – provision of alternatives, formulation of principles – to be augmented by a negative strategy, such as the restriction of capacity through closure of existing prisons and/or a moratorium on the building of new ones (Nagel, 1977; Rutherford, 1984), or the restriction of judicial sentencing discretion through legis-lation or a sentencing council (Ashworth, 1989b). Abolition of custody for trivial offences has been proposed consistently by deserts penologists, and for offenders unlikely to reoffend by incapacitation theorists.

Our by now considerable experience of reductionism should have convinced us that reasonable as it may sound, it is in fact far less realistic than some utopian-sounding agendas for at least partial abolitionism, because reductionism is unrealistic in the sense that it simply does not work. It produces, at best, a temporary dip in prison numbers. The strengthening of probation orders in England and Wales through greater use of day centre conditions, for example, contributed to a decrease in prison numbers from the mid-1980s peak, but numbers have risen again in the 1990s. Similarly, dissemination of new desert-based sentencing principles in Sweden, following on from liberalisation of parole measures in 1983, produced the desired effect of prison populations in the late 1980s being lower than in 1983, but by 1989 they were rising once more. In Denmark, in 1982, reduced maximum sentences were introduced for several classes of property offences, the rules for punishing drunken drivers were relaxed and the minimum time to be served before eligibility for parole was reduced, but once again the resulting decrease in prison use seems not to have been sustained (Mathiesen, 1990, pp. 153–4).

Whilst there has been much – probably perfectly sincere – lamentation on the part of politicians and criminal justice personnel over the failure to maintain prison rationing, there is little evidence of a rational feedback loop where these failures are properly analysed, appropriate implications drawn and consequent policy adjustments made. A rational response to rerising prison populations would surely be to start by analysing not just the numbers but the characteristics of the 'unwanted' prison population, by looking at prisoners in the criminality categories that policy has ordained should be decarcerated, to see what they have in common, in personal–social characteristics and in routes to custody. Amongst the population imprisoned for non-serious, less violent offences, even the most cursory examination would find the people who have been my concern throughout: the poor and unemployed, migrants, the mentally disordered, the disaffected, the destitute, in other words the marginalised or, as Mathiesen puts it, the expelled (ibid., 1974). This would be true of black and white, male and female prisoners, but especially where blacks and females are imprisoned for anything other than the more serious, violent offences, one would find a preponderance of these marginalised groups – impoverished, disordered or damaged individuals. The goal of prison rationing, of prison bifurcation along offence lines, can only be achieved if strategies more directly targeted at the decarceration of these groups of offenders are adopted.

The most a reductionist strategy seems able to achieve is a decrease in direct imprisonment of these people, in other words, immediate imprisonment following commission of a non-serious offence. Whether reductionism is approached through expansion of alternatives plus exhortation, or through sentencing principles, guidelines or laws, vulnerable people will continue to be imprisoned because of breach of

non-custodial orders, because of fine default, and whilst awaiting conviction or sentence. They will be imprisoned because their chances of
success on community corrections programmes are considered poor,
because they are caught in the revolving-door cycle of petty persistent
offending, or sometimes simply because there is nowhere else for
them to go.

Abolitionist strategies are the only way to ensure that prison becomes
the exceptionally severe penalty for exceptionally serious crime, that it
becomes residual, that it is reserved for those 'few from whom society
can be protected in no other way' (Blom-Cooper, 1988, p. 48). Wherever
policy draws the prison/non-prison line, only protection of the line by
abolitionism can ensure that it is held.

Partial or selective abolitionism has already been tried in relation
to offence types, for example, prostitution was supposedly made non-
imprisonable under the 1982 Criminal Justice Act; the much-vaunted
Minnesota Sentencing Guidelines stipulate non-imprisonment for the
least severe offences, no matter how many times they may be committed.
The Netherlands, Scandinavia, Germany and other places have made
certain minor offences *de jure* or *de facto* non-imprisonable. These
attempts at partial abolition are undermined when imprisonment is retained as a back-up sanction for non-completion of community penalties. Thus, prostitutes may no longer collect a 'go direct to jail' card
for prostitution, but they get one next time round the board for non-
payment of fines; minor fraudsters, shop-lifters and the like go to prison
for fine default and also for breach of probation, community service
or suspended sentence. This 'once removed' effect is well documented,
for example, early evaluations of suspended sentences in England and
Wales (Bottoms, 1981), of intensive probation and allied experiments
in America (Lerman, 1975). Even so, the idea that prison is a necessary
back-up sanction to induce compliance with community penalties per-
sists. The problems this deferred imprisonment occasions are sufficiently well known that they do not need detailed listing here, suffice it
to mention the inhibiting effects on probation officers and others who
might argue more strongly in 'risky' cases for community penalties,
were it not that they risk both their clients' liberty and their own success
rates if they obtain orders on people who fail to fulfil all the conditions
of the penalty. The temptation to play safe, by recommending probation,
community service, suspended sentence or fines only for those who
present the minimum risk of non-compliance as well as of reoffending,

or of trying to ignore compliance or offending problems which arise in the course of orders, is obviously great.

Whilst these arguments have been voiced regularly, one which is less frequently heard, but which might be more consistent with the spirit of the times, is drawn from the justice model itself. The objection to pre-guidelines penal practice that the penalty served should be derived from the offence committed rather than from behaviour as a prison inmate – compliance with treatment programmes, acquiescence with prison regimes, etc. – surely must in justice be applicable also to community penalties. Nothing but a further offence should occasion any new risk of imprisonment, and even then this should only be when the new offence itself is prisonworthy.

It is customarily objected by those wishing to retain imprisonment as a back-up sanction that the threat of custody is the only way to ensure that offenders take non-custodial penalties seriously enough, that they do not regard being allowed to remain in the community as having 'got away with it'. Respect for the law, they would argue further, demands that the penalty for disobeying an order of the court should be particularly severe: contempt of court in whatever form demands imprisonment. A different view is held by Swedish judges, who believe that showing tolerance and understanding of fine defaulters poses no danger to the authority of the court. Those cited by Peter Young in his study of the use of financial sanctions

> could not see why their lenient attitude necessarily led to disrespect for the court or the criminal law. Indeed it was forcibly contended that to pursue to the bitter end of imprisonment those who had defaulted on small fines was more liable to create disrespect because it is absurd. (Young, P., 1987, quoted in Carlen, 1989, p. 25)

Sweden uses distress warrants to deal with non-payment, and along with several other countries has been considering the use of short periods of community service. The work–money nexus of industrial capitalism makes this an obvious substitution, but does raise the anxiety that wilful refusers might be just as likely to default on community service as on the original fine, whilst those who cannot pay the fines would be unduly penalised.

Deliberation over non-compliance with any penalty brings us back to the fundamental issue of people: tariffs, reductionist strategies or partial abolitions will inevitably be undermined if they are aimed only at

offences or other legal categories, rather than at persons. The point here
is sentence feasibility in the sense of the term elaborated by Pat Carlen
in a series of works (Carlen, 1989, 1990), that is, people should have a
reasonable chance of compliance. Fines must be realistic in relation
to income as well as in relation to the value or monetary equivalent
of any harm committed. The unemployed are found by one study to
be four times as likely as the employed to fall behind with fine payments (Crow and Simon, 1987); other studies of imprisoned fine defaulters show them not only to be characteristically unemployed, but
often homeless too (Shaw, 1989). Fining the destitute clearly fails the
feasibility test, as does fining single mothers for financial misdemean-
ours such as non-payment of television licence fees, women who are
frequently burdened with multiple debts. A prerequisite for feasibility
of fines is moving from a flat-rate to a day-fine system as operated by
the Scandinavian countries, Germany, Austria, Belgium and Portugal
inter alia, and now being adopted by some American states. Here the
offender's means are built into the structure of the system, so cannot be
disregarded by sentencers (Thornstedt, 1975). A unit-fine system, which
shares some of the features of the day-fine system, has been introduced
into Britain in the 1991 Criminal Justice Act, and at the time of writing
we have yet to see whether this will raise the rate of fine usage and
reduce imprisonment for fine default.

Feasibility considerations apply equally to other community penalties, however. Offenders should not be given sentences which they have
no prospect of completing, whether for reasons of protection of the
public, penal equivalence to custody, credibility with sentencers, or any
other such buzz formula. People who are homeless, destitute, damaged
or disorganised cannot be expected to cope with lengthy community
service orders, very demanding probation conditions or the like – there
have even been instances of unemployed offenders losing benefit en-
titlement because the demands of probation orders made them fail
the availability for work test. Equally, even well-organised and well-
motivated offenders may find their efforts to attend regularly at probation centres or community service placements subverted by difficulties
with bus services, child-care facilities and the like, giving a new meaning
to 'justice by geography'. Pat Carlen's prescription that the courts should
only impose such conditions as are considered feasible by a probation
officer, with full knowledge of the defendant's circumstances, is thus an
indispensable requirement if community corrections are to have any real
hope of diverting non-dangerous offenders from prison.

Discretion also needs to be returned to probation officers and other corrections administrators over definition of non-compliance. A telephone call from a probationer to say s/he is not going to attend an appointment may be a flouting of the seriousness of the criminal justice system. On the other hand, it might be a significant step towards acknowledging such seriousness and towards a more socially responsible lifestyle by someone who until that point has led a completely disorganised life, never kept an appointment and never thought to explain themselves to anyone: the point is that only the probation officer can ascribe meaning to events such as telephoned postponements, irregular attendance, lack of engagement and unsatisfactory work. Again, only a further offence should occasion any new risk of custody, and then only if the offence warrants imprisonment of itself.

Feasibility becomes a two-edged sword, however, in the absence of abolition of imprisonment for certain categories of persons. Without abolition, there is an obvious danger that poor prognosis of an offender's success with community penalties tough enough to be regarded by the courts as having at least near equivalence to custody would lead to substitution of imprisonment as the original sentence. In other words, exactly what happens now would continue: any reductionist innovation, from bail information schemes to intensive probation, would be denied to the homeless, the indigent, the rootless, the disturbed, the hopeless and the hapless. With back-up imprisonment but without feasibility consideration the courts may well take more risks, as they would see it, but the risk for the offender would be of secondary imprisonment, and for the community corrections agency the risk would be of high failure rates. With feasibility but without abolition, and with or without back-up imprisonment, the result would be that more of the most disadvantaged offenders would go directly to jail.

What is needed, then, is the abolition of imprisonment for the kinds of people most vulnerable to 'poor risk' assessments, with the proviso of special case imprisonment for very serious offences. Pat Carlen presents a strong case for women's imprisonment to be the first, experimental case of such selective abolition (Carlen, 1990, p. 121). She contends that the very small number of women who are imprisoned for serious offences against the person means that special case imprisonment for such offences would still allow for decarceration of all but about one hundred women. Thus significant decarceration could be achieved without posing any physical danger to the public. Moreover, the high cost of keeping women in prison and also their children in care compared to the relatively low social cost of female crime presents a strong economic argument for abolition of imprisonment for all but a small number of untypically dangerous women. The number of women in prison is small enough to make the provision of accommodation, rehabilitative programmes and general support in the community practicable.

Abolition of women's imprisonment is undoubtedly a requirement of any reorientation of penal policy in the direction of social justice. Women prisoners are predominantly poor; many have histories of sexual abuse in childhood, physical abuse in adulthood; many are addicted, disordered, disowned; the proportions of black women prisoners are particularly high, as are proportions of other discriminated against minorities such as gypsies. Motivation is far more often survival than kicks, feeding hungry families rather than going along with delinquent friends. Even the most serious sounding crimes, for example drug-trafficking, amongst imprisoned women usually turn out to be the drug-carrying 'mules' who are occupying about a quarter of the spaces in the women's prisons of Britain and mainland Europe, women who are amateurs, unaware of the value of their cargo, unaware of the problem of addiction in Europe and North America, and unaware of the huge profits being made by the organisers of the trade (Green, 1991). Their imprisonment rarely leads to capture of the trade's professionals, it has scarcely any deterrent value since European sentencing practices are hardly common knowledge in the barrios of South America or the shanty towns of Africa and Asia, and there is little incapacitation effect beyond that produced by arrest, since a courier once spotted would be of no further use. There is, in short, virtually no return to the 'host' country bearing the costs of many years' imprisonment. The money spent on keeping these women in prison would be far better expended on efforts to catch the professionals or on foreign aid to reduce women's need to resort to such desperate measures to earn money.

Whilst entirely supporting Pat Carlen's call for at least an experimental abolition of imprisonment as a normally available response to women offenders, I would urge equally strongly the need for abolition of imprisonment for mentally disordered offenders, of either sex. As proposed for women offenders, there should only remain the possibility of detention for mentally disordered persons convicted of serious, specified offences, and in such cases confinement should be in hospitals rather than prisons. Specification of offences, and restriction of the list of detentionable offences to serious, violent crimes, is necessary to guard against abolition becoming nothing more than a change in nomenclature, incarceration in an institution called a secure hospital rather than called a prison. Mentally disordered persons convicted of offences not on the list of those liable to special case detention should be offered treatment, accommodation, social and financial support in the community. If their condition, rather than their offence, dictates institutional treatment, this should be on the same basis as non-criminal patients, according to mental health legislation rather than the criminal law. The criteria of good prospect of benefit from treatment urged by Gostin would be of utmost importance in the original decision to assign a mentally disordered offender to hospital rather than to out-patient treatment (Gostin, 1984). Of equal importance is that coming into psychiatric care by way of criminal justice processes rather than via medical or social work routes should not remove any rights of review, and should not facilitate any extension of the period for which compulsory detention is possible. Mentally disordered offenders needing institutional care should be assigned to hospitals within health services, not to psychiatric wings within prisons.

There will remain, of course, some people convicted of very serious offences whose psychiatric condition would make them dangerous if left at liberty, so that escape needs to be impossible and release unsanctionable without very firm and expert psychiatric evidence of improvement. Secure hospitals, special institutions are inevitable, but the number of such cases at any one time is likely to be quite small, and provision of such residual secure incarceration should not interfere with the general abolitionist contention that mentally disordered persons on desert grounds should not be imprisoned for minor offences because such cases would not meet gravity criteria, and even in more serious cases they would not meet culpability criteria. Very serious, very dangerous cases are unusual and therefore require unusual measures, the point is that it should be recognised that these cases are exceptional and should therefore be dealt without outside mainstream penal policy, outside the routine of criminal justice processes.

Whilst women and the mentally disordered are two categories of offenders for whom a general abolitionist policy should be adopted, there are other groups for whom very strict criteria should be applied before custodial sanctions are imposed, with desert/retributivist claims set aside unless considerations of culpability or dangerousness are especially strong. Addicts whose offending is linked to their addiction, for example, might be considered in much the same way as mentally disordered, as should also the very institutionalised. This reverses the policy of reserving community penalties for those with more favourable personal characteristics that applies in many countries, for example, it is almost the exact reversal of the conditions for non-custodial sanctions that have been applied in Belgium, mentioned in the first chapter. It also goes against the 'war on drugs' mentality of the USA, now spreading in Europe, so that even those countries like The Netherlands which have traditionally adopted tolerant or therapeutic policies towards addictions rather than penalisation are becoming more punitive. In England and Wales, there is no coherent policy about the sentencing of addicted persons, but there is in some sentencers a belief that being in prison will afford access to treatment, or at least force withdrawal from drugs or alcohol. Prisoners do, however, seem to have readier access to supplies than to treatment in prison – there have been continuous reports of drugs being readily obtainable in British penal institutions. In the case of addictions as in the case of mental illness, lack of therapeutic facilities outside prisons is not a good reason for incarceration.

Strict criteria for the imposition of further periods in custody on the heavily institutionalised would complement the introduction of criteria for first custodial sentences and custodial sentences for juveniles. The old lag, the offender who provokes arrest in order to gain a bed, regular meals or companionship at Christmas is far from being an apocryphal character, but is a regular performer in the lower courts. It is just this sort of person about whom there is almost universal agreement that imprisonment is inappropriate. These offenders are being disadvantaged by social policy which fails to provide a sufficient network of community care, and also by the policies of criminal justice agencies who are targeting their efforts and provisions on the more serious but apparently corrigible, mainly young, offenders.

These groups of people – women, the mentally disordered, the addicted and the institutionalised – are the very offenders at whom bifurcation and reductionist strategies are aimed. Policy-makers trying to achieve a bifurcated response to crime stress that seriousness and dangerousness should be the indicators for imprisonment. Reductionists point out the proportions of prison populations made up of fine defaulters, the inadequate, the petty persistent offenders and mentally disordered offenders, and say that we could reduce prison numbers significantly by providing adequate community programmes which would combine commensurate punishment for minor or intermediate gravity offences with help for the circumstances or conditions which prompted the criminality. Reductionist approaches have been given a fair run; it is surely now pragmatic and realistic to underpin them with partial abolitions.

State-obligated rehabilitation

Setting aside the primacy of the retributive tariff for some offenders, abolition of imprisonment for some, necessitates acknowledgement of other purposes of penalty than the infliction of commensurate punishment. Two issues raised in the previous chapter are brought to the fore: the necessity of differentiation in community sanctions, and the necessity of clarification of the penal value of the various non-custodial sanctions. Declaration that imprisonment is unsuitable for certain groups of offenders should logically entail that it is not appropriate for community disposals to replicate the features or pains of imprisonment – the punishment in the community model is rendered inapplicable. Rather than a unifying principle of punishment (such as restriction of liberty) which makes different penalties more nearly functionally equivalent, what is needed is differentiation to enable sentencers to choose a penalty according to its utility for whichever function may be most suitable or urgent in individual cases.

Although deserts theorists and neo-Kantian philosophers may contend that individuals should not be punished in order to achieve social goals, whilst it may be morally correct to insist that people should always be ends and never means, in fact of course criminal justice is public policy and as such the whole point of penal law is to serve social goals. To try to cast criminal justice as about individuals is patently nonsense: the aim of criminal justice is to redress wrongs done to society, to induce offenders to make restitution to society, to affirm that certain behaviours are not acceptable to society. Retribution is not for the individual's good, it logically must always be in service of, or linked to, utilitarian goals, and the ultimate justifying objective must be the control or prevention of crime. To say, as deserts theorists sometimes do (for example, Ashworth, 1991), that punishment has little to do with control or prevention of crime is to make penality a theology rather than a strand of public policy.

The only possible justification for any state infliction of pain or restriction of liberty is that it is necessary for the promotion of some social good or the prevention of some greater social harm: the modern state can have no justification for inflicting pain for its own sake. Punishment, pain, then, can never be 'deserved', it can only be socially necessary. Penal sanctions can, therefore, only involve retributive punishment if this contributes to the prevention of future crime, whether by the offender who is being punished or by others. Deserts theorists are correct in saying that utilitarian theories are not a sufficient basis for penal policy, because they imply no obvious limits to punishment, but this is not to say that they are not necessary. Moreover, deserts theorists are also correct in so far as they point out that the contribution of penalisation to prevention of further crime may be less than the contribution of detection, situational crime prevention, social policies to reduce inequality, and so forth, but this is not the same as denying that their defining objective is the prevention of further crime. Depending on the nature of the crime and the character of the criminal, the future crime prevention goal will be best served by deterrence – general or individual – or through prevention either by incapacitation or by reform or treatment. Penal policy must, in other words, acknowledge a single, justifying objective – the control or prevention of crime – which it will serve by mixed strategies of punishment, strategies of deterrence, incapacitation and reform (Hart, 1968).

Specific penalties, then, need to be designed to serve specific penal goals. For normal crimes, run-of-the-mill crimes which any of us can imagine ourselves committing given opportunity and absence or temporary loosening of moral/social constraints, and where the offending does not seem to have arisen from any medical or psychiatric conditions which would indicate need for treatment or any personal–social circumstances which would indicate need for help rather than punishment, simple deterrent penalties, aimed first and foremost at the offending individual but also with an eye to the general population of potential offenders, would suffice. Proportionality should govern the degree of punishment, guaranteeing an adequate but not excessive level of deterrence, a penal approach very much along the lines originally proposed by Beccaria (Roshier, 1989). Fines and community service are the obvious, uncomplicated deterrent punishments which can be commensurably graduated, with imprisonment reserved for the most serious, but still normal crimes, committed by normal criminals. Run-of-the-mill penalties for run-of-the-mill offences; rational sanctions for reasoning criminals, in other words. Both fines and community service are fairly straightforwardly punitive, with an element also of restitution or reparation to the community, and as long as there is a day-fine or unit-fine system, both can be finely calibrated to reflect the seriousness of the crime, degree of culpability, and level of deterrence thought necessary. The choice between them can sometimes be difficult; community service can too easily take on a 'forced labour' aspect for those without means. Money and labour are, of course, constantly exchanged in capitalist society, so their penal equivalence is reasonable in principle. Feasibility or even offender preference could be the basis for selection. Discharge is the other simple penalty which fits the bill of individual deterrence where the nature of the offence is such that the proportionality principle would dictate little or no punishment.

It is easy to see how probation would fit into this kind of pluralistic, differentiated penal policy. Probation without negative conditions would be the usual choice in cases where the offending behaviour could be shown to be linked with personal or social problems, so that the probation task would be to provide help with economic or social difficulties (accommodation, debt, relationships, training, employment) or to arrange treatment for problems such as alcohol abuse, drug addictions or psychiatric disorders. If effective transmission mechanisms to secure bifurcated sentencing, rationing of prison places to the most serious, culpable, offences and offenders, were actually to be achieved, then 'risk of custody' could become a much less important criteria for probation targeting than risk of reoffending, where the risk is posed by the persistence of conditions of life which make adherence to a non-criminal lifestyle difficult. Risk of reoffending because of social–personal–clinical circumstances would be the main reason for choosing probation rather than a simple penalty or discharge, and probation would have a very important task in assessment of both need and feasibility. With no risk of custody for any event other than commission of a further serious offence, there would be no danger of 'up-tariffing' by recommending probation at any stage in a criminal career.

What is now understood by the phrase 'punishment in the community' – negative conditions such as curfews, intensive reporting, etc. – would be reserved for cases where it can be demonstrated (through persistent offending, reoffending in spite of community service, fines or other simple penalties) that public protection through some degree of incapacitation is necessary, but where the offence is not so serious as to dictate custody. Again, twin-tracking through sentencing guidelines, and supported by selective abolitions, would eliminate the risk of up-tariffing, if these options were used for somewhat less serious offences than those for which imprisonment is reserved.

   This penal scenario, then, suggests community penalties which are primarily deterrent/restorative (fines, community service), some of which are primarily oriented to public protection (probation with negative conditions), and both these kinds of penalty would be experienced as retributive by offenders. It also contends that there should remain a place for sanctions which are not primarily retributive but rehabilitative, namely, probation without negative conditions, probation to provide help or treatment. Since the idea is not punishment, it follows that there would be no negative sanctions for non-completion of the order itself or any of the therapies being offered; only a further offence would occasion new penalties, and then the penalty would be linked to the present circumstances. There would be no add-on punishment for breach of probation.

   The argument that rehabilitation should have a place in penal policy is not, perhaps, too controversial. There would not be much disagreement with the view that some people find themselves convicted of crimes for whom the notion of punishment is inappropriate; whether through reduced culpability, extreme improbability of reoffending, triviality of offending, most of us are easily able to accept that there should be available non-punitive ways of responding to crime. Non-prosecution because of triviality of the act, discharge because of extreme improbability of reoffending are widely accepted, and rehabilitative disposals would seem to fit the reduced culpability case. Risk of reoffending offers a criterion to differentiate cases suitable for rehabilitative disposals, such as probation without negative conditions, from those which could be more appropriately and cost effectively dealt with by discharges, and would guard against net-strengthening, unnecessary interventiveness in the lives of lightly criminalised persons. State-obligated rehabilitation as proposed by the so-called 'new rehabilitationists', however, claims a much more central place for rehabilitation than that of being one among several penal aims, one among several alternative orientations of differentiated penalties. The term 'state-obligated rehabilitation' has been given slightly different meanings by its various advocates, but the essential argument is that although much has been made of the rehabilitative character of twentieth-century penal systems, in fact states have never acknowledged any obligation to provide therapeutic facilities to those whom they have brought within the orbit of punishment facilities. Prison inmates or probationers might have been judged by their progress towards rehabilitation, but although they might have been disadvantaged by non-involvement with rehabilitative programmes, these have only been available at the whim of the state – not continuously, uniformly or mandatorily (Cullen and Gilbert, 1982). First formulated in connection with prisons, the idea of state-obligated rehabilitation has been extended to community penalties, and it has been argued that a rehabilitative element should be included in all sentences unless the 'offender and court are agreed that a rehabilitative element would be redundant in a particular case' (Carlen, 1989, p. 20).

There are weak and strong meanings of 'rehabilitation' in this context. The strong meaning, which underpins both Cullen and Gilbert's and Carlen's models, rests on the belief that of all the various rationales for penal sanctions, only rehabilitation is clearly motivated by the aim of preventing future crime. Retributive punishment is looking to the past rather than the future; the deterrent effects of punishment are far from established; and incapacitation offers nothing to prevent further crime once inmates are eventually released or restrictions lifted. It is more crime deferment than crime prevention, so that although rehabilitation may be unsuccessful in particular instances, it is at least consistent with the basic principles of criminal law. In the absence of death, transportation or life imprisonment for almost all crimes, rehabilitation offers the best chance of reducing reoffending. Prevention of reoffending is a clearly understood, well-supported rationale for penality, complementary to situational and social-structural interventions to prevent primary offending. The state, then, on this account is obligated by its duty to society rather than by any duty to individual offenders, to include rehabilitative elements in penalties, and Carlen further argues that the offender is similarly obligated to participate, an obligation qualified only by the criterion of feasibility discussed above:

> so long as the state fulfilled its obligation to rehabilitate in a particular case the offender could be obliged to engage in any 'feasible' programme of rehabilitation or regulation (including, for instance, urine testing of drug-takers or electronic monitoring of other offenders). For *no* rehabilitative or regulatory programme would be rejected out of hand on the grounds of its being an essential violation of civil liberties or on the grounds of its being essentially lacking in feasibility. Rather, it would only be rejected on the grounds of its non-feasibility in a specific case. (ibid., italics in original)

Whilst I would query the elision of rehabilitation and regulation here, and would argue that regulatory techniques such as electronic monitoring will usually (but not necessarily always) have incapacitative rather than rehabilitative efficacy, the point is well made in both Carlen's formulation and that of Cullen and Gilbert that there must be a reciprocity of obligation between state and offender to work towards prevention of reoffending.

Inside the prison, new rehabilitationists demand something more positive than humane containment and minimum standards, although humanity in dealings with inmates, decent physical standards and an end to overcrowding are clearly prerequisites for any chance of reform of inmates. Prison sentences too, it is argued, should contain elements designed to prevent future crimes as well as to punish crimes already committed. Work release, training and education, the 'development of competences' are urged (Matthews, 1989, p. 148), so that prison can be a positive as well as a negative experience, developing potential for refraining from crime as well as demonstrating society's intolerance of the criminal acts committed. Advocates of prison rehabilitation programmes are careful to distinguish their proposals from the so-called rehabilitative regimes of the pre-1970s and 1980s sentencing reforms. Although there is some defence of the old-style rehabilitation as being the impetus behind the only humanitarian gains that have been achieved in prisons and some claim that the main problem was that rehabilitative facilities were only patchily or sporadically available (Cullen and Gilbert, 1982), the new rehabilitation model departs radically from the old in its insistence that rehabilitative progress should have no import for sentence length. Rehabilitation does not entail indeterminate sentencing; on the contrary, uncertainty over release date must be expected to be counter productive to rehabilitative efforts because of the anxiety and resentment generated. As I have argued in a previous work, if prison is antithetical to rehabilitation, if indeterminacy turns rehabilitation from help into coercion, then we would do better to avoid indeterminacy and restrict imprisonment rather than to give up on rehabilitation (Hudson, 1987, chapter 1). Whilst rehabilitation may have been used as a scapegoat for the evils of violent and overcrowded prisons and for the abuses of discretion in indeterminate sentencing systems, neither prison nor indeterminacy bears any necessary relation to rehabilitative goals (Rotman, 1990, p. x).

The wish to preserve the humanitarian impulse behind rehabilitation, the desire to help rather than hurt, to reintegrate rather than to segregate, or in Carlen's phrase 'sentencing to promote good rather than to impede evil' (Carlen, 1989, p. 20) without repeating the unintended coercive consequences of parole and indeterminacy, or raising impossible expectations for curing criminality, has prompted the new rehabilitationists to analyse carefully the principles behind their proposals and the circumstances in which the new agenda might succeed. Rotman distinguishes four different models of rehabilitation, which he says have succeeded each other during the historical development of the rehabilitative idea. He describes the penitentiary model, the therapeutic model, the social learning model, and the latest model, the rights model (Rotman, 1990, p. 59). The penitentiary model, reform through contemplation and through submission to the institutional regime, is subverted if it can be shown that enforced contemplation does not necessarily lead to penitence but perhaps to bitterness or insanity, or that the regime is not necessarily reformative, in other words it is discredited by the critique of the institution. The therapeutic and social learning models are undermined if the premises underlying them are faulty, in other words, they are as good or bad as the positivistic ideas about the causes of crime from which they are derived. All the models also share the problem of being withdrawn or imposed at will, with assessments of success also arbitrary and in the hands of the state. Even were any of them fully effective, they would be coercive if there were not an equality of obligation and freedom in states' and offenders' rights to offer, receive or refuse rehabilitation, and if their application was not limited by legislated restrictions on the power to punish.

The new model of rehabilitation, then, is consonant with contemporary penal discourse in that it is linked to rights. Rights of the state to punish and of criminals not to be punished unduly are best protected by rehabilitation being offered within a determinate sentence, fixed by considerations of desert or dangerousness. The weaker form of new rehabilitation theory would obligate the state on infliction of punishment, to provide rehabilitative facilities sufficient to ensure that the offender is not damaged beyond the intention of the penalty. A sentence of imprisonment is a sentence for the restriction of liberty, not a sentence to loose contact with families, to become deskilled, progressively less employable, to become dirty, squalid, to be brutalised or become depressed or psychotic. Prisoners, therefore, have rights to rehabilitative provisions to counteract these well-known effects of incarceration, the maintenance of competencies to counteract the manufacture of handicaps concomitant with imprisonment (Gallo and Ruggiero, 1991). At the very least, the condition known as prisonisation needs to be countered through rehabilitative efforts, as is acknowledged in some places. It is, for instance, written into the German penal code that the effect of penalties on the criminal should always be considered; home leaves and conjugal visits in Scandinavia, The Netherlands and elsewhere try to preserve family ties that may otherwise be weakened by imprisonment, and in England the Woolf report has recommended the building of smaller, community prisons to try to maintain prisoners' local ties (Woolf and Tumin, 1991).

Such minimalist rehabilitation policies accord with the prison standards movement: daily baths, integral sanitation, frequent changes of clothes are essential for dignity as well as for hygiene. It was pointed out in the preceding chapter that lack of such facilities has brought many US jurisdictions into conflict with constitutional law under the totality of conditions argument; Rotman considers whether or not the Supreme Court has upheld a right to rehabilitation as well as to freedom from cruel and unusual punishment. He concludes that the court has proclaimed the importance of rehabilitation in criminal justice, but has stopped short of holding a right to positive rehabilitation to be constitutionally guaranteed. The right to rehabilitation sufficient to prevent degeneration, loss of ties, etc., he argues was established by an application of the Eighth Amendment to the case of *Laaman and Helgemoe*, where the judgment stated among other things: 'Punishment for one crime, under conditions which spawn future crime and more punishment, serves no valid legislative purpose and is so totally without penological justification that it results in the gratuitous infliction of suffering in violation of the Eighth Amendment' (quoted by Rotman, 1990, pp. 81–2). This succinctly encapsulates the case for all punishment to have regard to utilitarian purposes, and although the argument is strongest in the case of imprisonment, it could apply equally to community punishments which are overly demanding, or which exacerbate family tensions, poverty, child-care problems, or in any way make the likelihood of reoffending more rather than less.

In England, the lack of any constitutionally guaranteed rights makes a right to rehabilitation impossible, but closer integration with Europe might make the European prison standards more relevant. Implementation of minimum standards, of the Woolf proposals including those for local prisons, for sentence contracts and planning for release remains at the discretion of the government of the day, and at the time of writing although the Home Office endorses the principles of the Woolf Report, it is making very few firm, date-specific commitments for their implementation. In a summary of their proposals for the prison service, for instance, Home Office officials write: 'The concept of community prisons will take many years to complete'. Moreover, although they acknowledge that when considering inmate activities, family links and preparation for release, 'Programmes must allow for work and provide access to education, training and other activities as well as visits' (Home Office, 1991b, pp. 6, 10), their proposals are couched in vague terms, talking of opportunities such as available resources allow, and suggesting only consideration of the scope for this, considering the scope of pilot schemes for the other. State-obligated rehabilitation is an idea gaining currency among reformers, then, but few states, and especially not England and Wales, have yet admitted the obligation. The language of minimum standards, humane containment, avoidance of cruel, unusual or degrading punishments does, however, accord with this minimalist idea of an obligation to provide sufficient rehabilitation to prevent unwilled damage being done by punishment, especially imprisonment. If this minimum position were accepted, rehabilitation, other than punishment, would become the unifying principle in penal sanctions.

To summarise, I am suggesting that in cases of low culpability – a notion which should have much wider application than a narrowly conceived insanity or diminished responsibility defence and should also include addictions, economic privation, emotional or social trauma – rehabilitation should be the primary objective and punishment should be kept to a minimum. In cases of trivial offences or improbability of further offending, positive rehabilitation would usually be unnecessary, and minimal punishment would mean that there would be little need for rehabilitation to counteract the ill effects of penalisation. Where imprisonment or other significant retributive or incapacitative penalty is imposed, what I have termed minimal or negative rehabilitation, rehabilitation in the weak sense of preventing deterioration should be an obligation of the state and a right of the offender, an obligation that is inherent in the notion of commensurability of penalty to offence – minimum rehabilitation is necessary to ensure that the suffering occasioned by punishment is no more than that pronounced by the court. Rehabilitation in the stronger sense of programmes to help the offender become less likely to offend than would have been the case in the absence of penalisation, is entailed as an obligation on the state by the overriding purpose of penal sanctions, that is to contribute to the reduction of crime through the prevention of reoffending. If the state takes to itself the right to punish, it must acknowledge the duty to use punishment for its proper purposes; limits on the state's right to punish and obligation to rehabilitate should be indicated by proportionality, feasibility and reasonable prospect of success. The criteria of good prospects of benefit from treatment that have been proposed for mentally disordered offenders could sensibly have a wider application. However, although there can never be guarantees of success, and although success of penal measures is notoriously difficult to measure, there are clear ethical objections to using offenders experimentally, and very strong moral objections to persistence with penal sanctions (such as 'short, sharp shock' detention regimes, or electronic tagging) out of ideological predeliction in the face of consistent evidence of failure.

The point of disagreement amongst new rehabilitationists themselves is the question of offenders' rights to refuse rehabilitation or treatment. To some extent, the right to refuse question assumes inflated importance because of conflation of 'rehabilitation' with 'treatment'. If rehabilitation is synonymous with treatment, and furthermore such treatment as is prescribed by a state official, as in the therapeutic or social learning models, then without a right to refuse, rehabilitation is coercive rather than enabling. The regimes commended by Rotman in Ringe, Denmark and Butner, North Carolina, as examples of conditions under which rehabilitation can succeed, are characterised by life inside the prisons being as near normal, that is, as near life on the outside, as possible, and part of that normality is autonomy (Rotman, 1990, chapter 5). Offenders in normalised regimes should have self-determination in almost everything except the decision that they be confined. Whether they work, take education classes, whom they see or correspond with, whether they take part in counselling sessions or seek medical treatment, should be personal decisions: for other people to make such decisions is to prescribe activities as treatment rather than to provide an environment that enhances self-determination. With rehabilitation conceived as the dyad of state obligation/offender right, the right to decline to participate seems clear. Do offenders, though, have parallel obligations to prevent further offending, obligations which would mean that refusal to participate in reasonable programmes (that is, programmes which satisfy the criteria of proportionality, feasibility and good prospect of success), could not be granted as a right?

Pat Carlen, as indicated above, would argue that this is indeed the case. Her view is that as society and the individual have usually both contributed to the commission of criminal acts, they have a common obligation to take steps to ensure that such acts are less likely in the future. Provided proposed rehabilitative elements meet her test of feasibility, on the grounds of shared obligation rather than a rights/ obligations dualism, there can be no right to refuse. On this view, the rights are held by society as (theoretical) victim and by non-criminal individuals as potential victims, and the obligations fall upon the state as represented by its penal system, and on offenders. These obligations are entailed by the crime control purpose of the penal system, and the obligations on the state to carry out this purpose extend to implementation as well as offer of rehabilitation. I find this argument persuasive, provided that my criteria of good prospect is included, and provided that the proposed rehabilitation is a component of a sanction of equal penal value to, but less negatively punitive than, an alternative penalty which would offer more public protection, which would be the choice in the absence of availability of or acceptance of the rehabilitation programme.

Once again, the importance of assigning penal values on a proportionality basis of different sanctions is revealed as of utmost importance, since this offers the possibility of fulfilling obligations towards society as victim without being overly oppressive of offenders or denying basic civil liberties. As things stand in most jurisdictions, offenders have to agree to probation or community service, but with the threat of a more severe penalty if they decline, this is hardly a real choice. A choice between sanctions of equal penal value, but with clear understanding that refusal of (positive) rehabilitative sanctions would lead to a penalty of similar commensurability value but of a purely retributive or incapacitative nature, would respect both proportionality and self-determination. Within prisons or restrictive community sanctions, refusal of rehabilitative facilities should not affect the duration or the intensity of punishment, and should not negate the state's obligation to seek minimal rehabilitation, the prevention of deterioration.

Integration and cooperation

Another idea whose time has come is interagency cooperation, greater integration of criminal justice agencies with each other, and with groups and agencies outside the formal criminal justice system. Attainment of selective abolition and the new rehabilitation both depend on much greater integration: under such a penal approach it would be unacceptable for judges to pronounce the tariff sentence and then forget about what happens to the offender post-sentence.

As already pointed out, choice of sanctions according to feasibility criteria needs consideration of a probation officer's report on what would be possible in a particular case. Choice of sanctions according to penal purpose would also need advice from a probation officer on the circumstances surrounding the offending behaviour, and the provision of rehabilitative elements would have to be coordinated by a probation officer, with other professionals, community resources and so on being utilised in actual delivery of the programme. Involvement of a wide range of community groups may well be an important factor in the chances of success in rehabilitative penalties (Currie, 1985). Prison rehabilitation would involve liaison with outside-the-walls agencies to maintain community links, provide work-, education- or treatment-release opportunities, whilst inside-the-walls teachers, trainers, therapists and welfare workers would need to be working as a much more integrated team with prison officers.

Feasibility and maintenance of reasonable standards both dictate that sentencers must constantly be kept aware of the resource implications of their decisions: impact considerations would need to be built into courtroom decision-making if proper standards of penal provision were to be upheld. We already know enough of the subversion of penal purposes that comes about through isolation of criminal justice agencies from each other. Impact-blind sentencing results in overcrowded prisons. Disparities in time served may result from some offenders having sentences reduced through emergency release schemes, some having more time at liberty before being called to prison, or even evading prison sentences altogether. Greater plea bargaining may arise through overloading in an uncoordinated system. Biles' study of the different effect on imprisonment rates in England and Wales and Australia, for example, showed that court loading because of increased cases resulted in acceptance of guilty pleas to lesser charges, to speed court throughput, with consequently less risk of imprisonment, in Australia, but the same situation of rising numbers of court cases resulted in more time being spent on remand in England and Wales (Biles, 1983). Speeded up, conveyor belt justice would not necessarily lead merely to reduced punishment, it might lead to functionally inappropriate penalties or inadequate investigation of feasibility, the risk being run by the probation service in England and Wales, undertaking to do more reports with shorter adjournment periods under the 1991 Criminal Justice Act.

As well as these distortions, unintended consequences may often come about through fragmentation – different sections of the system may misunderstand each other's purposes and possibilities. For example, lack of knowledge of what sort of work is available on community service placements, what happens in day centres or intensive probation programmes, may result in inappropriate referrals or lack of take-up by sentencers. Similarly, misunderstanding by probation officers of judicial perspectives may lead to lack of confidence in recommending non-custodial or rehabilitative disposals, up-tariffing may often come about because of lack of any sharing of perspectives between the judiciary and the programme providers. These are fairly obvious reasons for increasing cooperation between the formal criminal justice agencies, but there are more subtle concerns which bespeak the need to bring a wider range of agencies and groups into criminal justice forums. A rational response to crime can only emerge from a sharing of perspectives, any individual agency is bound to be influenced by its own organisational goals and problems, so that goal drift will inevitably occur which may undermine its efficacy for its allotted penal policy purposes. Interagency cooperation is necessary but not sufficient for the sort of policies advocated here to have reasonable chance of success. What is needed is something more than agencies informing each other about their policies and practices; agencies need to be contributing to a strategic, integrating body which sets itself objectives which are more than the sum of individual agency goals. Local crime commissions, along the lines suggested by Locke in his advocacy of strategic planning for crime control, come close to what is needed, provided they have some executive power and do not become merely comfortable meetings of the great and the good, with no authority *vis-à-vis* the constituent agencies (Locke, 1990).

The proposals made in this chapter could only be implemented if noncriminal justice system agencies and community groups were involved in integrated responses to offending. Providing care in the community for mentally disordered offenders, support in the community for women offenders, treating trivial or minimum culpability offenders nonpunitively depends on sufficient resources being available outside the criminal justice system. The problems of mentally disordered offenders, homeless and addicted offenders, can only be dealt with outside prisons or transcarceral institutions if there is both community provision and community tolerance. It is no use withdrawing penal provision if community provision is not available, the consequences of penal decarceration would not be reintegration and reduction of reoffending, but would be more likely to be the sort of deviance-inducing malign neglect that we have seen accompanying the closure of mental hospitals. Adopting a more humane and measured view of offenders cannot mean abandoning them to community intolerance. There is often strong local resistance to the siting of accommodation for offenders, treatment facilities and the like in residential neighbourhoods, and although offenders may be less visible than the more floridly symptomatic psychiatric patients, the stigma is none the less very strong. The success of law and order ideologies in creating stereotypes, sensationalised images of criminals as dangerous beasts, and casting crime as the number one menace to society, will take much work to undo. Any moves towards greater use of community sanctions and less reliance on prison, more rehabilitation and less punishment, will depend on recognition by all groups of crime as a community problem, something which cannot be solved by locking offenders out of sight or even by leaving them to the care of designated agencies, but as something which must be owned by local communities at all levels.

What Mathiesen describes as 'policy preparation', the work that can make ideas such as partial abolition and state-obligated rehabilitation acceptable, is indispensable (Mathiesen, 1990, p. 161). The ideology of exclusion has to be replaced by one of reintegration (Braithwaite, 1989). Criminals must continue to be acknowledged as part of society whether undergoing punishment or not, crime and punishment are inescapably community problems and responsibilities. As Mathiesen rightly tells us, the sort of social solidarity on which reintegrative responses to crime depend cannot be taken for granted but must be painstakingly built, and a *sine qua non* is an approach to crime as a community problem which does not appear to suggest that more humane penalties means taking criminality any less seriously. Adequate compensation and support to victims are essential, as are what he calls 'vulnerability relief' through crime prevention and 'anxiety relief' through better communication (ibid., pp. 164ff). The left realists are correct here in their insistence that a crucial element of a rational crime strategy is knowledge of what sorts of criminality neighbourhoods see as the most urgent problems, with police and other criminal justice agencies being more accountable in terms of community priorities rather than just organisational preferences and pressures (Matthews, 1987; Young, J., 1987).

Integration is needed with non-criminal justice agencies and other social policy domains not just to provide services for offenders and victims, but to help reduce crime. Without being unduly beguiled by arguments about links between poverty, unemployment, race and crime or leaping into positivistic-style theorising about causes in actual criminal instances, we can surely accept that societies with high levels of racism, isolation, marginalisation and material–social inequality generally tend to be high crime societies. We also know that societies with loose social bonds, little emphasis on morality and means of achievement (anomic societies, or as Braithwaite puts it, low-shame societies) are high crime societies (Braithwaite, 1989). Improved social provision, more support for families, action to reduce racism, sexism, unemployment, ghetto housing, poverty and homelessness are therefore vital in a strategic approach to crime prevention. Initiatives such as the French SOS Racisme, the *étés-jeunes* summer recreational programmes, deserve to be extended within France and copied outside it, as they offer hope of reducing crime rates without targeting and therefore stigmatising individuals as potential delinquents (Pitts, 1990). Whilst penal policy needs to be more individualised, crime prevention should be more collectivised, targeted at ameliorating criminogenic social conditions rather than attempting to identify particular people who are likely to succumb to criminality. French experience with local crime commissions has confirmed the need to integrate law enforcement with social crime prevention programmes. The multiparty commission of mayors set up in 1982 (the Bonnemaison Commission) thus recommended:

To be really effective in tackling crime, social prevention and law enforcement must be combined in a careful and controlled way. Its recommendations were guided by the need to establish local inter-agency co-operation and better use of current resources. As petty and common crime has not been stopped by the enforcement of laws and budgets could no longer be expanded, it was necessary to encourage the breakdown of bureaucratic barriers and encourage the reassessment of priorities to respond to crime problems more effectively at local level. The commission's report puts forward solutions concerned with housing, training for employment and problems of young immigrants. However, it also stresses the need to have a crime policy that is both concerned with the enforcement of the law and with tackling the root-causes of crime. The public should be involved, for instance, by working with young delinquents or with victims. This involvement will reduce public alienation from the system and combat the stereotypes generated by media sensationalism of events. (Liège, 1991, p. 128)

An integrated approach to criminal justice, therefore, needs to reintegrate criminals with their communities, to reintegrate penal policy with other aspects of crime policy, and to reintegrate criminal policy with other social policy, as well as reintegrating punishment with other penal purposes. Given adequate preparation, openness, sharing of responsibility, there is no need to believe that such an approach would be unpopular. Research has demonstrated that members of the public are more interested, more knowledgeable and less punitive than penal professionals generally assume; that there is more support for rehabilitation and prevention than for simple retribution, and that the more knowledge and contact people have of crime and with criminals, the less punitive they tend to become (Doob and Roberts, 1988; Gottfredson, Warner and Taylor, 1988; Van Dijk and Steinmetz, 1988; Walker, Collins and Wilson, 1987). A shared, community-based approach needs to be aware of just what penal purposes command public support, what are the public tolerance levels for leniency or severity. It also needs to probe behind these views to see what fears, what moral values or social attitudes condition them, otherwise public anxieties may be inflamed rather than allayed by information sharing and community approaches, and opposition may be forthcoming where cooperation would have been expected. Punitive attitudes towards offenders have been found, for example, to be derived at least partly from racial prejudice in white communities, but in black communities to be based more on fear of crime (Cohn, Barkan and Halteman, 1991). Attitudes to punishment may stem from fear of crime, from moral values about conduct, from stereotypes about offenders, and without knowing what lies behind expressed attitudes it is impossible to know what sort of information will help induce less fear and more tolerance, what sort of action will satisfy community needs.

Rational and humane penal policy, then, can only develop if crime is accepted as a social phenomenon, a problem of communities as a whole rather than of individual bad apples, and as a communal duty rather than appertaining solely to formal law enforcement and criminal justice agencies. Penal policy needs to consider people as well as acts, to acknowledge purposes other than simple retributive punishment, and to become more integrated with other aspects of crime and criminal justice policy and with social policy in the broadest sense. Criminal justice agencies need to integrate with each other, with social agencies, and with the communities they serve.

The 1991 Criminal Justice Act and the Woolf Report show that the ideas discussed in this chapter have to some extent penetrated official thinking, as well as achieving wide support in the academic/reform community. Only to a limited extent, however. Whilst the Criminal Justice Act clearly states the intention that imprisonment should be reserved for serious offenders, and whilst various official pronouncements have deplored the number of mentally disordered offenders in prison, the continued imprisonment of this group is envisaged by the requirement that a presentence report will be obtained before such persons are committed to custody. Section 25 of the Act which deals with mitigation and mentally disordered offenders states that whilst nothing in the section should be taken as *requiring* a court to pass a custodial sentence, equally nothing should be seen 'as restricting any power (whether under the 1983 Act or otherwise) which enables a court to deal with such an offender in the manner it considers to be most appropriate in all the circumstances' (Home Office, *Criminal Justice Act 1991*, s. 25).

Similarly, although conditions on the psychiatric wing at Brixton prison have been widely condemned as being the very opposite of therapeutic, a new psychiatric wing is being built in the prison rather than mentally ill prisoners being transferred to hospitals. Abolition of imprisonment for women is not being contemplated; the Woolf Report gives no consideration to the difficulties of women prisoners, indeed the only mention is to state that they are not within the scope of the enquiry. Imprisonment for fine default is not abolished by the Act. Section 22 provides for periods of between seven days' and three months' custody for non-payment of fines. In the case of unit fines – which are only applicable to fines imposed by magistrates' courts – the length of imprisonment is to be calculated according to the number of units, for flat-rate fines the length will relate to the amount of the fine. Provision is made for fines to be deducted directly from state benefit, but there is no guidance in the relevant section of the Act (section 22) as to when deduction of benefit is preferable to imprisonment in default.

There is no mention of other possible penalties for fine default, such as community service, or non-financial reparatory measures. We are, then, very far from even experimenting with selective or partial abolitions.

Rehabilitation is coming back on to the penal agenda, but very tentatively. Although the end of the 'nothing works era' has been proclaimed (Pitts, 1992), rehabilitation is clearly within the context of punishment. The Act mentions rehabilitation only in relation to probation orders (section 8.2), but the guidelines for the probation service that have been issued by the Home Office (Home Office, 1992), make clear that the level of interventiveness of a probation order is linked first and foremost to the seriousness of the offence, rather than the needs of the offender. It is said that 'the purposes of probation are a separate matter from the severity of punishment' (ibid., p. 20). Probation officers, therefore, will have to work for rehabilitative ends within a framework of severity that does not have regard to rehabilitative considerations.

As I have pointed out, although the Woolf Report talks of local prisons, compacts, contracts and constructive sentences, the White Paper in response makes no commitments to early implementation of these sections of the report. The Criminal Justice Act has sections referring to provision of services, but the services it discusses are prison escort duties, staffing remand prisons and the like (Part IV). There is no mention of provision of rehabilitative services.

The idea that does seem to have been enthusiastically adopted is that of interagency cooperation. Various reports, white papers and green papers have been advocating such cooperation, and the model of working in juvenile justice – where joint ownership of the delinquency problem and joint projects by police, probation, social services departments and voluntary agencies appears to have achieved reductions in both prosecution and custody – has been advocated first of all for the 17 to 21-year-old age group, and now for the whole of the criminal justice system. Interagency initiative is credited with a large measure of the reduction of custody in Germany (Feest, 1991), but the difference is that where that has been primarily practitioner led, interagency cooperation in the wake of the 1991 Act is government led. Criminal Justice Consultative Groups are, at the time of writing, being established in the various regions, but it is clear that their brief is the efficient management of the criminal justice system, rather than responding to community needs and wishes in problems of crime and criminal justice. It remains to be seen whether areas take the initiative to widen the membership and scope of these committees so as to become more responsive to their communities, and to attempt crime prevention and crime/justice public education along the lines called for by Mathiesen, as well as efficient management of the business of the courts. Even if criminal justice agencies do desire to involve themselves more with other social policy agencies and with communities, they do so at a time when the agencies of primary crime prevention – education, housing, mental health services, and of course, employment – are being further cut back. Local government, far from being given an enhanced role as a pivot of community solidarity, is having even more of its functions stripped.

Above all, these initiatives must take place at a time when, although there has been some effort to tackle fear of crime through publicising the British Crime Survey, through crime prevention documents issued by police authorities (though these have been subject to caustic criticism (Stanko, 1992)), crime is still being sensationalised, and blamed on individual wickedness rather than social conditions. Disturbances on housing estates in Oxford, Cardiff, Newcastle, Carlisle and other towns and cities in the summers of 1991 and 1992 are blamed on a hard core of individuals. In 1991, it was professional criminals who were said to be whipping up young people's resentment of police when incidents such as the deaths of young drivers of stolen cars being chased by police provided flashpoints; in 1992 it is anarchists, and fringe-left groups such as Class War, who are said to be coming into areas and stirring up trouble. The fact that the estates where troubles occur are regularly described as the most deprived in the area, with rates of unemployment far higher than the locality average, where community facilities are non-existent or closed down, is less frequently commented on by central government officials or law enforcement agents. If the ideas put forward in this chapter seem to be those whose time has come if one judges by the extent of assent they receive amongst theorists and penal reformers, reading legislation and the various reports and white/green papers that precedes legislation reveals that their influence is less than that of the desert lobby, and less than that of the get tough lobby. Furthermore, they are being advanced in a social–political context that can still best be described as the 'law and order society' (Hall, 1980), the 'exceptional state' (Ratner and McMullan, 1985) where government sees its task as the management of crisis rather than as the promotion of welfare.

6 Punishment, Justice and the Problem of Law

Throughout the preceding pages I have argued that contemporary penal practice fails to satisfy standards of social justice, and that it also fails to deliver criminal justice in the sense of justice as fairness and equity to offenders, treating like offences similarly, not penalising people for who or what they are, only for what they have done. Moreover, these shortcomings of penal practice are not only failings according to some utopian notion of a perfectly just social order, they are failings according to current, widespread penal policies. The social injustices of criminal justice are undermining attempts of legislators, policy-makers and other penal professionals to achieve agreed aims such as twin-tracking, rationing of imprisonment to serious offences, and equality of impact of penalties. Demonstrable overrepresentation of black offenders, foreign offenders, unemployed and impoverished offenders in prison populations leaves penal systems open to suspicion that they are not reserving incarceration for serious crimes, but that they continue to use prisons to repress the disaffected, coerce the indigent and corral the unwanted. The extreme differences in prison conditions and regimes even within the same jurisdiction affront notions of equality of impact of penalties or humane containment of prisoners. Moreover, the interventiveness and aggregation of the latest community sanctions come close to rendering the idea of bifurcation meaningless, and the continuing presence of mentally disordered and homeless offenders in prisons because they have nowhere to go rather than because they have perpetrated serious crimes, belies supposed commitment to proportionality of sentence to offence gravity and offender culpability.

In considering these penal dilemmas, the solutions proposed by policy-makers have been assessed as offering only limited scope for amelioration of these injustices. Pious pronouncements of race-, class- and gender-blindness in sentencing guidelines, restriction of judicial discretion or education of judicial sensibilities can at best reduce direct discrimination, but can do nothing to diminish the indirect discrimination which comes about by linking tariffs and guidelines to the very factors most highly correlated with race, class or gender. Policy statements which (sincerely) deplore the numbers of mentally disordered

178

prisoners, similarly can have little impact if more community mental health facilities, especially residential facilities for the chronic mentally ill, are not provided and unless communities become more tolerant of the nuisance and disturbance occasioned by the disordered. Community penalties cannot be effective if they are imposed without assessments of appropriateness and feasibility; they cannot be a non-prison track if they are expected to replicate the pains of imprisonment outside the institution; there can be no equality of penal impact inside the prison if problems of maintenance of order and morale among long-serving inmates are not dealt with more constructively than by punishment blocks and control units. If it remains confined within its present parameters, penal discourse offers little real hope of altering the differential impact of penal policy on rich and poor, black and white, conventional and unconventional. Just as penal policy can only have minimal impact on crime without broader social strategies of crime prevention, so it can have little impact on justice without broader policies to reduce inequalities and social divisions, and to increase social provision.

The previous chapter considered proposals by criminologists to redress some of these blatant injustices of penal policy: reductionism, selective abolitionism, and the new rehabilitation agenda. These are agendas which either seemed unrealistically radical until quite recently, or in the case of rehabilitation were against the penological mainstream, but which the persistence of overcrowding and eruptions of serious disorder within prisons, together with ever increasing crime rates, in spite of unprecedented levels of penal innovation and expenditure, have brought to the edges of official acceptability. What has made such ideas more appealing to officials are partly pragmatic considerations of costs and management of institutions, but also growing acknowledgement that to wish for something is not necessarily to make it so. If prison rationing, fair punishment and respect for the criminal justice system are to be achieved, then more positive action than pronouncement of principles is called for; either proposals such as these must be adopted or judicial independence must be radically breached. The only options available are reductionism, buttressed by abolitions where necessary, or binding sentencing schedules laid out either by governments or sentencing councils. In other words, the policies and the transmission mechanisms must be taken forward together.

If the laws or guidelines strategy were to be adopted in those places where it is not so already, or if the content of existing laws and guidelines were to be made more consistent with social justice, then the brief of commissions or councils would have to be broadened considerably to allow for much less race- and class-bound assessment of which harms are to be most severely punished. In addition, there would need to be much more attention paid to the race-, class- and gender-bound operation of the filtering mechanisms between the penalising circuit and other regulatory circuits.

In sum, the penal system and criminal law must be subject to reform, and must also listen more attentively to the suggestions of extra-system reformers.

The reform proposals put forward in the last chapter are eminently reasonable – they do not call into question the fundamental right of the state to enforce laws, to punish; they do not contest the social significance of crime; they are consistent with declared official policies – but are they at all achievable? To the extent that they are not, this is because they are beset by the same problem that besets any consideration of a more rational penal policy, namely, the problem of punishment. The notion of punishment so often acts as a closure in discussions of criminal justice. Crimes, it is perennially objected, cannot go unpunished, and the proposals in the last chapter such as abolition of imprisonment for fine default or for failure to complete other non-custodial penalties, making considerations of feasibility more central to criminal justice decision-making, still more the idea of making rehabilitation (really, this time round) the unifying principle of penality, all involve some relinquishing of the power to punish. Even more are the claims of commensurate retribution questioned by the more radical possibilities hinted at earlier, particularly categorial leniency for crimes with high correlations with the various dimensions of disadvantage. Setting aside the claims of the tariff for women in poverty, mentally disordered offenders, addicted or abused offenders, means prioritising help over punishment, and prioritising people over acts. Yet the jurisprudential discourse which so dominates thinking about crime today is uncritically committed to the primacy of punishment, and to the denial of individuality to the legal subject. It is to this problem – the problem of jurisprudence – that I turn in this final chapter.

Decentring punishment

Reductionism and partial abolitionism cannot achieve their goals if the primacy of punishment is left unchallenged. Opposition to the extensive use of imprisonment without opposition to punishment per se means that reductionists are forced to concede that alternatives to custody may have to be as punitive as imprisonment if they are to be used in its place. Many reductionists do concede this, sometimes overtly, more often implicitly in their calls for 'tough', 'sensible' or 'realistic' community penalties (for example, Matthews, 1987). In the words of a Home Office Minister of State, 'probation must be as tough as prison for Jack the Lad' (Patten, 1987). In which case, one might ask what it is about prison that the reductionists object to. If it is prison conditions, prison overcrowding, lack of rehabilitative opportunities, loss of personal responsibility along with loss of personal liberty, these objections could all be overcome by increasing capacity, by implementing minimum standards, and by bringing in more constructive regimes. Indeed, the reductionists do espouse campaigns for so-called positive custody, and support prison-based new rehabilitation agendas (Cullen and Gilbert, 1982; Matthews, 1989), although most are opposed to any extensions of prison capacity (Rutherford, 1984). Standards, and the minimal new rehabilitationist aim of avoiding deterioration of prisoners, restricting any penalisation that is beyond loss of liberty itself, are compatible with the primacy of punishment, but support for such improvements is usually combined with a call for actual reduction in the use of imprisonment. The point is, then, that the basis for the call for curbing imprisonment rather than improving prisons in such formulations is unclear.

If the idea of punishment is unchallenged, imprisonment might seem to have several advantages. Provided equity could be guaranteed between rich and poor, male and female, black and white in such matters as assignment to closed or open prisons, therapeutic or warehouse prisons, close-to-home or distant prisons, equity of penal impact is more approachable than with many other forms of penalty. It could be argued that it would be, if anything, favourable to the disadvantaged, in that exchanging a comfortable home, loving family and full lifestyle for a prison cell is a more drastic reversal of fortune than moving from a halfway house or a doorway, empty days with time to kill and only the company of hostile strangers. Imprisonment also has the advantage that it can be finely graded to the seriousness of crimes, calculated in days and months which have the same meaning for all much more nearly than do the monetary units of fines. It is hardly surprising that deserts theorists have found it easier to come up with ordinally graduated schedules of imprisonment than to provide guidance on the use of non-custodial penalties.

Partial or selective abolitionists, too, must make clear their stance on punishment. If their objection to imprisonment of women, the mentally disordered or the addicted is because of lack of suitable facilities, again this objection could be countered by improved health services, more local prisons, etc. With juveniles and young people, the objection to their incarceration has often been that they are inappropriately confined in adult prisons, and here again we have seen the answer in practice of building more youth prisons, rather than abolishing youth imprisonment. Rather than marking any new penological departure, the development of more youth institutions, more therapeutic institutions, more facilities for women with babies, continues the modernist penal project of moving from the mingling, undifferentiated teeming populace of the pre-reform prison towards the classification and segregation inherent in modern punishments.

If arguments for penal reform, then, are based on degraded conditions and lack of facilities, then more and better imprisonment would seem to answer the case. And yet by definition, the last thing reductionists subscribe to is expansionism! Ambiguities in reductionist, left realist discussions of penalties – do they wish to restrict imprisonment, and if so, why; how far are they willing to go in replicating the characteristics of imprisonment in community penalties? – stem from their equivocation over the problem of punishment *per se*. Although some who urge adoption of a reductionist or selective abolition programme do confront the problem of punishment and argue for the substitution or prioritisation of other goals in the categories they select for abolition (for instance, Carlen, 1989, 1990), others espouse the crime-and-punishment ethos of the age by calling for more penalisation of domestic violence, sexual offending, corporate crime, environmental pollution and the like. Though action no doubt needs to be taken to prevent abuses of vulnerable groups and abuse by the powerful, the worrying point is that many sectors of left/progressivist social movements seem to see the criminal law and the penal system as the obvious way of 'doing something about' undesirable behaviour, in a way that mirrors the right's use of penal law to repress behaviour they define as unconscionable (Scheerer, 1986). Thinking about penal reform without thinking about punishment, then, leads to muddle and ambiguity, and leaves any apparent progress prone to unintended but predictable consequences of either strengthening segregative institutions or extending segregative traits in supposedly non-carceral sanctions.

Abolitionists acknowledge this closure of mainstream reform discourse at the point of punishment, they see that one cannot get rid of or significantly reduce imprisonment, or encourage functional diversity in non-carceral sanctions, if the overriding aim of criminal sanctions must always be punishment. Whenever the demands of other objectives – such as reform or help – clash with those of punishment, punishment will undermine these if its necessity is always taken for granted. Although there are differences in just what abolitionists seek to abolish and how they propose to achieve their ends (Folter, 1986), there is general agreement among them that the penalising response to crime should be replaced by a more restorative approach. Instead of punishing offenders via the penal law, crimes should, according to the abolitionists, occasion a forum where the grievances of both the victim and the offender can be heard, where recompense to the victims can be made, and where the balance of relationships between victim, offender and community can be restored.

While some are content to see restorative justice as an adjunct to penalising justice, others would seek to replace retributive justice with restorative justice entirely, and while some see acts of restoration as a more appropriate way than state punishment for the offender to acknowledge responsibility and pay social dues, others presume no necessary ascription of blame following a rule-transgression, merely that the existence of a problem situation should be recognised (Hulsman and Bernat de Celis, 1982). A restorative, reconciliatory response to crime was, in the 1970s and 1980s, assumed by some observers to be the next major trend. Restoring a sense of participation to victims, restoring a sense of self-worth to offenders, restoring a sense of morality and acceptance of limits to action to communities, was thought to be the next advance for modern societies in coping with deviance. Observers claimed to be able to discern a definite 'trend away from formal law towards justice based on equity (intuitive sense of justice in the particular case) and solidarity (procedures concerned primarily with reconciling the parties) . . . and developing moral ideas' (Unger, 1976, p. 204). As we saw in Chapter 1, however, moves towards informal, restorative justice were either subverted or incorporated into the formal criminal justice system, and the interpretation of justice as equity that has prevailed has moved away from intuition in particular cases to implementing tariffs drawn up for cases in general.

The reason for this is the same as that for the subvertion of alternatives to custody and minimum intervention strategies into punishment in the community with its multiple orders, house arrest and the like, the same as the reason for lack of progress on abolishing imprisonment for the mentally disordered and for women, and the same as the reason for ruling consideration of racism and structural inequalities out of court; that is, uncritical acceptance of the necessity for punishment. Many of the suggestions of the reductionists and partial abolitionists for a combination of prevention, compensation and rehabilitation might be more widely acceptable were it not for the judicial addiction to punishment, in a society where judicial discourse enjoys so much authority: decentring punishment may make common sense, but it does not make juridical sense (Steinhert, 1986). Since abolitionist and also other, ostensibly more pragmatic, agendas for making penal policy better serve ideals of justice involve minimising or relinquishing the power to punish, we need to understand the strength of arguments in favour of the necessity of punishment if we are to have any hope of countering them.

Much thinking about punishment presupposes its necessity or ultimate justification, so that the question 'why punish?' is usually dealt with not as though it were 'whether punish?', but as though it were 'how punish?' or 'to what end punish?' Discussions of the justification of punishment are generally about the philosophical or empirical advantages or disadvantages of retributivist or utilitarian rationales *vis-à-vis* each other, rather than attempts to justify punishment *ex nihilo* (Honderich, 1984; Walker, 1991). Retributivists often sound as though they are engaging with philosophical fundamentals, but in fact they close off 'whether punish' questions by making punishment justified almost as a matter of definition. In fact deserts theory in legal discourse is a theory of allocation of punishments rather than an argument for its necessity, as is made clear by the subtitle of Von Hirsch's statement of the new retributionist perspective – *The Choice of Punishments* (Von Hirsch, 1976). Utilitarian theory in most of its variants similarly presupposes punishment, and is engaged with questions of how much punishment, what kind of punishment?

Since legal theory itself assumes punishment, it must turn to other disciplines if it wishes to engage reflexively with the necessity of or justification for it, usually moral or political philosophy. Whilst there has been some modishness in attempts to base the need for punishment on non-teleological moral philosophies such as Kantian forms of desert theory and on intuitionism (people instinctively feel an urge to punish; there is a general moral sentiment that punishment is the appropriate response to crime), most theories are consequentialist, in some way following Rawls in seeking to show that punishment is an essential component of, or can contribute to the realisation of, a just social order (Rawls, 1972). The contribution of punishment is usually conceptualised either at a societal level of securing compliance with the rules necessary for the survival of the social order, or at an individual level, restoring the balance of rights disturbed by the commission of an offence. These functions of punishment are obviously complementary, since equilibrium of rights is one of the social goods to be defended by the criminal law. In some contemporary consequentialist formulations, there is more positive conception of the goals which should be served by specification of behaviours as crimes and by enforcement of criminal law, using terms such as the promotion of welfare, empowerment and autonomy (Lacey, 1988), and dominion (Braithwaite and Pettit, 1990). These contemporary consequentialists are happy to incorporate retributivism in its role of setter of limits to punishment.

The necessity of punishment to enforce criminal law is proposed both empirically and conceptually. Empirically, it is argued that it would be naive to suppose people would obey rules in the absence of penalties for rule-breaking – in such an ideal society, criminal law would not be necessary. (The same reasoning urges retention of imprisonment for fine default, breaches of probation or community service.) Conceptually, it is contended that the very notion of law entails mechanisms to ensure compliance, and punishment is the mechanism intrinsic to criminal law. Nicola Lacey, for example, in her defence of punishment, argues this conceptual entailment by defining criminal law as 'a set of public norms generally backed up by the threat of punishment for breach' (Lacey, 1988, p. 176), and this reasoning is familiar to criminologists, many of whom would draw on the presence of punitive sanctions to distinguish crime from other forms of deviance. Some abolitionists have argued that this conceptual linkage of punishment to criminal law mistakenly assumes identity between sanction and punishment. By defining punishment as the intentional infliction of pain or loss rather than as sanctions invoked for rule breaking, they argue that it would be possible to imagine a criminal law that was backed up by sanctions but not by punishments (De Haan, 1988). Other abolitionists grant the definitional relationship between crime and punishment, and the more usual abolitionist position is acceptance that abolishing punishment means abolishing criminal law, though this, of course, is not the same as abolishing the whole idea of social rules.

Lacey gives us a valuable lead in her definition of criminal law as involving threat of punishment, leaving open the question of its actual application. Her suggestions for the rationing of actual punishment go somewhat beyond those usually found in desert theory, proposing that punishment should only be for those for whom it is deserved not just according to a capacity concept of responsibility or culpability, that is, that the offender knew what s/he was doing and was not prevented by insanity, loss of conscience through drugs, alcohol, provocation, etc. from choosing to refrain from the act, but also that there should be a further, 'dispositional' concept of responsibility. Arguing that capacity formulations depend upon too strong an idea of free will, she proposes that punishment be reserved for those who demonstrate a conscious opposition to social norms, those 'whose actions exhibit a considered, settled rejection of community values or some aspect of them' (Lacey, 1988, p. 190).

The other claim for punishment made by legal theorists is that it restores the balance of advantage and disadvantage, rights and obligations, disturbed by a crime. If someone has gained advantage – property, power – unfairly, s/he should suffer some compensatory loss or deprivation, to return the equilibrium of advantage to the *status quo ante*. This concept has drawn the objection that the equilibrium of advantage is not restored by punishment but further disturbed by the addition of the pain or loss caused by the punishment to that caused by the crime (Wasserstrom, 1980). This disagreement about the effect of punishment seems to me to reflect the difference between legal theory and social– political theory. For social or political theorists, punishment is a positive, an additional infliction of pain, which must be justified in the context of utilitarian/social contract precepts of the duty of government to reduce the total of pain in society, whereas legal theory is looking to the duality of rights and obligations, which sees the duty of law as ensuring that obligations are honoured, and that rights are not seized without concomitant obligations. Legal theory, then, sees punishment not so much as the addition of something (pain), but as the removal of something unfairly gained, removal effected by punishment-as-deprivation (of liberty, money, time).

Both views raise some dilemmas. The legal formulation has in its favour that it would seem to dictate commensurability, that the punishment should be no more than is necessary to negate the advantage gained by the crime, but it has the difficulty that it is not easy to see how it could apply in a seriously unequal society. It leads back to the penological cliché of how there can be justice in an unjust society. If rights are not evenly distributed, how can obligations be evenly exacted? The social–

political approach has the enormous disadvantage that it makes general deterrence the most plausible justification for punishment, since the additional suffering occasioned by punishment could only be countenanced if it prevents the suffering occasioned by further offending, and hence it gives no limit to punishment that derives from the original offence, thereby opening the way for severe penalties on the expectation of deterrence. On the other hand, it has the (for me) enormous advantage that by recognising punishment as additional infliction of pain it does acknowledge that it (always?) requires justification, and the utilitarian perspective allows for the view that since the deterrent effect of punishments may not be realised but the pain to offenders is real and immediate, following the minimisation of pain formula could indicate compensation to the victim rather than punishment for the offender. The way out of this utilitarian dilemma for legal theory has, of course, been to cast society as the victim of crime rather than the individual whose person has been attacked or whose property has been damaged or stolen, so that punishment can be cast as restitution to society.

There are many books which deal comprehensively and penetratingly with these issues, and my purpose here is not to rework these albeit (to my mind, at least) fascinating debates, but to make the point that penal reformers must take some stance on the issue of punishment. Because it involves the deliberate infliction of suffering, and especially because the suffering is inflicted by the state upon individuals, punishment stands in need of justification, so that the abolitionists' case is stronger than critics generally allow, simply in insisting on punishment as problematic. On the other hand, the presumption of punishment is so strong that even if, with De Haan, we grant that a strong case could be made on rational grounds for a punishment-free society (De Haan, 1988), the pragmatists are right to see that agendas for change in the way we deal with rule breakers must accommodate to the fact that for the foreseeable future at least, we will continue to rely on state punishment as a defence both against unacceptable levels of anti-social behaviour and against private vengeance.

In writing a book on penal policy, I am obviously assuming the continuance of criminal law and the penal system. I am persuaded by the definitional link between criminal law and the existence of penal sanctions, and I am therefore persuaded that abolitionism is a case of ideal theory. We would not need punishment only if we did not need criminal law, and it is only in an ideal society that one can imagine not needing criminal law. The idea of a punishment-free society under anything like present conditions is also counter-intuitive: people do wish offenders to be punished and the abolition of state punishment would in all probability lead not to communal redress but to vigilante vengeance. None the less, the abolitionist lens is valuable for looking at punishment more rationally. Punishment, rather than non-punitive responses, needs to be justified in actual cases; as Lacey says, it is the threat of punishment that is entailed by criminal law, not anything like its blanket application. There is no need, therefore, to accept that 'realistic' non-custodial sanctions must be sanctions that are punitively equivalent to custody; there is no need to accept that punishment itself, rather than imprisonment, cannot be waived or kept to a minimum in individual cases or even in categories of cases. Punishment must be continuously rejustified because it:

1. involves deliberate infliction of pain;
2. may not be the most effective way to achieve ends such as prevention of further crime or restoring social equilibrium;
3. is an expensive resource.

As well as being morally difficult, punishment is costly, and therefore should be treated as a scarce resource. The need to ration punishment itself, then, arises not just through squeamishness, desert or efficacy, but because societies have limited capacity to punish (Pontell, 1984). I would fully endorse Lacey's contention that the actual application of punishment should be reserved for those cases where it is consistent with desert and consequentialist justifications (that is, it should only be inflicted on competent, guilty persons and that it should be of a nature that is consistent with the ends of preventing further offending and demonstrating disapproval of the criminal behaviour), and further that there should be a stable, deliberate disregard for a generally shared social norm for actual punishment to be provoked. This raises the problem of how to make such decisions, especially the latter decision of dispositional culpability, and brings us back to my central concern of how to respond to the crimes of the disadvantaged.

Standpoints and legal theory

This approach to punishment poses as central questions for criminal justice decision-making:

1. How are we to decide when punishment will have less utilitarian value than help, redress or other non-punitive responses?
2. How are we to decide who is both capacity-responsible and disposition-responsible?

Accepting the relevance and legitimacy of the questions, let alone providing answers, takes us beyond the normal parameters of legal theory. A perspective on legal reasoning which recognises the importance of these kinds of questions and offers some prospect of generating answers is the body of knowledge which, as it has become more systematised, has come to be known as feminist legal theory, or feminist jurisprudence.

Feminist approaches to law consist primarily in applying three methods as well as or instead of the usual legal reasoning processes, methods which allow for inclusion or illumination of facets of problem situations which would otherwise be excluded or passed over:

> One method, asking the woman question, is designed to expose how the substance of law silently and without justification submerges the perspectives of women and other excluded groups. Another method, feminist practical reasoning, expands traditional notions of legal relevance to make legal decision-making more sensitive to the features of a case not already reflected in legal doctrine. A third method, consciousness-raising, offers a means of testing the validity of accepted legal principles through the lens of the personal experience of those directly affected by those principles. (Bartlett, 1990, p. 836)

The first method, asking the woman question, generally means examining whether concepts and principles that are assumed to be gender-neutral are in fact masculine. In law, 'asking the woman question' inevitably reveals that the 'reasonable person' who is the legal subject is in fact male; it is the male way of being in the world that guides assumptions of reason, motive, rights and obligations. An obvious example of relevance at the time of writing concerns the conditions for a defence of self-defence or provocation in homicide cases: action taken out of provocation or in self-defence must be immediate and spontaneous, whereas most women, out of a reasonable fear that they would come off worst if they retaliated there and then to an act or threat of violence, must hold on to their fear and anger until an opportunity presents itself for ridding themselves of the source of attack. Other examples would be laws on rape and prostitution which presume the generalised male sex drive but female sexual arousal within relationships.

Feminist consciousness-raising, a well-known activity of women's movements, in the sphere of criminal law is usually taken to mean women lawyers and jurists bringing their own experiences as women to bear on legal proceedings, empathising with women victims, understanding the impact of fear of crime on women's lives, as well as imagining the effects on women offenders of separation from children because of imprisonment. It means being able to envisage situations such as having to confront the machismo culture of a probation day-centre, or the trouble that may be forthcoming from male partners if women have to spend a lot of time with other men because of the requirements of a community sanction.

These feminist legal methods also widen the scope of concern for the impact of penalties on male offenders – the impact on female partners and children caused by home confinement with curfews and electronic monitoring, as well as the impact on families of imprisonment of men. They have also highlighted the social construction of masculinity in our societies as a very significant factor in criminality given the gender difference in male and female crime rates, and something that needs to be tackled if male offenders are to become less likely to reoffend. Together these methods would lead to progress towards a so-called woman-wise penality, which would have as its essential requirements:

1   That the penal regulation of female law-breakers does not increase their oppression *as women* still further.
2   That the penal regulation of law-breaking men does not brutalize them and make them even more violently or ideologically oppressive towards women in the future. (Carlen, 1990, p. 114; italics in original)

The other element of feminist law – feminist practical reasoning – has aroused the most controversy. It has been claimed that feminist reasoning is of a different kind from male reasoning, applying itself to different goals, using different processes, admitting different factors as relevant. Feminist reasoning, it is said, is more concerned with concrete situations than with abstract principles, and it seeks the resolution of conflicts rather than the triumph of right. With regard to law, the main differences are said to be that resolving present disputes becomes more important than following established precedents or correctly interpreting rules, and that the legal subject is seen as the centre of a network of relationships rather than as an individual standing alone and individually responsible (Bartlett, 1990). Carol Gilligan's book *In a Different Voice* suggested distinct masculine and feminine moral sensibilities, examining the cognitive psychology of Kohlberg to argue that what is generally taken to be 'advanced' or 'correct' moral reasoning, is in fact male moral reasoning (Gilligan, 1982). She terms the masculinist, abstract, rule-bound moral reasoning the 'logic of justice' as opposed to the feminine, relational, problem-solving 'ethic of care', and says that the latter principle is either absent from law, or else is heard in law in a position much subordinated to the masculine voice. Other writers draw on Gilligan's ideas to criticise law and criminal justice practices. Frances Heidensohn, for example, characterises the rival approaches to dispute resolution not as a male voice and a female voice, but as the Portia model and the Persephone model (Heidensohn, 1986). She says that where the Portia model valorises rationality, individualism, formal rules, formal equality and upholding of rights, the Persephone model emphasises cooperation, mutual responsibility, informal processes and relational networks. Heidensohn claims that the Portia model (which corresponds with the due process, just deserts orientation) is predominant in contemporary criminal justice processes, at the expense of the more caring, Persephone model.

A key point in the formulations of Gilligan and those who have used a similar framework is the individualism of the masculine voice, compared with the relationalism of the feminine voice. Here, it can easily be objected that legal discourse is all too relational, the problem is not individualism but the recognition of only certain relationships, and these relationships are conceived not only with a masculinist view of the world, but also with class-, race- and sexuality-bound world-views. Relationships within the heterosexual, nuclear family are reinforced by law whilst homosexual, non-marital relationships struggle for recognition; laws of trespass, squatting and so on consistently favour owners; race relations and equal opportunity legislation has too many exceptions to make any significant difference on social inequalities; immigration legislation favours white and handicaps black migrants. Women have striven for the right to legal individualism rather than being seen always as the property of fathers or husbands, and whatever progress they may have made in achieving formal individualism, their treatment at law continues to be influenced by judgements about their performance as daughters, wives and mothers.

Critics of this different voice, alternate models approach object that

such dichotomised approaches cannot be distinguished in judicial processes, that to the extent that they can it is misleading to ascribe them
to essentialist male and female reasoning processes, and they both play
their part in criminal justice and penal practice (Daly, 1988). For me, the
value of configuring legal and penal policy ideas into two distinct
models is not so much to make points about gender-correlated reasoning
processes, but to highlight the fact that there are different ways of
looking at penal questions, and that it is not a matter of one, be it Portia
or Persephone, justice or care, having better understanding of the consequences of crime or the purposes of law, but that there are different
values which rightly have bearing on criminal justice decision-making.
Whilst, with Daly, we can find both the logic of justice and the ethic of
care at work in criminal justice and penal practice, it is the balance
between them that matters. In the last several years the logic of justice
has become more and more predominant, and it has even been espoused
by those who might be expected to represent the ethic of care more
wholeheartedly. It has been my argument throughout, and in previous
works, that no one perspective should be allowed to become too
dominant. The justice approach was valuable when and where the
care/rehabilitation approach had become too institutionalised or had
become distorted by indeterminate sentencing or by uncontrolled net-
widening, but when the logic of justice voice itself becomes unchallenged in assertions of the benefits of punishments proportional to crimes,
the voice urging attention to the plight of offenders needs to make
sure it can still be heard.

Without getting too embroiled in debates within feminist legal scholarship, the common strands would seem to be that constructions cannot
be assumed to be gender neutral, that people appearing before the courts
need to have their individuality recognised, but also to be seen in the
context of the relationships and circumstances that are important to
them and germane to the problem to be resolved, that applying abstract
rules might not always be the best way of solving concrete problems.
Feminist jurisprudence is relevant to my question of the rationing of
punishment because of its acknowledgement that punishment might
not always have the greatest utility in dealing with a crime problem, in
some cases the purposes of criminal law might better be served by
compensation, reconciliation or help. It also has relevance to the question of attributing dispositional responsibility and assessing the extent
of obligation through its espousal of an epistemology of standpoints.

Assessments of feminist contributions to law, criminology and other branches of social science have chronicled the progress from add-on empiricism, to standpoint feminism, to an emerging, postmodernist recognition of standpoints (Bartlett, 1990; Cain, 1989, 1990; Kerruish, 1991; Smart, 1990). Briefly, feminist scholarship has gone from asking questions about females from within a (male) traditional frame of reference, to making claims for the superiority of knowledge gained from a female vantage point. Standpoint feminism argues that the male or established perspective on social institutions, social processes and social relationships is inadequate because the assumptions used in seeking knowledge are so consistent with the assumptions used to maintain the phenomena under observation that too much is inevitably left unquestioned; because women are on the downside, they question more and therefore can achieve fuller understanding. In particular, since in most social formations men are in the positions of power, they rarely recognise the power dimensions in social formations.

In its latest, postmodernist phase, feminist writers see that 'woman' itself is not a unitary concept, but that gender consciousness and gendered experience are mediated through race, class, age, location and so forth, and that therefore there can be no unitary 'feminist standpoint'. To urge the superiority of a particular standpoint, moreover, recreates the self-enclosed, uncritical viewpoints of masculine knowledge, and therefore must itself become flawed and partial. Claims of standpoint superiority are, crucially, incongruent with the emancipatory intent of (the) feminist epistemological project. What remains of value is recognition of the positionality of knowledge and insistence (in common with other critical theories) that knowledge which does not incorporate an awareness of its standpoint must be ideological. Espousal of an epistemology of standpoints, rather than (a) standpoint epistemology, then, opens the way to consideration of how to assess dispositional capacity and how to deal with crimes of the disadvantaged, because it admits of the validity of standpoints of persons other than those with positions of legal power; it opens up criminal justice decision-making to perspectives other than the juridical.

Difference and legal theory

Even if definitions of crime and rankings of seriousness were to become less class-, race- or gender-correlated, even if provision of psychiatric facilities were to be greatly expanded, even if unemployment and homelessness were to be reduced, everything we know about the social role of criminal law and the operation of the filtering mechanisms between the penalising circuit and other regulatory circuits would lead us to expect that numbers of the disadvantaged and disordered would continue to appear before the criminal courts. We cannot, therefore, expect ever to be able to avoid dilemmas of difference: difference in levels of capacity, difference in opportunities to acquire possessions, excitement, status or mere survival in non-criminal ways, and therefore differences in levels of obligations, differences in appropriate responses to law-breaking. To do justice, we need to be alert not just to disparities arising from the unlike treatment of sameness, but also to discrimination in the like treatment of difference.

Difference cannot but be problematic for legal theory. Having rules depends on there being classes of cases to which those rules apply: legal discourse must be constructed so that individual instances can be sub-sumed within general categories. Codes, and precedents and the devel-opment of tariffs in non-code legal systems, work precisely to prescribe the judicial task as deciding which general category the particular case belongs to, and then applying the relevant rule, imposing the relevant sanction. Other discourses – psychiatry, social work – may be allowed a presence to represent particularity, but the juridical perspective is gener-ality and, again, the more dominant the juridical voice becomes, the more is concern for difference suppressed. Whereas the role of these other discourses in criminal justice processes is to illuminate individual-ity from out of generalist definitions of offences, the juridical goal is the opposite – it is to identify generality in spite of the individuality of the offender. In order to be able to apply general rules, legal theory has to specify criteria for sameness and difference. To apply the same penalties in different cases, juridical reasoning must demonstrate that on the criteria that matter, the cases are 'relevantly the same' (Kerruish, 1991, p. 110). For criminal justice decisions, the criteria that matter are usually offence type, previous record, current court orders and for some categories of crime, variables such as whether carrying a gun, whether violating a relationship of trust, whether violating public or private property. Gender, race and class are ruled unimportant, but factors which may be highly correlated to these variables, such as employment status, responsibility for children, may be granted some circumstantial rel-evance. Availability of non-criminal options, still more, perception of availability of non-criminal options, are ruled irrelevant, as are experi-ences of racism, sexism, class discrimination. Regardless of differences of biography, social location or life-chances, people are considered the same in the most relevant respect of all – freedom to choose not to commit crimes. That individuals have choices is a basic legal assumption; that circumstances constrain choices is not.

Legal theory cannot appreciate that this existential view of the world as an arena for the acting out of free choices is a perspective of the privileged, and that potential for self-actualisation is far from apparent to those whose lives are constricted by material and ideological handicaps. This kind of empathetic grasp of others' world-view is usually only available to those who have themselves been conscious of some restraint upon their freedom of choice, whether because of gender, age, class, race or disability. In other words, freedom of choice in the very strong sense in which is it is fundamental to legal theory is a standpoint relative concept, and jurisprudence has no conception of standpoint relativity. Not only does jurisprudence have no such conception, its very *raison d'être* denies it such a possibility. Since its task is to lay down and interpret rules for the whole society, it can only claim authority by convincing us that its one voice is able to speak for all. Its claim is that law is a unitary, objective, rationally superior perspective and therefore it cannot admit any notion of a plurality of perspectives.

Law cannot, then, concede that the meaning of 'the same' act could be different to people acting out of different motives, from different social situations, with different degrees of power in social relationships. The juridical voice has, indeed, been remarkably successful in persuading us all that whatever the scale of the unemployment problem, however rampant racism and sexism might be, however despairing are the marginalised, there is no excuse, the law is still the law and a crime is still a crime. Legal theory itself, not just the law-and-order ideology of the Reagan–Thatcher era, persuades us of the importance of not excusing crime, it helps us lose sight of the difference between condoning the act and sympathising with the offender. It has also lately persuaded us that rather than social workers, probation officers and psychiatrists writing about personal biographies and social-structural circumstances in ways that might counter judicial prejudice or ignorance, such things are irrelevant, what matters is to concentrate on the offence.

Against the substantive inequalities which make it difficult to maintain that those who derive so few of society's benefits should endure an equal portion of its pains if they transgress its laws, legal theory gives us procedural equality. Legal theory does not accommodate to actual subjects, but constructs for us a legal subject who is indeed identical to all other legal subjects. In her incisive analysis of supposedly different legal theory traditions, Valerie Kerruish shows us how they all share this foundational presumption of identity of legal subjects, and explains the importance of using the term 'equality' to explain the status of legal subjects *vis-à-vis* each other, rather than 'identity': 'Equality avoids the insult to individualist egos which sameness as identity implies. It also carries with it a link to freedom' (Kerruish, 1991, p. 110).

We are procedurally equal in that we have an individual relationship to the state, and since our inequality is in our relationships with each other, substantive inequality is irrelevant to law. Since our relationship to the state is defined as one of mutual rights and obligations, then it follows that legal subjects must be equal in their legal rights and obligations, whatever inequalities may exist in social rights and obligations. By implication, any conceivable stream of legal thought would be committed to equality (sameness) rather than difference. Modern legal forms have developed first and foremost to regulate the relationship between the individual and the state, to delimit their respective rights and obligations. Replacing private vengeance with state retribution necessarily entails displacement of subject–subject relationships in favour of state–individual relationships, and therefore the dichotomy of the individual and the social which we find in legal theory is not some unfortunate misconception, but it is the very foundation of jurisprudence in constitutional society. It is not just that 'Each text . . . develops a form of individualist social theory and constructs authority and obligation as central categories of legality' (ibid., p. 86), it is that any jurisprudential text is bound to do so.

Conclusion – challenging the dominance of jurisprudence

I have argued that while criminal justice decision-making must pay attention to sameness (it is unjust to punish the same crimes differently), it must also be alert to difference. We cannot know that acts are really the same unless we apprehend meaning, motive, circumstances and range of choices as well as behaviour. I have argued in this latter section, however, that jurisprudence is a discourse of sameness, its purpose is to assign acts to categories to enable the application of rules, which purpose it achieves by constructing identity through the specification of criteria of relevance, and thereby ruling out difference. It is not surprising, therefore, that the legal conscience should be troubled by evidence of disparity, by excess or abuse of discretion: the rationalising tendency of legal reasoning is to strain towards ever more sameness (which in legal practice it calls 'consistency').

The success of legal ideology in enforcing equality of obligation in a materially unequal society has led to the growth of fundamental questioning of juridical concepts, principally from within the Critical Legal Studies movement (Fitzpatrick and Hunt, 1987). In particular, the idea of rights as defined in liberal legal discourse has been subjected to much critical analysis. Formal ascription of legal rights, the argument goes, has no meaning for people who do not have the wealth or power either to define which rights should be guaranteed by law, to secure for themselves rights which are specified, or to secure redress against violations of rights. We have considered in Chapter 3 the effect of prioritisation of rights over needs in the case of the mentally disordered; we can see in the case of the homeless which rights are upheld (the right to protection of property from intrusion), and which are not (the right to shelter); we can see in any courtroom on any day of the week the difference being able to pay for a good lawyer to defend one's rights can make. So, do rights have any value for the less advantaged, and if not, can the less advantaged have any corresponding obligations? If the constructs of rights and obligations do not serve social justice, should we dismantle formal law and jurisprudence? Or to pose the question another way, does legal theory's inescapable standpoint blindness make it incapable of reform of a kind that would make it more useful to those suffering deficits of power and benefit? The question of rights is central: can we broaden the notion of rights to include elements of welfare, can we reconceptualise rights to take cognisance of their root in social relationships, or must we continue with what Kerruish calls the fetishism of rights in modern legal theory, an account of rights which sees them as natural, universal and self-evident rather than being contingent on power-structured social relationships? If the idea of rights as conceived in legal theory is jettisoned or severely damaged, then the law's claims to regulate conflict must correspondingly be severely restricted. Without rights there can be no correlative obligations; if it can be shown that certain groups are excluded from rights, then they must also be excluded from obligations.

Kerruish argues that although legal theory's representation of rights masks reality in some very important ways, the idea of rights is important of itself. Even where rights are not supported in practice, even where support for rights is unevenly distributed, then differences between equality of rights in theory and partiality of rights in practice should be corrected, rather than the idea of rights discarded. In spite of their criticisms of law in practice, Kerruish and Lacey both maintain that even those who derive least benefit from the existence of law are better off with it than without it, and therefore there is a general obligation to obey the law, which justifies, as Lacey claims, a general threat of punishment. But just as rights may exist equally for all persons in theory but not be supported for everyone in practice, so punishment may be available in theory for all cases, but should not be inflicted in every case, only in cases where the offender has an effective share of social benefits, and an effective freedom of choice.

Jurisprudential discourse, then, defines rights and obligations, specifies rules and provides for sanctions. More than this is, however, needed to make decisions in actual criminal cases. Legal theory is formulated in terms of generality, of relationships between state and individual, of procedural equality, of protection of rights, whereas crimes are problems that need understanding of particularity, of relationships between people, of substantive inequality, of feasible solutions. Responding to crimes needs a variety of perspectives; legal reasoning by itself is insufficient to arrive at the best solution. The difficulty is that the more that crime problems are constructed only as legal problems, the less likely it is that other perspectives will be drawn upon. Legal theory is very exclusive – apparently different traditions in legal theory are agreed that it is lawyers and lawyers alone who have answers to questions which are assigned to the realm of law. Legal empiricism, the tradition represented by Hart, says that the law is what previous legal decisions say it is, while the seemingly more open, hermeneutic formulation of Dworkin says that the 'one right answer' is that which will be arrived at by rational debate, coherent with the established culture (Dworkin, 1986). Apart from the problem that the prevailing culture might be racist, sexist and classist, it is of course lawyers who are seen here as the carriers of culture, it is they who are party to the debate.

Although other perspectives are allowed a say (probation officers, psychiatrists and others write reports, address the court, give evidence), this is entirely at the behest of the judiciary. They are confined to the space allotted to them by the judicial processes, and they must present their evidence in quasi-juridical format. At present the influence of these complementary discourses has been reduced too far, and their participants have lost too much confidence in their own professional perspectives, and have accepted juridical dominance too compliantly. Criminal justice decision-making needs to take account of the motivation and circumstances of offenders, of the feasibility of sentences, of the possibility that in any particular case waiving punishment in favour of help or treatment may be more effective in preventing future crime. Account must also be taken of the contingencies that have funnelled the offender into the penal circuit: would help or treatment be better provided under a medical or a welfare rather than a judicial aegis; could earlier inappropriate entry into the penalising subsystem be corrected by an exit at the present stage; have circumstances changed so that someone assigned to the penal system needs to be reassigned to the welfare or medical system (for instance, are facilities available that were not previously, has an offender's clinical condition deteriorated, have employment prospects improved?). Or, would the anticipated gains from the crime still have left the offender with a significant benefit deficit, so that an additional penal burden would be unfair?

A discourse of individual rights is, however, worth defending. Apart from the fact that given jurisprudential dominance, its deconstruction could only be a theoretical activity and its persistence must be assumed, its existence is of value, provided it could be counterbalanced by alternative perspectives of equal weight. The penological reflection of legal discourse that we find in deserts theory is a safeguard against misapplications or abuses of welfare discourses, but in turn welfare discourse needs to be strengthened and accorded equal status if it is to function as a safeguard against insensitive applications of rights discourse. Although participants in criminal justice processes cannot be expected to be polyglot experts in all the relevant discourses, they should be expected at least to appreciate the importance of perspectives other than their own. If judges continue to be recruited from the legal profession, then they should receive sufficient grounding in disciplines such as psychiatry and sociology to give them some purchase on those aspects of a case which are extraneous to jurisprudence, as Downes tells us is the case in The Netherlands (Downes, 1988). They should be at least sufficiently attuned to other perspectives to appreciate advice given, and to be able to accept that such advice is from a standpoint other than their own, that that is its purpose and value.

This is no doubt much easier in non-adversarial jurisdictions, where the (legal) facts of the case do not so completely dominate proceedings, but more separation between conviction proceedings and sentencing proceedings could improve matters in adversarial systems. Instead, we are moving in the opposite direction, with more stand-down reports, less time for reports when cases are adjourned. And rather than judges and magistrates becoming more versed in psychiatric and social work perspectives, the contemporary trend is for social workers, probation officers and other non-lawyers to be trained in judicial perspectives. Reciprocal familiarity of perspectives is all to the good; dominance of one perspective and near abdication of the other is very different. The same importance should be given to investigating social facts as legal facts, and the same weight given to the resulting evidence.

In sum, crime is a complex, human social event and needs to be responded to as such. Contemporary criminal justice is best adapted to deal with run-of-the-mill offences, committed by perfectly free, perfectly rational agents, with other possibilities open to them, offending for instrumental reasons. Tariff sentencing, the legal perspective, suits such cases well, but unfortunately such cases are by no means the majority of those that come before the courts. As long as the filtering mechanisms do not work more justly to funnel out those who commit crimes because of economic urgency, or who are provoked by racism, physical abuse, helplessness or despair, illness or addiction, but to the contrary filter into the penalising circuit the disturbed and the dispossessed, this rational, consistent legal justice cannot by itself fulfil the requirements of social justice. Legal reasoning may tell us the penalty for an act, but cannot by itself give us the best solution for a person, and after all 'acts cannot be punished, only persons. We do not sentence acts, only persons – consequences fall on the person and are, in the main, not directed to the act' (Mohr, 1980, p. 21).

The balance between rights and needs, punishment and help, the legal and the social, the individual and the collective, must become more equal. Legal theory needs to bear in mind that the purpose of law is to help secure the well-being of citizens; penal policy should bear in mind that it is but one strand of social policy and that all social policy should be directed towards the attainment of social justice.

Bibliography

Abel, R. L. (1982) (ed.) *The Politics of Informal Justice, Vol. 1: The American Experience* (New York: Academic Press).

Abramson, M. (1972) 'The Criminalization of Mentally Disordered Behaviour: Possible Side Effects of a New Mental Health Law', *Hospital and Community Psychiatry*, vol. 23, no. 4, pp. 101–5.

Acres, D. (1987) 'Consistently Achieving Our Sentencing Aims', in D. C. Pennington and S. Lloyd-Bostock (eds), *The Psychology of Sentencing: Approaches to Consistency and Disparity* (Oxford: Centre for Socio-Legal Studies).

Adler, M. and Longhurst, B. (1989) *Towards a New Sociology of Imprisonment: Prison Discourse Today*, paper given to the British Criminology Conference, Bristol Polytechnic, 17–20 July.

Albrecht, H.–J. (1987) 'Foreign Minorities in the Criminal Justice System in the Federal Republic of Germany', *Howard Journal*, vol. 26, no. 4, pp. 272–286.

—— (1989) 'Commentary', in R. Hood (ed.) *Crime and Criminal Policy in Europe* (Oxford: Centre for Criminological Research).

Allen, H. (1987) *Justice Unbalanced: Gender, Psychiatry and Judicial Decisions* (Milton Keynes: Open University Press).

American Friends Service Committee (1972) *Struggle for Justice* (New York: Hill & Wang).

Ancel, M. (1987) *Social Defense: The Future of Penal Reform*, trans. Thorsten Sellin (Littleton, Colorado: Rothman).

Antilla, I. (1986) 'Trends in Criminal Law', in J. Van Dijk *et al.* (eds) *Criminal Law in Action: An Overview of Current Issues in Western Society* (Arnhem: Gouda Quint).

Ashworth, A. (1983) *Sentencing and Penal Policy* (London: Weidenfeld & Nicolson).

—— (1989a) 'Criminal Justice and Deserved Sentences', *Criminal Law Review*, May, pp. 340–55.

—— (1989b) *Custody Reconsidered* (London: Centre for Policy Studies).

—— (1991) *Principles of Criminal Law* (Oxford: Clarendon Press).

—— (1992) 'Non-Custodial Sentences', *Criminal Law Review*, April, pp. 242–51.

Audit Commission (1980) *Making a Reality of Community Care* (London: HMSO).

Austin, J. and Krisberg, B. (1981) 'Wider, Stronger and Different Nets: The Dialectics of Criminal Justice Reform', *Journal of Research in Crime and Delinquency*, vol. 18, no. 1, pp. 165–96.

—— and Krisberg, B. (1982) 'The Unmet Promise of Alternatives to Incarceration', *Crime and Delinquency*, vol. 28, no. 3, pp. 374–409.

—— and Krisberg, B. (1985) 'Incarceration in the United States: The Extent and Future of the Problem', *Annals of the American Academy of Political Science: Our Crowded Prisons*, vol. 478, pp. 15–30.

Baldock, J. C. (1980) 'Why the Prison Population Has Grown Larger and Younger', *Howard Journal*, vol. XIX, pp. 142–55.

Ball, R. A. and Lilley, J. R. (1985) 'Home Incarceration: An International Alternative to Institutional Incarceration', *International Journal of Comparative and Applied Criminal Justice*, vol. 9, no. 2, pp. 85–97.

—— and Lilley, J. R. (1988) 'Home Incarceration with Electronic Monitoring', in J. E. Scott and T. Hirschi (eds) *Controversial Issues in Crime and Justice* (Newbury Park, Cal.: Sage).

Barak, G. and Bohm, R. M. (1989) 'The Crimes of the Homeless or the Crime of Homelessness? On the Dialectics of Criminalization, Decriminalization and Victimization', *Contemporary Crises*, vol. 13, pp. 275–88.

Bartlett, K. T. (1990) 'Feminist Legal Methods', *Harvard Law Review*, vol 103, pp. 829–88.

Bean, P. (1976) *Rehabilitation and Deviance* (London: Routledge & Kegan Paul).

Beck, B. (1979) 'The Limits of Deinstitutionalization', in M. Lewis (ed.) *Research in Social Problems and Public Policy (1)* (Greenwich, Conn.: JAI Press).

Becker, H. (1966) *Outsiders* (New York: The Free Press).

Biles, D. (1983) 'Crime and Imprisonment: A Two Decade Comparison Between England and Australia', *British Journal of Criminology*, vol. 23, no. 2, pp. 166–72.

—— (1986) 'Prisons and their Problems', in D. Chappell and P. Wilson (eds) *The Australian Criminal Justice System, the Mid 1980s* (Sydney: Butterworths).

—— and Mulligan, G. (1973) 'Mad or Bad? – The Enduring Dilemma', *British Journal of Criminology*, vol. 13, no. 3, pp. 275–9.

Bishop, N. (1988) *Non-custodial Alternatives in Europe* (Helsinki: HEUNI (Helsinki Institute for Crime Prevention and Control)).

Blagg, H. and Smith, D. (1989) *Crime, Penal Policy and Social Work* (Harlow: Longman).

Blomberg, T. G. (1987) 'Criminal Justice Reform and Social Control: Are We Becoming a Minimum Security Society?', in J. Lowman, R. J. Menzies and T. S. Palys (eds) *Transcarceration: Essays in the Sociology of Social Control* (Aldershot: Gower).

Blom-Cooper, L. (1988) *The Penalty of Imprisonment* (London: Prison Reform Trust and Howard League for Penal Reform).

Blumstein, A. (1987) 'Sentencing and the Prison Crowding Problem', in S. D. Gottfredson and S. McConville (eds) *America's Correctional Crisis: Prison Populations and Public Policy* (Westport, Conn: Greenword Press).

—— Cohen, J. and Miller, H. D. (1980) 'Demographically Disaggregated Projections of Prison Popuations', *Journal of Criminal Justice*, vol. 8, pp. 1–26.

Bottomley, A. K. and Coleman, C. (1980) 'Law and Order: Crime Problem, Moral Panic or Penal Crisis', in A. E. Bottoms and R. H. Preston (eds) *The Coming Penal Crisis* (Edinburgh: Scottish Academic Press).

—— and Pease, K. (1986) *Crime and Punishment: Interpreting the Data* (Milton Keynes: Open University Press).

Bottoms, A. E. (1977) 'Reflections on the Renaissance of Dangerousness', *Howard Journal*, vol. 16, pp. 70–97.

—— (1981) 'The Suspended Sentence in England 1967–1978', *British Journal of Criminology*, vol. 21, no. 1, pp. 1–26.

—— (1983) 'Neglected Features of Contemporary Penal Systems', in D. Garland and P. Young (eds) *The Power to Punish* (London: Heinemann).

—— (1987) 'Limiting Prison Use: Experience in England and Wales', *Howard Journal*, vol. 26, pp. 177–202.

—— and Brownsword, R. (1983) 'Dangerousness and Rights', in J. Hinton (ed.) *Dangerousness: Problems of Assessment and Prediction* (London: Allen & Unwin).

—— and Light, R. (1987) 'Introduction', in A. E. Bottoms and R. Light (eds) *Problems of Long-term Imprisonment* (Aldershot: Gower).

—— and McWilliams, W. (1979) 'A Non-Treatment Paradigm for Probation Practice', *British Journal of Social Work*, vol. 9, no. 2, pp. 159–202.

—— and Preston, R. (1980) (eds) *The Coming Penal Crisis: A Criminological and Theological Exploration* (Edinburgh: Scottish Academic Press).

Bowlby, J. (1946) *Forty-four Juvenile Thieves* (Eastbourne: Ballière, Tindall).

Box, S. (1981) *Deviance, Reality and Society*, 2nd edn (London: Cassell).

—— (1983) *Power, Crime and Mystification* (London: Tavistock).

—— (1987) *Recession, Crime and Punishment* (Basingstoke: Macmillan).

—— and Hale, C. (1982) 'Economic Crisis and the Rising Prisoner Population', *Crime and Social Justice*, vol. 17, pp. 20–35.

—— and Hale, C. (1985) 'Unemployment, Imprisonment and Prison Overcrowding', *Contemporary Crises*, vol. 9, pp. 209–28.

Box-Grainger, J. (1986) 'Sentencing Rapists', in R. Matthews and J. Young (eds) *Confronting Crime* (London: Sage).

Braithwaite, J. (1989) *Crime, Shame and Reintegration* (Cambridge: Cambridge University Press).

—— (1991) *The Political Agenda of Republican Criminology*, paper given to the British Criminology Conference, University of York, 27–29 July.

Braithwaite, R. and Pettit, P. (1990) *Not Just Deserts* (Oxford: Oxford University Press).

Brand-Koolen, M. J. M. (1987) 'The Dutch Penal System and Its Prisons – An Introductory Note', in M. J. M. Brand-Koolen (ed.) *Studies on the Dutch Prison System* (Amstelveen: Kugler).

Browne, D. (1990) *Black People, Mental Health and the Courts* (London: NACRO).

Burney, E. (1985) *Sentencing Young People: What Went Wrong with the Criminal Justice Act 1982?* (Aldershot: Gower).

Burton, M. (1983) 'Understanding Mental Health Services: Theory and Practice', *Critical Social Policy*, vol. 7, pp. 54–74.

Busfield, J. (1986) *Managing Madness: Changing Ideas and Practice* (London: Unwin Hyman).

Byrne, J. M. (1990) 'The Future of Intensive Probation Supervision and the New Intermediate Sanctions', *Crime and Delinquency*, vol. 36, no. 1, pp. 6–41.

Cain, M. (1985) 'Beyond Informal Justice', *Contemporary Crises*, vol. 9, no. 4, pp. 335–73.

—— (1986) 'Realism, Feminism, Methodology and Law', *International Journal of the Sociology of Law*, vol. 14, pp. 255–67.

—— (1990) 'Realist Philosophy and Standpoint Epistemologies or Feminist Criminology as a Successor Science', in L. Gelsthorpe and A. Morris (eds) *Feminist Perspectives in Criminology* (Milton Keynes: Open University Press).

Carlen, P. (1983) *Women's Imprisonment* (London: Routledge & Kegan Paul).

—— (1989) 'Crime, Inequality and Sentencing', in P. Carlen and D. Cook (eds) *Paying for Crime* (Milton Keynes: Open University Press).

—— (1990) *Alternatives to Women's Imprisonment* (Milton Keynes: Open University Press).

Carr-Hill, R. (1987) 'O Bring Me Your Poor: Immigrants in the French System of Criminal Justice', *Howard Journal*, vol. 26, no. 4, pp. 287–302.

Centre for Contemporary Cultural Studies (1982) *The Empire Strikes Back* (London: Hutchinson).

Chaiken, J. M. and Chaiken, M. R. (1982) *Varieties of Criminal Behaviour* (Santa Monica, Cal.: Rand).

Chambliss, W. J. (1969) *Crime and the Legal Process* (New York: McGraw Hill).

Chan, J. B. C. and Ericson, R. (1981) *Decarceration and the Economy of Penal Reform* (Toronto: University of Toronto, Centre for Criminology).

Cheadle, J. and Ditchfield, J. (1982) *Sentenced Mentally Ill Offenders* (London: Home Office Research and Planning Unit).

Chigwada, R. (1989) 'The Criminalization and Imprisonment of Black Women', *Probation Journal*, vol. 36, no. 3, pp. 100–5.

Chiricos, J. G. (1987) 'Rates of Crime and Unemployment: An Analysis of Aggregate Research Evidence', *Social Problems*, vol. 34, pp. 187–212.

Christie, N. (1977) 'Conflicts as Property', *British Journal of Criminology*, vol. 17, pp. 1–15.

—— (1982) *Limits to Pain* (Oxford: Martin Robertson).

Cipollini, R., Faccioli, F. and Pitch, T. (1989) 'Gypsy Girls in an Italian Juvenile Court', in M. Cain (ed.) *Growing Up Good* (London: Sage).

Clear, T., Flynn, S. and Shapiro, C. (1987) 'Intensive Supervision in Probation: Comparison of Three Projects', in B. McCarthy (ed.) *Intermediate Punishments: Intensive Supervision, Home Confinement and Electronic Surveillance* (Monsey, NY: Willow Press).

—— and Hardyman, P. (1990) 'The New Intensive Supervision Movement', *Crime and Delinquency*, vol. 36, no. 1, pp. 42–60.

Cohen, J. (1983) 'Incapacitation as a Strategy for Crime Control: Possibilities and Pitfalls', in M. H. Tonry and N. Morris (eds) *Crime and Justice: An Annual Review of Research, vol. 5* (Chicago: University of Chicago Press), pp. 1–84.

Cohen, S. (1977) 'Prisons and the Future of Control Systems: From Concentration to Dispersal', in M. Fitzgerald *et al.* (eds) *Welfare in Action* (London: Routledge & Kegan Paul).

—— (1979) 'The Punitive City: Notes on the Dispersal of Social Control', *Contemporary Crises*, vol. 3, pp. 339–63.

—— (1985) *Visions of Social Control: Crime, Punishment and Classification* (Cambridge: Polity Press).

Cohn, S. F., Barkan, S. E. and Halteman, W. A. (1991) 'Punitive Attitudes Towards Criminals: Racial Consciousness or Racial Conflict', *Social Problems*, vol. 38, no. 2, pp. 287–96.

Cook, D. (1989) *Rich Law, Poor Law: Different Responses to Tax and Supplementary Benefit Fraud* (Milton Keynes: Open University Press).

Cooke, R. K. (1987) 'Practical Aims of the Sentencer', in D. C. Pennington and S. Lloyd Bostock (eds) *The Psychology of Sentencing: Approaches to Consistency and Disparity* (Oxford: Centre for Socio-Legal Studies).

Cooper, D. (1967) *Psychiatry and Anti-Psychiatry* (Harmondsworth: Penguin).

Cornish, D. and Clarke, R. (1986) *The Reasoning Criminal: Rational Choice Perspectives in Offending* (New York: Springer-Verlag).

Cornwell, D. J. and Arendesen, R. L. E. (1991) *The Prosecution and Post-Conviction Disposal of Serious Child Sexual Abusers in England and Wales and The Netherlands: An International Comparison of Philosophies and Outcomes*, paper given to the British Criminology Conference, University of York, 27–29 July.

Council of Europe (1985) *Economic Crisis and Crime* (Strasbourg: European Committee on Crime Problems).

—— (1987) *Prison Information Bulletin No. 9* (Strasbourg: Directorate of Legal Affairs).

Craft, M. (1984) 'Who Are Mentally Abnormal Offenders?' in M. Craft and A. Craft (eds) *Mentally Abnormal Offenders* (Eastbourne: Ballière Tindall).

Criminal Law Review (1982) *Criminal Justice Act 1991* April, whole issue.

Crow, I. and Simon, F. (1987) *Unemployment and Magistrates' Courts* (London: NACRO).

Cullen, F. and Gilbert, K. (1982) *Reaffirming Rehabilitation* (Cincinatti: Anderson).

Currie, E. (1985) *Confronting Crime: An American Challenge* (New York: Pantheon Books).

Daly, K. (1989) 'Criminal Justice Ideologies and Practices in Different Voices: Some Feminist Questions about Justice', *International Journal of the Sociology of Law*, vol. 17, pp. 1–18.

Dear, M. and Wolch, J. (1987) *Landscapes of Despair: From Deinstitutionalization to Homelessness* (Cambridge: Polity Press).

De Haan, W. (1988) 'The Necessity of Punishment in a Just Social Order: A Critical Appraisal', *International Journal of the Sociology of Law*, vol. 16, pp. 433–53.

—— (1990) *The Politics of Redress: Crime, Punishment and Penal Abolition* (London: Unwin Hyman).

Dell, S. (1984) *Murder into Manslaughter* (Maudsley Monograph no. 27) (Oxford: Oxford University Press).

Ditchfield, J. A. (1976) *Police Cautioning in England and Wales*, Home Office Research Study no. 37 (London: HMSO).

Donzelot, J. (1975) 'The Prison Movement in France', in H. Bianchi, M. Simondi and I. Taylor (eds) *Deviance and Control in Europe* (New York: John Wiley).

Donzelot, J. (1980) *The Policing of Families* (London: Hutchinson).

Doob, A. N. and Roberts, J. (1988) 'Public Punitiveness and Public Knowledge of the Facts: Some Canadian Examples', in M. Hough and N. Walker (eds) *Public Attitudes to Sentencing: Surveys from Five Countries* (Aldershot: Gower).

Downes, D. (1988) *Contrasts in Tolerance: Post-War Penal Policy in The Netherlands and England and Wales* (Oxford: Clarendon Press).

Dworkin, R. (1977) *Taking Rights Seriously* (London: Duckworth).
—— (1986) *Law's Empire* (London: Fontana).
Eratt, S. and Neudek, K. (1992) *The Life Sentence Prisoner* (Vienna: United Nations Crime Prevention and Criminal Justice Branch).
Ericson, R. V. (1987) 'The State and Criminal Justice Reform', in R. S. Ratner and J. L. McMullan (eds) *State Control: Criminal Justice Politics in Canada* (Vancouver: University of British Columbia Press).
Esteves, A. M. (1990) 'Electronic Incarceration in Massachusetts: A Critical Analysis', *Social Justice*, vol. 17, no. 4, pp. 76–105.
Farrington, D. P. (1987) 'Predicting Individual Crime Rates', in D. M. Gottfredson and M. H. Tonry (eds) *Prediction and Classification: Criminal Justice Decision Making* (Chicago: University of Chicago Press).
Faugeron, C. (1989) 'The Problems of Imprisonment', in R. Hood (ed.) *Crime and Criminal Policy in Europe* (Oxford: Centre for Criminological Research).
Feest, J. (1991) 'Reducing the Prison Population: Lessons from the West German Experience', in J. Muncie and R. Sparks (eds) *Imprisonment: European Perspectives* (Hemel Hempstead: Harvester Wheatsheaf).
Feinberg, J. (1981) 'The Expressive Function of Punishment', in H. Goss and A. Von Hirsch (eds) *Sentencing* (Oxford: Oxford University Press).
Fitzgerald, M. and Sim, J. (1982) *British Prisons*, 2nd edn (Oxford: Basil Blackwell).
Fitzmaurice, C. and Pease, K. .(1982) 'Prison Sentences and Populations: A Comparison of Some European Countries', *Justice of the Peace*, vol. 46.
Fitzpatrick, P. and Hunt, A. (1987) *Critical Legal Studies* (Oxford: Basil Blackwell).
Flowers, R. B. (1988) *Minorities and Criminality* (New York: Greenwood Press).
Fludger, N. (1981) *Ethnic Minorities in Borstal* (London: HMSO).
Fogel, D. (1975) *We are the Living Proof: The Justice Model of Corrections* (Cincinatti: Anderson).
Folter, R. S. (1986) 'On the Methodological Foundation of the Abolitionist Approach to the Criminal Justice System', *Contemporary Crises*, vol. 10, pp. 39–62.
Foucault, M. (1977) *Discipline and Punish: The Birth of the Prison* (London: Allen Lane).
—— (1978) *I, Pierre Rivière, Having Slaughtered My Mother, My Sister and My Brother* (Harmondsworth: Penguin).
Franke, H. (1990) 'Dutch Tolerance: Facts and Fables', *British Journal of Criminology*, vol. 30, no. 1, pp. 81–93.
Frankel, M. E. (1973) *Criminal Sentences* (New York: Hill and Wang).
Galanter, M. (1985) 'The Legal Malaise, or Justice Observed', *Law and Society Review*, vol. 19, no. 4, pp. 537–56.
Gallo, E. and Ruggiero, V. (1991) 'The Immaterial Prison: Custody as a Factory for the Manufacture of Handicaps', *International Journal of the Sociology of Law*, vol. 19, pp. 273–91.
Garland, D. (1985) *Punishment and Welfare* (Aldershot: Gower).
Gaylin, W. *et al.* (1978) *Doing Good: The Limits of Benevolence* (New York: Pantheon Books).

Genders, E. and Player, E. (1989) *Race Relations in Prisons* (Oxford: Clarendon Press).

Gewirth, A. (1978) *Reason and Morality* (Chicago: University of Chicago Press).

Gilligan, C. (1982) *In a Different Voice* (Cambridge, Mass.: Harvard University Press).

Gilroy, P. (1987) 'The Myth of Black Criminality', in P. Scraton (ed.) *Law, Order and the Authoritarian State* (Milton Keynes: Open University Press).

Goffman E. (1968) *Asylums: Essays on the Social Situation of Mental Patients and Other Inmates* (Harmondsworth: Penguin).

Gordon, R. A. (1977) 'A Critique of the Evaluation of Patuxent Institution', *Bulletin of the Academy of Psychiatry and the Law*, vol. 5, no. 2, p. 210.

Gostin, L. (1984) 'Towards the Development of Principles for Sentencing and Detaining Mentally Abnormal Offenders', in M. Craft and A. Craft (eds) *Mentally Abnormal Offenders* (Eastbourne: Ballière Tindall).

Gottfredson, S. D. (1987) 'Prediction: An Overview of Selected Methodological Issues', in D. M. Gottfredson and M. H. Tonry (eds) *Prediction and Classification: Criminal Justice Decision Making* (Chicago: University of Chicago Press).

—— and Gottfredson, D. M. (1985) 'Selective Incapacitation', *Annals of the American Academy of Political and Social Science*, vol. 478, pp. 135–49.

—— Warner, B. and Taylor, R. B. (1988) 'Conflict and Consensus about Criminal Justice in Maryland', in M. Hough and N. Walker (eds) *Public Attitudes to Sentencing: Surveys from Five Countries* (Aldershot: Gower).

Green, P. (1991) *Drug Couriers* (London: Howard League for Penal Reform).

Greenberg, D. (1975) 'Problems in Community Corrections', *Issues in Criminology*, vol. 19, pp. 1–34.

—— (1990) 'The Cost-Benefit Analysis of Imprisonment', *Social Justice*, vol. 17, no. 4, pp. 49–65.

Greenwood, P. W. (1983) 'Controlling the Crime Rate through Imprisonment', in J. Q. Wilson (ed.) *Crime and Public Policy* (San Francisco: Institute for Contemporary Studies).

—— and Abrahamse, A. (1982) *Selective Incapacitation* (Santa Monica: Rand).

Griffiths, R. (1988) *Community Care: Agenda for Action* (London: HMSO).

Grounds, A. (1991) 'The Transfer of Sentenced Prisoners to Hospital, 1960–1983', *British Journal of Criminology*, vol. 31, no. 1, pp. 54–71.

Gwynne Lloyd, M. (1991) 'Early Release of Prisoners in France: plus ça change, plus c'est la même chose', *Howard Journal*, vol. 30, no. 3, pp. 231–7.

Hale, C. (1989) 'Economy, Punishment and Imprisonment', *Contemporary Crises*, vol. 13, pp. 327–49.

Hall, S. (1980) *Drifting into a Law and Order Society* (London: Cobden Trust).

Hall S. *et al.* (1978) *Policing the Crisis* (London: Macmillan).

Halleck, S. L. (1987) *The Mentally Disordered Offender* (Washington, DC: American Psychiatric Press).

Harrington, C. (1985) *Shadow Justice? The Ideology and Institutionalization of Alernatives to Court* (Westport, Conn.: Greenwood Press).

Harris, M. K. (1987) 'A Brief for De-escalating Criminal Sanctions', in S. D. Gottfredson and S. McConville (eds) *America's Correctional Crisis: Prison Populations and Public Policy* (Westport, Conn.: Greenwood Press).

Hart, H. L. A. (1968) *Punishment and Responsibility: Essays in the Philosophy of Law* (Oxford: Oxford University Press).

Hawkins, D. F. and Hardy, K. A. (1989) 'Black–White Imprisonment Rates: A State-by-State Analysis', *Social Justice*, vol. 16 no. 4, pp. 75–93.

Headley, B. D. (1989) Introduction: Crime, Justice and Powerless Racial Groups', *Social Justice*, vol. 16, no. 4, pp. 1–9.

Heidensohn, F. (1986) "Models of Justice: Portia or Persephone? Some Thoughts on Equality, Fairness and Gender in the Field of Criminal Justice', *International Journal of the Sociology of Law*, vol. 14, pp. 287–98.

Higgins, J. (1984) 'The Mentally Abnormal Offender and His Society', in M. Craft and A. Craft (eds) *Mentally Abnormal Offenders* (Eastbourne: Ballière Tindall).

Hill, M. and Bramley, G. (1986) *Analysing Social Policy* (Oxford: Basil Blackwell).

Hogarth, J. (1971) *Sentencing as a Human Process* (Toronto: University of Toronto Press).

Hogg, R. (1988) 'Taking Crime Seriously: Left Realism and Australian Criminology', in M. Findlay and R. Hogg (eds) *Understanding Crime and Criminal Justice* (Sydney: The Law Book Co.).

Home Office (1978) *The Sentence of the Court*, 3rd edition (London: HMSO).

—— (1986) *The Ethnic Origin of Prisoners: The Prison Population on 30 June 1985 and Persons Received, July 1984–March 1985*, Statistical Bulletin 17/86, (London: HMSO).

—— (1988) *Punishment, Custody and the Community*, Cmnd 424 (London: HMSO).

—— (1990a) *Criminal Statistics for England and Wales 1989*, Cmnd 1322 (London: HMSO).

—— (1990b) *Prison Statistics England and Wales 1989* Cmnd 1221 (London: HMSO).

—— (1991a) *The Response to Racial Attacks: Sustaining the Momentum* (London: HMSO).

—— (1991b) *Custody, Care and Justice: The Way Ahead for the Prison Service in England and Wales* (London: HMSO).

—— (1992) *Criminal Justice Act 1991. A Quick Reference Guide for the Probation Service* (London: Probation Service Division).

Honderich, T. (1984) *Punishment: The Supposed Justifications*, rev. edn (Harmondsworth: Penguin).

Hood, R. G. (1978) 'Tolerance and the Tariff: Some Reflections on Fixing the Time Prisoners Serve in Custody', in J. Baldwin and A. K. Bottomley (eds) *Criminal Justice* (London: Martin Robertson).

Hudson, A. (1989) 'Troublesome Girls', in M. Cain (ed) *Growing Up Good* (London: Sage).

Hudson, B. (1984) 'The Rising Use of Imprisonment: The Impact of 'Decarceration' Policies', *Critical Social Policy*, vol. 11, pp. 46–59.

—— (1985) 'Intermittent Custody: A Response to the Green Paper', *Howard Journal*, vol. 25, no. 1, pp. 40–51.

—— (1987) *Justice through Punishment: A Critique of the 'Justice' Model of Corrections* (Basingstoke: Macmillan).

—— (1989) 'Discrimination and Disparity: The Influence of Race on Sentencing', *New Community*, vol. 16, no. 1, pp. 23–34.

—— (1990) *Preventing Crime: Good Practice in Europe*, paper given to the Annual Conference of the Howard League for Penal Reform, University of Oxford, September.

Hulsman, L. and Bernat de Celis, J. (1982) *Peines perdues: Le système penal en question* (Paris: Lelenturion).

Hunt, A. (1987) 'The Critique of Law: What is "Critical" about Critical Legal Theory?', in P. Fitzpatrick and A. Hunt (eds) *Critical Legal Studies* (Oxford: Basil Blackwell).

Ignatieff, M. (1978) *A Just Measure of Pain: The Penitentiary in the Industrial Revolution* (London: Macmillan).

Ingram, B. L. and Wellford, C. F. (1987) 'The Totality of Conditions Test in Eight Amendment Legislation', in S. D. Gottfredson and S. McConville (eds) *America's Correctional Crisis: Prison Populations and Public Policy* (Westport, Conn.: Greenwood Press).

Inniss, L. and Feagin, J. R. (1989) 'The Black "Underclass" Ideology in Race Relations Analysis', *Social Justice*, vol. 16, no. 4, pp. 13–34.

Invernizzi, I. (1975) 'Class Struggle in the Prisons: Practical and Theoretical Problems', in H. Bianchi, M. Simondi and I. Taylor (eds) *Deviance and Control in Europe* (London: John Wiley).

Irwin, J. (1985) *The Jail: Managing the Underclass in American Society* (Berkeley: University of California Press).

Jacobs, J. B. (1977) 'Macrosociology and Imprisonment', in D. F. Greenberg (ed.) *Corrections and Punishment* (Beverly Hills, Cal.: Sage).

—— (1983) *New Perspectives on Prisons and Imprisonment* (Ithaca: Cornell University Press).

Jankovic, I. (1977) 'Labour Markets and Imprisonment', *Crime and Social Justice*, vol. 8, pp. 17–31.

Jareborg, N. (1986) 'The Coherence of the Penal System', in J. Van Dijk *et al.* (eds) *Criminal Law in Action* (Arnhem: Gouda Quint).

Jefferson, T., Sim, J. and Walklate, S. (1991) *Europe, the Left and Criminology in the 1990s: Accountability, Control and the Social Construction of the Consumer*, paper presented to the British Criminology Conference, University of York, 27–29 July.

Jenkins, W. I. (1978) *Policy Analysis: A Political and Organisational Perspective* (London: Martin Robertson).

Jessop, B. (1990) *State Theory: Putting Capitalist States in Their Place* (Cambridge: Polity Press).

Jobson, K. (1980) 'Reforming Sentencing Laws: A Canadian Perspective', in B. A. Grosman (ed.) *New Directions in Sentencing* (Toronto: Butterworths).

Junger, M. (1988) 'Racial Discrimination in The Netherlands', *Sociology and Social Research*, vol. 72, pp. 211–16.

—— (1989) 'Ethnic Minorities, Crime and Public Policy', in R. Hood (ed.) *Crime and Criminal Policy in Europe* (Oxford: Centre for Criminological Research).

Junger-Tas, J. (1986) 'Community Service in The Netherlands', *Community Service Newsletter*, parts I and II.

Kalmthout, A. M. van and Tak, P. J. (1988) *Sanction Systems in the Member States of the Council of Europe. Part 1 Deprivation of Liberty, Community Service and Other Substitutes* (Deventer: Kluwer).

Keat, R. and Urry, J. (1982) *Social Theory as Science*, 2nd edn (London: Routledge & Kegan Paul).

Kerruish, V. (1991) *Jurisprudence as Ideology* (London: Routledge).

King, R. and McDermott, K. (1989) 'British Prisons, 1970–1987: The Ever-deepening Crisis', *British Journal of Criminology*, vol. 29, no. 2, pp. 107–28.

King, R. D. and Morgan, R. (1980) *The Future of the Prison System* (Aldershot: Gower).

Kittrie, N. N. (1973) *The Right to be Different* (New York: Penguin).

—— (1980) 'The Dangers of the New Directions in American Sentencing', in B. A. Grosman (ed.) *New Directions in Sentencing* (Toronto: Butterworths).

Kleck, G. (1981) 'Racial Discrimination in Criminal Sentencing: A Critical Evaluation of the Evidence with Additional Evidence on the Death Penalty', *American Sociological Review*, vol. 46, pp. 783–805.

—— (1985) 'Life Support for Ailing Hypotheses: Modes of Summarizing the Evidence for Racial Discrimination in Sentencing', *Law and Human Behaviour*, vol. 9, no. 3, pp. 271–85.

Knapp, K. (1984) 'What Sentencing Reform in Minnesota Has and Has Not Accomplished', *Judicature*, vol. 68, pp. 181–9.

Koenraadt, F. (1983) 'Forensic Psychiatric Expertise and Enforced Treatment in The Netherlands', *Contemporary Crises*, vol. 7, pp. 171–82.

Kozol, H. L. *et al.* (1972) 'The Diagnosis and Treatment of Dangerousness', *Crime and Delinquency*, vol. 18, no. 4, pp. 371–92.

Kramer, J. H. and Lubitz, R. L. (1985) 'Pennsylvania's Sentencing Reform: The Impact of Commission-Established Guidelines', *Crime and Delinquency*, vol. 31, pp. 481–500.

Kress, J. M. (1980) 'Reforming Sentencing Laws: An American Perspective', in B. A. Grosman (ed.) *New Directions in Sentencing* (Toronto: Butterworths).

Krisberg, B. (undated) *Youth in Confinement: Justice by Geography* (San Francisco: National Council for Crime and Delinquency).

Lacey, N. (1988) *State Punishment* (London: Routledge).

Laffargue, B. and Godefroy, T. (1989) 'Economic Cycles and Punishment: Unemployment and Imprisonment', *Contemporary Crises*, vol. 13, pp. 371–404.

Laing, R. D. (1967) *The Politics of Experience* (Harmondsworth: Penguin).

Langan, M. (1990) 'Community Care in the 1990s: The Community Care White Paper: "Caring For People"', *Critical Social Policy*, vol. 29, pp. 58–70.

Lea, J. and Young, J. (1984) *What Is To Be Done About Law And Order?* (Harmondsworth: Penguin).

Lemert, E. (1951) *Social Pathology* (New York: McGraw-Hill).

—— (1970) *Social Action and Legal Change: Revolution within the Juvenile Court* (Chicago: Aldine).

—— (1981) 'Diversion in Juvenile Justice: What Hath Been Wrought' *Journal of Research in Crime and Delinquency*, vol. 18, no. 1, pp. 34–46.

Lerman, P. (1975) *Community Treatment and Social Control* (Chicago: University of Chicago Press).

Liège, M.-P. de (1991) 'Social Development and the Prevention of Crime in France', in F. Heidensohn and M. Farrell (eds) *Crime in Europe* (London: Routledge).

Locke, T. (1990) *New Approaches to Crime in the 1990s* (Harlow: Longman).

Lowman, J. and Maclean, B. (1991) 'Prisons and Protest in Canada', *Social Justice*, vol. 18, no. 3, pp. 130–54.

—— Menzies, R. J. and Palys, T. S. (1987) 'Transcarceration and the Modern State of Penality', introduction to J. Lowman, R. J. Menzies and T. S. Palys (eds) *Transcarceration: Essays in the Sociology of Social Control* (Aldershot: Gower).

Lynch, J. P. (1988) 'A Comparison of Prison Use in England, Canada, West Germany and the United States: A Limited Test of the Punitive Hypothesis', *Journal of Criminal Law and Criminology*, vol. 79, no. 1, pp. 180–219.

Maguire, M. (1980) 'The Impact of Burglary on Victims', *British Journal of Criminology*, vol. 20, p. 261.

Mair, G. (1991) 'What Works – Nothing or Everything?', *Research Bulletin no. 30* (London: Home Office).

Marshall, T. F. (1988) 'Out of Court: More or Less Justice?', in R. Matthews (ed.) *Informal Justice* (London: Sage).

Martinson, R. (1974) 'What Works? – Questions and Answers about Prison Reform', *The Public Interest*, vol. 35 (Spring), p. 22.

Mathiesen, T. (1974) *The Politics of Abolition* (Oxford: Martin Robertson).

—— (1980) *Law, Society and Political Action: Towards a Strategy under Late Capitalism* (London: Academic Press).

—— (1990) *Prison on Trial: A Critical Assessment* (London: Sage).

Matthews, R. (1979) 'Decarceration and the Fiscal Crisis', in B. Fine, *et al.* (eds) *Capitalism and the Rule of Law* (London: Hutchinson).

—— (1987) 'Taking Realist Criminology Seriously', *Contemporary Crises*, vol. 11, pp. 371–401.

—— (1988) 'Reassessing Informal Justice', in R. Matthews (ed.) *Informal Justice* (London: Sage).

—— (1989) 'Alternatives to and in Prisons: A Realist Approach', in P. Carlen and D. Cook (eds) *Paying for Crime* (Milton Keynes: Open University Press).

Matza, D. (1964) *Delinquency and Drift* (New York: John Wiley).

Melossi, D. (1985) 'Punishment and Social Action: Changing Vocabularies of Motive within a Political Business Cycle', *Current Perspectives in Social Theory*, vol. 6, pp. 169–97.

Melossi, D. and Pavarini, M. (1981) *The Prison and the Factory: Origins of the Penitentiary System* (London: Macmillan).

Michalowski, R. J. and Pearson, M. A. (1987) 'Crime, Fiscal Crisis and Decarceration: Financing Corrections at the State Level', in J. Lowman, R. J. Menzies and T. S. Palys (eds) *Transcarceration: Essays in the Sociology of Social Control* (London: Gower).

Milanovic, D. and Henry, S. (1991) 'Constitutive Penology', *Social Justice*, vol. 18, no. 3, pp. 204–24.

Minnesota Sentencing Guidelines Commission (1980) *Minnesota Sentencing Guidelines* (St. Paul: Minnesota Sentencing Guidelines Commission).

Mitford, J. (1974) *The American Prison Business* (London: Allen & Unwin).

Moffat, K. (H.) (1991) 'Creating Choices or Repeating History: Canadian Female Offenders and Correctional Reform', *Social Justice*, vol. 18, no. 3, pp. 184–203.

Mohr, J. W. (1980) 'New Directions in Sentencing', in B. Grosman (ed.) *New Directions in Sentencing* (Toronto: Butterworths).

Morris, A. and Giller, H. (1983) *Providing Justice for Juveniles* (London: Edward Arnold).

Morris, N. (1982) *Madness and the Criminal Law* (Chicago: University of Chicago Press).

Moxon, D. (1988) *Sentencing Practice in the Crown Courts*, research study no. 103 (London: Home Office).

Muncie, J. and Sparks, R. (1991) 'Expansion and Contraction in European Penal Systems', in J. Muncie and R. Sparks (eds) *Imprisonment: European Perspectives* (Hemel Hempstead: Harvester Wheatsheaf).

NACRO (National Association for Care and Resettlement of Offenders) (1986) *The Prison Medical Service* (London: NACRO).

—— (1988) *Imprisonment in Europe* (London: NACRO).

—— (1989) *Imprisonment in Western Europe, Some Facts and Figures*, Briefing no. 25 (London: NACRO).

—— (1992) *Criminal Justice Act 1991. Sentencing: The New Framework* (London: NACRO).

Nagel, I. H. (1990) 'Structuring Sentencing Discretion: The New Federal Sentencing Guidelines', *Journal of Criminal Law and Criminology*, vol. 80, no. 4, pp. 883–943.

Nagel, W. G. (1977) 'On Behalf of a Moratorium on Prison Construction', *Crime and Delinquency*, vol. 23, no. 2, pp. 154–72.

Nagin, D. (1978) 'Crime Rates, Sanction Levels and Constraints on Prison Populations', *Law and Society Review*, vol. 12, pp. 341–66.

NITFED (National Intermediate Treatment Federation) (1986) *Anti-Racist Practice for Intermediate Treatment* (London: NITFED).

O'Mahoney, B. (1988) *A Capital Offence: The Plight of the Young Single Homeless in London* (Barkingside: Barnardos).

Parker, E. and Tennent, G. (1979) 'The 1959 Mental Health Act and Mentally Abnormal Offenders: A Comparative Study', *Medicine, Science and the Law*, vol. 19, pp. 29–38.

Paternoster, R. and Bynum, T. (1982) 'The Justice Model as Ideology: A Critical Look at the Impetus for Sentencing Reform', *Contemporary Crises*, vol. 6, pp. 7–24.

Patten, J. (1987) Address to the Association of Chief Officers of Probation biennial conference, University of York.

Pearson, F. (1988) 'Evaluation of New Jersey's Intensive Supervision Program', *Crime and Delinquency*, vol. 34, no. 4, pp. 437–48.

Peters, A. A. G. (1986) 'Main Currents in Criminal Law Theory', in J. Van Dijk *et al.* (eds) *Criminal Law in Action* (Arnhem: Gouda Quint).

Petersilia, J. (1985) 'Racial Disparities in the Criminal Justice System: A Summary', *Crime and Delinquency*, vol. 31, pp. 15–34.

—— (1989) 'Implementing Randomized Experiments: Lessons from BJA's Intensive Supervision Project', *Evaluation Review*, vol. 13, no. 5, pp. 435–59.

—— and Turner, S. (1987) 'Prediction and Racial Minorities', in D. M. Gottfredson and M. H. Tonry (eds) *Prediction and Classification: Criminal Justice Decision Making* (Chicago: University of Chicago Press).

Pfeiffer, C. (1991) Address to the British Criminology Conference, University of York, 27–29 July.

Phillpotts, G. J. O. and Lanucki, L. B. (1979) *Previous Convictions, Sentence and Reconvictions*, Home Office Research Study no. 53 (London: HMSO).

Pilling, J. (1992) 'The Director General and Penal Reform', *Prison Service Journal*, vol. 85, pp. 31–6.

Pitts, J. (1986) 'Black Young People and Juvenile Crime: Some Unanswered Questions', in R. Matthews and J. Young (eds) *Confronting Crime* (London: Sage).

—— (1990) *Working with Young Offenders* (Basingstoke: Macmillan).

—— (1992) 'The End of an Era', *Howard Journal*, vol. 31, no. 2, pp. 133–49.

Platt, T. (1981) 'Street Crime', in P. Tagaki (ed.) *Crime and Social Justice* (London: Macmillan).

Pontell, H. N. (1984) *A Capacity to Punish* (Bloomington: Indiana University Press).

Pratt, J. (1989) 'Corporatism: The Third Model of Juvenile Justice', *British Journal of Criminology*, vol. 29, no. 3, pp. 236–54.

Quinney, R. (1977) *Class, State and Crime: On the Theory and Practice of Criminal Justice* (New York: David McKay).

Ratner, R. S. (1987) 'Mandatory Supervision and the Penal Economy', in J. Lowman, R. J. Menzies and T. S. Palys (eds) *Transcarceration: Essays in the Sociology of Social Control* (Aldershot: Gower).

—— and McMullan, J. L. (1985) 'Social Control and the Rise of the "Exceptional State" in Britain, the United States and Canada', in T. Fleming (ed.) *The New Criminologies in Canada* (Toronto: Oxford University Press).

—— and McMullan, J. L. (1987) (eds) *State Control: Criminal Justice Politics in Canada* (Vancouver: University of British Columbia Press).

Rawls, J. (1972) *A Theory of Justice* (Oxford: Oxford University Press).

Rawnsley, K. (1984) Foreword in M. Craft and A. Craft (eds) *Mentally Abnormal Offenders* (Eastbourne: Ballière Tindall).

Raynor, P. (1985) *Social Work, Justice and Control* (Oxford: Basil Blackwell).

—— (1988) *Probation as an Alternative to Custody: A Case Study* (Aldershot: Gower).

Reiman, J. H. (1979) *The Rich Get Richer and the Poor Get Prison* (New York: John Wiley).

Richey Mann, C. (1989) 'Minority and Female: A Criminal Justice Double Bind', *Social Justice*, vol. 16, no. 4, pp. 95–112.

Richman, A. and Harris, P. (1983) 'Mental Hospital Deinstitutionalization in Canada', *International Journal of Mental Health*, vol. 11 (Winter), pp. 64–83.

Roberts, C. (1987) 'The Probation Officer's Dilemma: Preparing Social Enquiry Reports', in D. C. Pennington and S. Lloyd-Bostock (eds) *The Psychology of Sentencing: Approaches to Consistency and Disparity* (Oxford: Centre for Socio-Legal Studies).

Robertson, G. (1984) 'Changes in the Use of the Criminal Provisions of the 1959 Mental Health Act', in T. Williams, E. Alves and J. Shapland (eds) *Options for the Mentally Abnormal Offender: Issues in Criminological and Legal Psychology no. 6* (Leicester: British Psychological Society).

Rogers, A. (1989) 'Young Black People and the Juvenile Justice System', *New Community*, vol. 16, no. 1, pp. 49–60.

Roshier, B. (1989) *Controlling Crime: The Classical Perspective in Criminology* (Milton Keynes: Open University Press).

Roth, R. T. and Lerner, J. (1982) 'Sex-Based Discrimination in the Mental Institutionalization of Women', in D. K. Weisberg (ed.) *Women and the Law: A Historical Perspective, vol. 1* (Cambridge, Mass.: Schenkman).

Rothman, D. (1971) *The Discovery of the Asylum: Social Order and Disorder in the New Republic* (Boston: Little Brown).

—— (1980) *Conscience and Convenience: The Asylum and its Alternatives in Progressive America* (Boston: Little Brown).

Rotman, E. (1990) *Beyond Punishment: A New View of the Rehabilitation of Offenders* (Westport, Conn.: Greenwood Press).

Rusche, G. and Kirchheimer, O. (1939) *Punishment and Social Structure* (New York: Russell & Russell).

Rutherford, A. (1984) *Prisons and the Process of Justice: The Reductionist Challenge* (London: Heinemann).

—— (1986) *Growing Out of Crime: Society and Young People in Trouble* (Harmondsworth: Penguin).

—— (1987) 'Discussant – the Control Review Committee Report', in A. E. Bottoms and R. Light (eds) *Problems of Long-term Imprisonment* (Aldershot: Gower).

—— *et al.* (1977) *Prison Population and Policy Choices* (Washington, DC: National Institute of Law Enforcement and Criminal Justice).

—— and McDermott, R. (1976) *Juvenile Diversion* (Washington, DC: National Institute of Law Enforcement and Criminal Justice).

Sabol, W. J. (1989) 'Racially Disproportionate Prison Populations in the United States: An Overview of Historical Patterns and Review of Contemporary Issues', *Contemporary Crises*, vol. 13, pp. 405–32.

Samson, C. (1990) 'Inequality, the New Right and Mental Health Care Delivery in the United States in the Reagan Era', *Critical Social Policy*, vol. 29, pp. 40–57.

Samuels, A. (1987) 'Consistency in Sentencing', in D. C. Pennington and S. Lloyd-Bostock (eds) *The Psychology of Sentencing: Approaches to Consistency and Disparity* (Oxford: Centre for Socio-Legal Studies).

Santos, B. de Souza (1979) 'Popular Justice, Dual Power and Socialist Strategy', in B. Fine *et al.* (eds) *Capitalism and the Rule of Law* (London: Heinemann).

Scheerer, S. (1986) 'Towards Abolitionism', *Contemporary Crises*, vol. 10, pp. 5–20.

Schuerman, L. A. and Kobrin, S. (1984) 'Exposure of Community Mental Health Clients to the Criminal Justice System', in L. A. Teplin (ed.) *Mental Health and Criminal Justice* (Beverly Hills: Sage).

Schur, E. (1973) *Radical Nonintervention: Rethinking the Delinquency Problem* (Englewood Cliffs, N.J.: Prentice-Hall).

Scraton, P. (1987) (ed.) *Law, Order and the Authoritarian State* (Milton Keynes: Open University Press).

Scull, A. (1977) *Decarceration: Community Treatment and the Deviant – A Radical View* (Englewood Cliffs, NJ: Pentice-Hall).

—— (1983) 'Community Corrections: Panacea, Progress or Pretence', in D. Garland and P. Young (eds) *The Power to Punish* (London: Heinemann).

—— (1984) *Decarceration: Community Treatment and the Deviant – A Radical View*, 2nd edn (Cambridge: Polity Press).

—— (1989) *Social Order/Mental Disorder* (London: Routledge).

Sedgwick, P. (1982) *Psycho-Politics* (London: Pluto).

Shaw, S. (1989) 'Monetary Penalties and Imprisonment: The Realistic Alternatives', in P. Carlen and D. Cook (eds) *Paying for Crime* (Milton Keynes: Open University Press).

Shelden, R. G. (1982) *Criminal Justice in America: A Sociological Approach* (Boston: Little Brown).

Sherman, M. and Hawkins, G. (1981) *Imprisonment in America: Choosing the Future* (Chicago: University of Chicago Press).

Sim, J. (1987) 'Working for the Clampdown', in P. Scraton (ed.) *Law, Order and the Authoritarian State* (Milton Keynes: Open University Press).

—— (1990) *Medical Power in Prisons* (Milton Keynes: Open University Press).

—— (1991a) 'We Are Not Animals, We Are Human Beings': Prisons, Protest and Politics in England and Wales, 1969–1990', *Social Justice*, vol. 18, no. 3, pp. 107–29.

—— (1991b) *'When You Aint Got Nothing You Aint Got Nothing To Lose': The Peterhead Rebellion, the State and the Case for Prison Abolition*, paper presented to the British Criminology Conference, University of York, 27–29 July.

—— (1992 forthcoming) 'Reforming the Penal Wasteland: A Critical Review of the Woolf Report', in E. Player and M. Jenkins (eds) *The Future of Prisons* (London: Routledge).

Smart, C. (1989) *Feminism and the Power of Law* (London: Routledge).

—— (1990) 'Feminist Approaches to Criminology or Postmodern Woman Meets Atavistic Man', in L. Gelsthorpe and A. Morris (eds) *Feminist Perspectives in Criminology* (Milton Keynes: Open University Press).

Social Justice, editorial (1990) 'Ideology and Penal Reform in the 1990s', *Social Justice*, vol. 17, no. 4, pp. 1–6.

Spitzer, S. (1975) 'Toward a Marxian Theory of Deviance', *Social Problems*, vol. 22, no. 5, pp. 638–51.

Squires, P. (1990) *Anti-Social Policy: Welfare, Ideology and the Disciplinary State* (Hemel Hempstead: Harvester Wheatsheaf).

Stack, S. (1984) 'Income Inequality and Property Crime', *Criminology*, vol. 22, pp. 229–58.

Stanko, E. (1992) address to Newcastle Polytechnic Conference, Durham, 28 March.

Steadman, H. J. *et al.* (1984) 'The Impact of State Mental Hospital Deinstitutionalization on United States Prison Populations, 1968–1978', *Journal of Criminal Law and Criminology*, vol. 75, no. 2, pp. 474–90.

Steadman, H. J. and Mórrissey, J. P. (1987) 'The Impact of Deinstitutionalization on the Criminal Justice System, in J. Lowman, R. J. Menzies at T. S. Palys (eds) *Decarceration* (Aldershot: Gower).

Steinhert, H. (1986) 'Beyond Crime and Punishment', *Contemporary Crises*, vol. 10, pp. 21–38.

Svensson, B. (1986) 'Punishment in Moderation', in J. Van Dijk *et al.* (eds) *Criminal Law in Action* (Arnhem: Gouda Quint).

Taylor, I. (1981) *Law and Order: Arguments for Socialism* (London: Macmillian).

—— Walton, P. and Young, J. (eds) (1977) *The New Criminology* (London: Routledge & Kegan Paul).

Taylor, W. (1982) 'Black Youth, White Man's Justice', *Youth and Society*, November.

Teplin, L. A. (1983) 'The Criminalization of the Mentally Ill: Speculation in Search of Data', *Psychological Bulletin*, vol. 94, no. 1, pp. 54–67.

—— (1984) 'Managing Disorder: Police Handling of the Mentally Ill', in L. A. Teplin (ed.) *Mental Health and Criminal Justice* (Beverly Hills, Cal.: Sage).

Thomas, D. (1979) *Principles of Sentencing*, 2nd edn (London: Heinemann).

—— (1992) 'Criminal Justice Act 1991. (1) Custodial Sentences', *Criminal Law Review*, April, pp. 232–41.

Thornstedt, H. (1975) 'The Day Fine System in Sweden', *Criminal Law Review*, pp. 307–12.

Thorpe, D. *et al.* (1980) *Out of Care: The Community Support of Juvenile Offenders* (London: Allen & Unwin).

Tuck, M. (1992) 'Some Reflections on the Woolf Inquiry into Prison Disturbances', *Prison Service Journal*, vol. 85, pp. 37–44.

—— and Riley, D. (1986) 'The Theory of Reasoned Action: A Decision Theory of Crime', in D. B. Cornish and R. V. Clarke (eds) *The Reasoning Criminal* (New York: Springer-Verlag).

Tutt, N. (1978) 'Introduction', in N. Tutt (ed.) *Alternative Strategies for Coping with Crime* (Oxford: Basil Blackwell; London: Martin Robertson).

Unger, R. (1976) *Law in Modern Society: Towards a Criticism of Social Theory* (New York: The Free Press).

United Nations Secretariat (1983) *Alternatives to Imprisonment: International Review of Criminal Policy no. 36, 1980* (New York: United Nations).

Van Den Haag, E. (1975) *Punishing Criminals* (New York: Basic Books).

Van Dijk, J. J. M. (1990) 'More Than a Matter of Security: Trends in Crime Prevention in Europe', in F. Heidensohn and M. Farrell (eds) *Crime in Europe* (London: Routledge).

—— and Steinmetz, C. H. D. (1988) 'Pragmatism, Ideology and Crime Control: Three Dutch Surveys', in M. Hough and N. Walker (eds) *Public Attitudes to Sentencing: Surveys from Five Countries* (Aldershot: Gower).

Vass, A. A. (1990) *Alternatives to Prison: Punishment, Custody and the Community* (London: Sage).

Von Hirsch, A. (1976) *Doing Justice: The Choice of Punishments* (New York: Hill & Wang).

—— (1985) *Past or Future Crimes: Deservedness and Dangerousness in the Sentencing of Criminals* (Manchester: Manchester University Press).

—— (1990a) 'The Politics of Just Deserts', *Canadian Journal of Criminology*, vol. 32, pp. 397–413.

—— (1990b) 'The Ethics of Community-based Sanctions', *Crime and Delinquency*, vol. 36, no. 1, pp. 162–73.

—— and Hanrahan, K. (1981) 'Determinate Penalty Systems in America: An Overview', *Crime and Delinquency*, vol. 27, pp. 289–316.

—— and Jareborg, N. (1991) 'Gauging Harm to Others: A Living Standard Analysis', *Oxford Journal of Legal Studies*, vol. 11, no. 1, pp. 1–38.

Walker, H. and Beaumont, B. (1981) *Probation Work: Critical Theory and Socialist Practice* (Oxford: Basil Blackwell).

Walker, J., Collins, M. and Wilson, P. (1987) *How the Public Sees Sentencing: An Australian Survey* (Canberra: Australian Institute of Criminology).

Walker, M. (1991) 'Sentencing System Blights Land of the Free', *Guardian Weekly*, 30 June, p. 10, Manchester.

Walker, N. (1985) *Sentencing: Theory, Law and Practice* (London: Butterworths).

—— (1991) *Why Punish?* (Oxford: Oxford University Press).

—— and Marsh, C. (1988) 'Does the Severity of Sentences Affect Public Disapproval? An Experiment in England', in N. Walker and M. Hough (eds) *Public Attitudes to Sentencing: Surveys from Five Countries* (Aldershot: Gower).

Walmsley, R. (1984) 'Recorded Incidence and Sentencing Practice for Sexual Offences', in M. Craft and A. Craft (eds) *Mentally Abnormal Offenders* (Eastbourne: Ballière Tindall).

Ward, D. (1987) 'Control Strategies for Problem Prisoners in American Penal Systems', in A. E. Bottoms and R. Light (eds) *Problems of Long-term Imprisonment* (Aldershot: Gower).

Wasik, M. (1992) 'Arrangements for Early Release', *Criminal Law Review*, April, pp. 251–61.

—— and Pease, K. (1987) *Sentencing Reform: Guidance or Guidelines* (Manchester: Manchester University Press).

—— and Taylor, R. D. (1991) *Guide to the Criminal Justice Act 1991* (London: Blackstone Press).

—— and Von Hirsch, A. (1988) 'Non-Custodial Penalties and the Principles of Desert', *Criminal Law Review*, pp. 555–72.

Wasserstrom, R. (1980) *Philosophy and Social Issues: Five Studies* (Notre Dame: Notre Dame University Press).

Wells, C. (1983) 'Whither Insanity?' *Criminal Law Review*, pp. 787–97.

Whitmer, G. E. (1980) 'From Hospitals to Jails: The Fate of California's Deinstitutionalized Mentally Ill', *American Journal of Orthopsychiatry*, vol. 50, no. 1, pp. 65–75.

Wilson, J. Q. (1975) *Thinking About Crime* (New York: Basic Books).

—— (1983) *Thinking About Crime*, rev. edn (New York: Basic Books).

WHO (1980) *Changing Patterns in Mental Health Care* (Copenhagen: World Health Organization, Regional Office for Europe).

Wolfensberger, W. (1980) 'A Brief Overview of the Principle of Normalization', in R. J. Flynn and K. F. Nitsch (eds) *Normalization, Social Integration and Community Services* (Baltimore: Maryland University Press).

Woolf, H. and Tumin, S. (1991) *Prison Disturbances April 1990*, Cmnd 1456 (London: HMSO).

Wright, R. and Logie, R. H. (1988) 'How Young House Burglars Choose Targets', *Howard Journal*, vol. 27, no. 2, pp. 92–104.

Young, A. (1991) *Feminism and the Body of Criminology*, paper given to the British Criminology Conference, University of York, 27–29 July.

Young, J. (1986) 'The Failure of Criminology: The Need for a Radical Realism', in R. Matthews and J. Young (eds) *Confronting Crime* (London: Sage).

—— (1987) 'The Tasks Facing Realist Criminology', *Contemporary Crises*, vol. 11, pp. 337–50.

—— (1988) 'Radical Criminology in Britain: The Emergence of a Competing Paradigm', *British Journal of Criminology*, vol. 28, no. 2, pp. 159–83.

—— and Matthews, R. (1992) 'Questioning Left Realism', in R. Matthews and J. Young (eds) *Issues in Realist Criminology* (London: Sage).

Index